Ethics in Nonprofit Organizations

Theory and Practice

Third Edition

Gary M. Grobman

White Hat **Communications**

Harrisburg, Pennsylvania

Ethics in Nonprofit Organizations
Theory and Practice
Third Edition

White Hat Communications
PO Box 5390
Harrisburg, PA 17110-0390
(717) 238-3787
(717) 238-2090 (fax)
Web Site: http://shop.whitehatcommunications.com

Some of the material in Chapter 2 was written by Gerald Kaufman, and adapted from *Introduction to the Nonprofit Sector: A Practical Approach for the 21st Century, 4th Edition* (2015, White Hat Communications).

DISCLAIMER: This publication is intended to provide general information and should not be construed as legal advice or legal opinions concerning any specific facts or circumstances. Consult an experienced attorney if advice is required concerning any specific situation or legal matter. Neither the author nor the publisher make any warranties, expressed or implied, with respect to the information in this publication. The author and publisher shall not be liable for any incidental or consequential damages in connection with, or arising out of, the use of this book.

Contact the author in care of White Hat Communications, or by email at:
gary.grobman@gmail.com

Printed in the United States of America.

ISBN: 9781929109-71-5

Table of Contents

FOREWORD

by David Horton Smith

The issue of ethics and its opposite outcomes, misconduct and crime, are crucial in the understanding, leadership, and management of nonprofit organizations (NPOs). As Smith et al. (2016: 273) summarize,

> "Philanthropy has a 'dark side' or 'darker side,' just as does any other human activity, individual or collective. Smith (2016 [now 2018]) argues that the 'angelic' nonprofit sector, including foundations and other charitable organizations, can be a site of deviance, crime, and ethical misconduct. The underlying reason is simple: as well as being able to act from altruism and philanthropic concerns, humans in any context, organized or informal, often also act out of egotism and self-interest. Humans can also create dysfunctions or negative outcomes through ignorance and incompetence, as unintended consequences of their actions."

Light (2008) reports on an American national survey of the adult public that showed only 15% of the people interviewed had a "great deal of confidence" in charitable organizations. In the same survey, an amazing 70% said charities waste "a great deal" or a "fair amount" of money; and only about 10% felt that charities were doing "a very good job" spending money wisely. The latter variable had the strongest statistical effect on a respondent's overall confidence versus non-confidence in charities. Another public survey showed that Americans' trust in NPOs dropped precipitously from 90% in 2001 to 64% in 2008 (Mead, 2008). The many public charity scandals in this period are often cited as a key reason for this dramatic percentage drop in confidence and for other evidence of increasingly negative public attitudes in the USA toward NPOs (e.g., Rhode and Packel 2009:8).

Because attitudes have significant effects on behavior, it is likely that philanthropic giving to NPOs in the USA is sub-optimal and will decline relatively in the future as a result of these growing negative attitudes, even though such giving continues to grow in absolute terms (Light, 2008; Mead, 2008). Research shows that NPO efficiency perceptions, especially the percent of total revenues/expenses going to fund-raising, have little effect on donors and contributions, and NPOs that spend more on fund-raising get more donations (Frumkin & Kim, 2000, p.16). Only the widespread notoriety of misconduct by many NPOs as publicized in selected media scandals, often involving revered specific NPOs, seems to account for the rapid growth of negative attitudes towards NPOs generally in the USA (Vail, 2008).

The reality of misconduct by US NPOs is irrefutable, given so much empirical evidence cited here (see Eng et al. 2016; Smith 2011, 2017, 2018a, 2018b; Smith, Eng, and Albertson 2016) and available elsewhere for all US organizations, especially businesses (e.g., Plinio, Young, & Lavery 2010). Further, studies of NPO paid staff suggest that serious lapses of ethics among the paid staff are crucial underlying causal factors. The 2007 National Nonprofit Ethics Survey (see Light, 2008; Mead, 2008) involved telephone interviews with paid staff of a random representative national sample of NPOs with two or more paid employees. The results show that NPOs have slightly more ethics than businesses or government agencies, but only barely so, and that NPOs generally lack strong ethics: Only 11% of NPOs were rated as having a strong ethical culture, as contrasted with 9% of businesses and 8% of government agencies. Weak ethical cultures in NPOs are also increasing over time, so the future prognosis for NPO misconduct is clearly poor.

Misconduct observed by NPO employees was at its highest level since 2000 (the first date of a relevant survey), with 55% of NPO employees reporting that they personally observed one or more acts of misconduct in the prior year (see Light, 2008). This is essentially the same as in businesses and government agencies, contrary to earlier surveys where NPO employees were significantly less likely to observe misconduct than the employees in other two key sectors. Financial fraud was observed by 8% of employees in NPOs in 2007—significantly greater than in business and government. Some 14% of NPO employees had also observed lying to customers, vendors, or the public (the same as for businesses and governments), while 21% of employees reported observing lying to employees (similar to businesses and governments). The study identifies severe risk of five types of misconduct in NPOs on average: conflicts of interest, lying to employees, misreporting hours worked, abusive behavior, and Internet abuse. These risks in NPOs were similar to risks in businesses and governments, and reported evaluation of the ethical behavior of employees by NPOs.

Given this generally sorry state of affairs, many experts have suggested potential remedies for foundations and other NPOs (Frumkin & Andre-Clark, 1999; Light, 2008; Mead, 2008; Pynes, 2013; Vail, 2008). One positive finding from the National Ethics Survey (see Light, 2008; Mead, 2008) was that when four key aspects of a strong ethical culture were implemented, internal NPO misconduct was markedly reduced, or even eliminated in certain misconduct areas. Such stronger ethics programs also reduced the growth of misconduct over the past decade. The four aspects were ethical leadership, supervisor reinforcement of ethics, peer commitment to ethics, and embedded ethical values.

In sum, whatever new laws, rules, and standards or monitoring bodies are put in place externally, improvements in NPO ethical behavior and reductions in NPO-related misconduct are unlikely—unless and until the roots of these problems are addressed at the level of individual employees (and also volunteers) in NPOs or other types of organizations in U.S. society. This is likely to be the case in other nations as well. Putting self-interest above the public interest is pervasive, and may be seen as normal for humans, as for other animals. Altruism and the philanthropic impulse/spirit exist, but they very much need to be nurtured to have a broad and positive impact on society.

This fine book can be an intensive self-study or teaching tool for NPO leaders, executives, paid staff, and even volunteers. Hence, this book permits addressing ethics in detail at the level of individual employees (and also volunteers) in NPOs. For this very basic reason the present book is incredibly valuable to anyone concerned with learning the details of NPO ethics.

References

Eng, S., et al. (2016.) Crime, misconduct, and dysfunctions in and by associations. In Smith, D. H., Stebbins, R.A., & Grotz, J. (eds.), *Palgrave handbook of volunteering, civic participation, and nonprofit associations.* Basingstoke, UK: Palgrave Macmillan.

Frumkin, P. & Kim, M. (2000). *Strategic positioning and the financing of nonprofit organizations: Is efficiency rewarded in the contributions marketplace?* Cambridge, MA: Harvard University, Hauser Center for Nonprofit Organizations, Working Paper No. 2.

Light, P. (2008). *How Americans view charities: A report on charitable confidence, 2008: Executive summary.* Issues in governance studies, No. 18. Washington, DC: The Brookings Institution.

Mead, J. (2008). Confidence in the nonprofit sector through Sarbanes-Oxley-style reforms. *Michigan Law Review,* Vol 106: 881-900.

Plinio A., Young, J. & Lavery, L. (2010). The state of ethics in our society: A clear call for action. *International Journal of Disclosure and Governance*, 7(3): 172-197.

Pynes, J. (2013). *Human resources management for public and nonprofit organizations.* New York, NY: Wiley.

Rhode, D. & Packel, K. (2009). Ethics and nonprofits. *Stanford Social Innovation Review* 7(3): 8-16.

Smith, D. H. (1995 November). *Deviant voluntary groups: Ideology, accountability, and subcultures of deviance in nonprofits.* Paper presented (in absentia) by Prof. Marsha Rose. Annual Conference of ARNOVA in Cleveland, OH.

Smith, D. H. (2008). *Comparative study of fundamentally deviant nonprofit groups and their role in global civil society and democratic cultures as a new frontier for third sector research: Evidence for prevalence of the false 'angelic nonprofit groups flat-earth paradigm.'* Paper presented at the Biennial Conference of The International Society for Third Sector Research, Barcelona, Spain, July 9-12.

Smith, D. H. (2008). *Accepting and understanding the 'dark side' of the nonprofit sector: One key part of building a healthier civil society.* Paper presented at the Annual Conference of The Association for Research on Nonprofit Organizations and Voluntary Action, Philadelphia, Pennsylvania, USA, November 20-22.

Smith D. H., & Stebbins, R. (2009). *Developing a grounded theory of deviant nonprofit group structural aspects.* Annual Conference of The Association for Research on Nonprofit Organizations and Voluntary Action, Cleveland, Ohio, November 19-21, 2009.

Smith, D. H. (2011). *Foreword. [On deviance and misconduct in the nonprofit sector.]* Pp. vii-xviii in Corbett, C., *Advancing nonprofit stewardship through self-regulation: Translating principles into practice.* Sterling, VA: Kumarian Press.

Smith, D. H. (in press). *Misconduct and deviance in nonprofit organizations.* Chapter in *Global encyclopedia of public administration, public policy, and governance,* by Farazmand, A. (Ed.). New York, NY: Springer.

Smith, D. H. (forthcoming). (2018a). *Deviant voluntary associations as leadership and management challenges: Understanding and dealing with potential nonprofit misconduct.* Bradenton, FL: David Horton Smith International.

Smith, D. H. (forthcoming). (2018b). *Method in their madness: Developing an empirically supported theory of deviant voluntary associations.* Bradenton, FL: David Horton Smith International.

Smith, D. H., with Eng, S. & Albertson, K. (2016). *The darker side of philanthropy: How self-interest and incompetence can overcome a love of mankind and serving the public interest,* pp. 273-286 in Jung, T., Phillips, S., & Harrow, J. (eds.), *The Routledge Companion to Philanthropy.* London: Routledge.

Preface

In January 2013, the New York Chapters of the National Association for the Advancement of Colored People (NAACP) and the Hispanic Federation publicly opposed a City of New York law that banned over-sized sugary drinks. The source of this opposition raised some eyebrows, as the intent of the law was to help reduce the incidence of obesity and diabetes, which public health officials report disproportionately affect minority communities. One might have expected both organizations would be by the side of Mayor Michael Bloomberg, who spearheaded the crusade against these health-damaging products.

In response to questions about why these organizations filed court motions to oppose the March 2013 implementation of the law, reporters were sent a joint statement from the NAACP, Hispanic Federation, and the American Beverage Association—the trade association that represents the soft drink industry, which is the target of the law. As one might have guessed, the association's members are some of the largest financial supporters of both of these nonprofit organizations, as documented by the media.[1]

Did the NAACP and Hispanic Federation join the American Beverage Association as a quid pro quo for donations they received? If so, this is likely legal in New York, or perhaps in any other state, but most "reasonable" people would consider this to be unethical behavior by these two organizations. Other "reasonable" people might disagree.

Ethical issues come up all of the time in nonprofit organizations, and board and staff may spend hours deciding the "right" approach to take and passionately argue compelling, but opposite, positions.

The purpose of this book is to explore in some detail what it means to take the "right," or ethical, approach. Included in this book are some common, and some not so common, situations that have ethical implications for nonprofits. For some of these situations, there may be no obvious right answer. And in some situations, each apparent option may have drawbacks that may violate competing principles—creating ethical dilemmas. Even the most ethical people will have differing opinions on how one should deal with any particular issue. Some of this disagreement may occur because they take differing approaches to ethics.

Our initial exposure to ethics concepts and principles comes from many sources early in our lives, but principally from our parents or others who take care of us. Common examples we may have heard as youngsters might include: "Don't hit your brother." "Don't wake Daddy." "Give your aunt a kiss." "Share your toys." "Don't waste your food (there are millions of starving children in China)."

Later, we learn behavioral concepts from our teachers, the popular media, and our classmates. Examples: "Wait your turn." "Don't lie." "Play fair." "Don't steal." "Say you're sorry."

1 http://www.guardian.co.uk/lifeandstyle/2013/jan/23/naacp-fights-bloomberg-new-york-soda-ban

Many of us have been exposed to age-old ethical concepts from our spiritual advisors: "Honor your parents." "Do not covet." "Do not commit adultery." "Do not murder." Many of these ethical concepts are universal, adopted by many different religions and by those who do not profess to have any religion.

And still later, we learn more from our professors and our work supervisors. Examples: "Be loyal to your organization." "Don't cover up misconduct." "Be a good leader and a good follower." "Do your share of the work, and don't take credit for the work of others." "Don't criticize people in front of others, and praise them when they are in front of others."

There is little debate that our ethical perspective is affected by the media. Television has always had a strong influence on how behavior is portrayed as millions watch and are influenced. Some of the most popular television shows today focus on main characters behaving badly—CSI, NCIS, *Breaking Bad,* and almost every reality TV show come to mind. Newspapers and radio give their interpretation of behavior and whether it is good or bad. Lately, I would include blogs and social media (i.e., Facebook, and other popular social networking sites), as participants seem to feel free to bare their souls to (almost) perfect strangers and perfunctorily chronicle personal behavior they would be embarrassed to share with their mothers. They fail to recognize that doing so may have as much or more permanence than what may have been on the Rosetta Stone.

So, as both a species and a culture, we have developed a loosely ordered system of cooperation with rules, some written (and often codified into law) and some unwritten. There is certainly debate on the origins of these rules—some may feel they are divinely granted, and others insist they come solely from the human imagination. Some may be hard-wired into our brains, again, either through Divine act or through evolution, in a way that improves our ability to survive as a species (see pages 67-68).

Why I Wrote This Book

The purpose of this textbook is not to delve into these esoteric questions, but rather to convey information about the ethical concepts and fundamental ethical principles relating to nonprofit organizations. Each nonprofit organization has as its purpose some discrete mission that is intended to improve the quality of life in some way for others who may or may not have any direct affiliation with that organization. When everyone is solely seeking to fulfill his or her own needs at the expense of others, perhaps through trial and error, ancient man has learned that no one's needs, or almost no one's needs, can be satisfied. Fortunately for nonprofit organizations, being selfish is considered unethical. The nonprofit sector requires individuals who put others' needs above their own; who volunteer; and who share their wealth, wisdom, and time. They need ethical leaders.

My Personal Interest in Nonprofit Ethics

I was never required to take an ethics course of any kind to fulfill my requirements for my undergraduate science program, or in my Master's or Ph.D. programs in public administration. And I never elected to take an ethics or ethics-related course during my academic career.

My first professional job after college was working for a U.S. Congressman, a "man of the cloth." He was a Methodist minister who arrived in Washington with a mission to stop the Vietnam War, beginning a 12-year stint in the U.S. House of Representatives with an implausible election victory that was directly attributable to the Watergate scandal. There was a perception by voters in his Congressional district that the local political machine was corrupt. The topic of ethics was high on the agenda then, and with good reason. In those days, members of Congress, even with safe districts, could (and did) raise hundreds of thousands of dollars in campaign contributions from special interest lobbyists, put the contributions into an account, and then, when they retired, legally put the money into their personal accounts!

Only a scant few years before, female employees were at high risk of being considered a part of the personal harem of the member of Congress for whom they worked. It was not unusual (and perhaps this is still true) for members of Congress to use their staffs for personal tasks. Members of Congress thought nothing was wrong with trading their vote for campaign contributions, or for "earmarks" that would fund projects in their districts and help them with re-election efforts.

I came to understand that my employer's ethical behavior with respect to his "politics" was mirrored by his ethical behavior toward everything else. I remember that he would circulate the office telephone bill to all staff. Attached would be his personal check in the amount of the cost of all of the personal calls he had made from the office telephone line, with his calls on the bill marked in yellow highlighter. He refused to be a bystander to injustice, and he was a persistent voice for those who did not have a voice in the halls of power—the aged, the poor, the sick, the marginalized. His ethical example influenced me, as well as others who worked with him, for many years afterwards.

After obtaining my Master's degree, I was hired as the executive director of a statewide Jewish advocacy organization. It was a 501(c)(4) tax-exempt nonprofit organization and the first nonprofit to employ me after seven years of serving in government and the for-profit sector. I remained the executive director for 13 years. One of my projects was developing a Holocaust education guide for teachers, which was funded by a grant from the Pennsylvania Department of Education. It was during that project that I became intimately exposed to the history of how an entire society (with minimal pockets of heroic exceptions) participated with zeal in perhaps the most heinous, unethical behavior in the history of mankind. Millions participated in genocide, applauded it, or looked away unmoved. Germany was, at the time, perhaps the most technologically advanced culture on the planet. How could this have happened?

Yehuda Bauer's short summary of the lessons of the Holocaust influenced me: *Don't be a perpetrator. Don't be a victim. Don't be a bystander.* Also influencing me was an oft-quoted speech by Martin Niemöller, an Anti-Nazi Lutheran pastor who had been imprisoned in the Dachau concentration camp. He summed up the consequences of being a bystander in the face of injustice (note: this is one of several versions of this quote):

First they came for the socialists, and I didn't speak out because I wasn't a socialist.

Then they came for the trade unionists, and I didn't speak out because I wasn't a trade unionist.

Then they came for the Jews, and I didn't speak out because I wasn't a Jew.

Then they came for me, and there was no one left to speak for me.[2]

I placed this quote prominently on the back cover of *The Holocaust: A Guide for Teachers.* In 1994, this book became one of the first to appear on the Internet for free in full text. It still may be accessed at: *http://www.remember.org/guide*

Years later, I found myself defending my doctoral dissertation. By some strange turn of events, my original dissertation chair had gone on sabbatical, and he had turned me over to the faculty member who taught ethics. After nine months of futile effort trying to satisfy my first chair, I decided to start from scratch with a new dissertation topic and chose to write about ethics codes of particular nonprofit organizations, those that are associations. It was at this point that I became exposed to ethics theory and practice relating to the nonprofit sector. This journey was not without its trials and frustrations. One moment I remember vividly was standing before my committee defending my dissertation, and feeling that I was "in the zone." There was nothing they could ask for which I was unprepared. Then, my chair asked me this question: *If you were asked to put together a syllabus for an ethics course, what would be in it?*

My mind went blank. I mumbled something, likely incoherent. But I survived.

Interestingly enough, several years later, I received a call from a university asking me to do just that—put together a syllabus for a nonprofit ethics course and teach it.

Former President Barack Obama, in his second inaugural address, said:

We, the people, declare today that the most evident of truths—that all of us are created equal—is the star that guides us still; just as it guided our forebears through Seneca Falls, and Selma, and Stonewall...

As I re-read his words, I cannot help noticing that much of what he said that day relates to ethics.

He talked about our behavior toward certain demographic populations. He emphasized the benefits we all accrue when everyone can participate in pursuing the American dream rather than being marginalized, as women, minorities, and homosexuals have been for centuries. He talked about how we treat our old and infirm. He talked about "fair" rules with respect to the free market, obligations to future generations, and preservation of the environment. Martin Luther King, Jr., once said, a person "will not be judged by the color

2 http://www.history.ucsb.edu/faculty/marcuse/niem.htm

of their skin, but by the content of their character." The former president, himself, is a success story of what can be achieved by creating a level playing field where everyone has the opportunity to achieve greatness.

I am a graduate of some of the "best" educational institutions, with the highest level of educational attainment. Yet, as I have shared above, I never had an ethics course. This just doesn't make any sense!

Nonprofit Ethics in the News

Nonprofit ethics cases can regularly be found in newspaper headlines. In 2012, some of my classroom ethics discussion, including written assignments, focused on a major scandal involving Penn State University and a loosely affiliated charity, the Second Mile. This charity was founded by Penn State football assistant coach Jerry Sandusky, now serving a long prison term for his conviction on child sex-abuse charges. This scandal evolved into one of the top general news stories of the year[3], resulting in the Second Mile charity having to liquidate and forcing the firing of a university's president and its revered football coach. It severely tarnished the reputation of a highly respected institution. William Aramony of United Way, John Bennett, Jr., of The New Era Foundation, and Bernie Madoff of Bernard L. Madoff Investment Securities, might be charter members of any Nonprofit Hall of Shame. It would be naïve to think that such a mythical shrine would have any difficulty finding new members to induct each year.

Each term, I started off with a short written assignment, requiring my students to review their local newspapers and analyze articles that relate to ethics in the nonprofit sector. My students often submitted stories of trusted employees caught embezzling funds from their organizations or using organizational credit cards to pay for personal expenses. There were stories of nepotism, conflicts of interest, and raising funds for purposes other than accomplishing an organization's mission.

Some recent national news stories involved nonprofit organizations in ethical lapses that were more complex than these topics.

In November 2012, the Lance Armstrong Foundation severed its ties with its organization's founder and chief spokesperson, Lance Armstrong, and changed its name to the Livestrong Foundation. Armstrong was forced out as Chairman of the board of directors a month prior to that. In mid-January 2013, Armstrong publicly admitted his involvement in the much-publicized bike doping scandal and lying about it under oath. Foundation leadership expected a strong decline to its fundraising attributable to the scandal, despite its courageous action to sever all ties with its founder. It reduced its spending budget by more than 10%.[4]

In June 2013, CNN reported on a major investigation into how funds raised by some major charities were being diverted for purposes other than the organization's mission.[5]

---

3 http://www.usatoday.com/story/news/2012/12/20/year-top-news/1783303/
4 Corrie MacLaggan (16 January 2013). "We expect Lance to be completely truthful": Livestrong". News Daily. Retrieved 23 January 2013.)
5 http://www.cnn.com/2013/06/13/us/worst-charities

Also that month, one of the most respected charities, Susan G. Komen for the Cure, formerly known as the Susan G. Komen Breast Cancer Foundation, decided to scale back one major fundraiser, a 3-day, 60-mile walk in seven major cities, because of a 37% decline in participation. Much of this decline was attributed to charges that the organization, founded in 1982, bowed to political pressure from pro-life advocates from within and outside the organization and withdrew its funding for Planned Parenthood in January 2012. After enduring a strident backlash for this, the organization restored its funding after four days of heated controversy—but not until several organization officials, including the CEO, were ousted from leadership positions.

Also during 2012-2013, there was one other salient story of questionable ethics involving a nonprofit organization, or as some might characterize Penn State University, a government-nonprofit hybrid.

Graham Spanier, president of Penn State University during the Jerry Sandusky child sex-abuse scandal, was fired by the board of directors in 2012. At the time of his firing, he was earning a reported $700,000 annually, not including benefits. He was charged with several crimes, including endangering the welfare of children, perjury, and obstruction of justice. At a preliminary hearing in July 2013, a judge cleared the way for a trial on these charges. On June 2, 2017, Dr. Spanier was sentenced to serve 4-12 months in prison, with a minimum of two months in jail and two months under house arrest. In addition, his sentence provided for two years probation, $7,500 in fines, and 200 hours of community service.

Spanier's inaction against the since convicted perpetrator not only caused pain and suffering to scores of victims, but ruined the reputation of the university and tens of millions of dollars in fines and likely multi-million dollar settlement payments to victims. Yet, newspapers reported that he was provided with a golden parachute worth more than $3 million.[6]

On May 19, 2015, the Federal Trade Commission (FTC) joined all 50 states and the District of Columbia in accusing four so-called cancer "charities" of fraudulently raising $187 million in donations. Among other charges, the FTC noted in a press release (see: *https://www.ftc.gov/news-events/press-releases/2015/05/ftc-all-50-states-dc-charge-four-cancer-charities-bilking-over*) that—

> *...the defendants used the organizations for lucrative employment for family members and friends, and spent consumer donations on cars, trips, luxury cruises, college tuition, gym memberships, jet ski outings, sporting event and concert tickets, and dating site memberships. They hired professional fundraisers who often received 85 percent or more of every donation.*
>
> *The complaint alleges that, to hide their high administrative and fundraising costs from donors and regulators, the defendants falsely inflated their revenues*

6 http://www.pennlive.com/opinion/index.ssf/2012/12/graham_spanier_golden_parachute.html

7 https://www.stripes.com/wounded-warrior-project-donations-drop-70-million-but-ceo-says-charity-is-on-the-re and *https://www.philanthropy.com/article/Wounded-Warrior-Project-Chided/240158 bound-1.467376#.WS7ItnJRHjo*

by reporting in publicly filed financial documents more than $223 million in donated "gifts in kind" which they claimed to distribute to international recipients. In fact, the defendants were merely pass-through agents for such goods. By reporting the inflated "gift in kind" donations, the defendants created the illusion that they were larger and more efficient with donors' dollars than they actually were. Thirty-five states alleged that the defendants filed false and misleading financial statements with state charities regulators....

In August 2016, the National Vietnam Veterans Foundation, the focus of a CNN investigation a few months earlier, announced it was shutting down completely. Over a 4-year period, the charity allegedly raised $29 million with only 2% allocated for veterans—the rest going to fundraisers and telemarketers.[8]

In September 2016, Ohio University announced it was returning a $500,000 gift made in 2007 by Roger Ailes, and removing his name from the school's newsroom, as a result of sexual harassment allegations against the former Fox News chairman.[9]

During the 2016 presidential general election campaign, allegations of improprieties by the family foundations of both major presidential candidates were front page news. The office of the New York State Attorney General on September 30 accused the Donald J. Trump Foundation of not registering with the state as required by law when it began soliciting outside donations in excess of $25,000 and ordered it to cease fundraising in New York (see: *http://www.nytimes.com/2016/10/04/us/politics/trump-foundation-money.html*). The 2015 tax return of the Foundation filed with the Internal Revenue Service included an admission that it violated a legal prohibition against "self-dealing", which prevents certain leaders of nonprofit organizations from using tax-exempt money to benefit themselves, their businesses, or their families—but without providing specifics of any violation or whether the foundation complied with procedures required when such violations occur.

Investigations by the *New York Times* and *Washington Post* provided some more detail about how assets of the Trump Foundation may have been diverted for purposes not permitted by law, such as covering personal expenses of Mr. Trump, paying business expenses of Trump companies, making political contributions, and supporting the candidate's campaign (see: *https://www.washingtonpost.com/politics/trump-foundation-apparently-admits-to-violating-ban-on-self-dealing-new-filing-to-irs-shows/2016/11/22/893f6508-b0a9-11e6-8616-52b15787add0_story.html?utm_term=.a7c1a7796957*).

On December 24, President-elect Trump announced that he intended to dissolve his foundation. However, the New York Attorney General's Office responded the same day that this would not be permitted until that office completed its investigation of the Foundation (see: *http://www.npr.org/sections/thetwo-way/2016/12/24/506852411/trump-plans-to-dissolve-his-foundation-n-y-attorney-general-pushes-back*). As Mr. Trump was preparing to take office, his transition team attorneys were scrambling to minimize, if not eliminate,

---

8 Drew Griffin and David Fitzpatrick, September 1, 2016, Veterans charity gave less than 2% of revenue to veterans closes its doors for good, CNN, retrieved September 12, 2016 from http://www.cnn.com/2016/08/31/politics/national-vietnam-veterans-foundation-charity-out-of-business/

conflicts of interest that affected charitable interests controlled by Mr. Trump and his family members—some of whom were expected to be in decision-making capacities in the Trump White House. In June 2017, *Forbes Magazine* published an extensive investigative feature article about conflicts of interest and spending practices of the Eric Trump Foundation, which alleged that hundreds of thousands of dollars of charitable donations were diverted to the Trump Organization, and additional hundreds of thousands of dollars were diverted to charities other than those for which the donations were given. "All of this seems to defy federal tax rules and state laws that ban self-dealing and misleading donors," the article suggested.[9] The New York Attorney General's Office announced in June 2017 that it was "looking into the issues raised by (the *Forbes'*) report," confirming that the foundations of both father and son were targets of investigations. For its part, the Eric Trump Foundation restructured its board, removing most of its members who had direct ties to Donald Trump, which at the time constituted a majority. Eric Trump agreed in December 2016 to no longer participate in fundraising for the foundation, and the organization filed to change its name to Curetivity in June 2017.[10]

Ms. Clinton's family charity, the Bill, Hillary, and Chelsea Clinton Foundation (formerly the William J. Clinton Foundation), was also in the news during the campaign, amid allegations that preferential treatment was afforded to foundation donors while she was serving as Secretary of State. In February 2015, the State Department acknowledged that the Foundation failed to comply with the terms of an agreement relating to donor disclosure that was designed to address potential conflicts of interest (see: *http://www.msnbc.com/ msnbc/state-acknowledges-issue-hillary-clinton-foundation-donation*). The Foundation was also criticized by the Trump campaign for Ms. Clinton's willingness to accept large donations from foreign governments that have public policies, particularly relating to women's rights, that are anathema to traditional American values. Despite some political damage from the negative publicity, no government action was taken against Ms. Clinton or the foundation.

Donor confidence in one of the nation's best known charities, the Wounded Warrior Project, is just beginning to turn the corner after a disastrous 2016. That year saw high-profile media investigations alleging lavish travel and staff conference spending not related to programming, culminating in the board firing both the CEO and COO. The organization's revenue declined from $398.9 million in FY 2015 fiscal year to $321.8 million in FY 2016, directly attributable to the scandal (Cahn, 2017; Sandoval, 2017). An inquiry into the allegations against the charity was led by Sen. Charles Grassley (R-IA) on behalf of the Senate Judiciary and Finance Committees. A nearly 500-page report released by the Senator on May 25, 2017, validated many of the charges against the charity, concluding that the organization was spending only about 68% of its donations on veterans' programs, that there were serious management deficiencies, that donors were being misled about how their donations were being used, and that some spending priorities were inappropriate.[11]

9 http://www.huffingtonpost.com/entry/roger-ailes-ohio-university-newsroom-campus-gift_
us_57d7a63fe4b0aa4b722c4c0d

10 https://www.forbes.com/sites/danalexander/2017/06/09/new-york-attorney-general-looking-into-eric-trump-founda-tion/#3621b2311075

11 http://www.huffingtonpost.com/entry/roger-ailes-ohio-university-newsroom-campus-gift_
us_57d7a63fe4b0aa4b722c4c0d

Perhaps if some of these nonprofit leaders had been required to take an ethics course or training of some kind, we would be reading more positive stories in the newspapers about the nonprofit sector.

Nonprofit Ethics Scenarios

In my classes, there was often spirited debate about various behaviors, and whether they might be "ethical" or "unethical." I have capsulized some of these behaviors in 120 short vignettes that are included in this book. There is not always a consensus about the answer to this question, and many of these situations are purposely ambiguous. I often pointed out to my students that it is often easy to justify a particular behavior, depending on which ethical approach one uses. Even more interesting, many behaviors can be justified or condemned, using *either* of the two major ethical approaches, the deontological approach (based on principles without regard to consequences of any behavior) and the teleological approach (based on the consequences of the behavior). I provide more details about this in the *Introduction to Ethics* chapter.

Complicating one's analysis of whether behavior might be unethical is the difficulty of distinguishing between ethical violations that are trivial, and those that become more worthy of scrutiny because of the matter of scale. For example, no one is likely to be fired summarily for committing the unethical transgression of making a single personal copy on the organization's copy machine, although most of us would agree that doing this is not ethical. When a nonprofit organization employee puts an advertisement in the paper offering to make copies for the public and collects money for this, and uses the organization's copy machine to make thousands of copies for this purpose, hardly anyone would dispute that this would be unethical (and criminal) behavior. What is problematic is where the line is drawn between so-called "de minimus" violations that might be appropriately overlooked and those that should be sanctioned to one degree or another. Each year, I pose a discussion question along the lines of this dilemma, and my students were often passionate—and often disagreed—about what they felt was worthy of punishment and what might not.

All of the scenarios included in this book are fictional, although some are based on actual cases that I have experienced either firsthand or secondhand. Many that have their origins in actual events have been exaggerated beyond recognition. All have been disguised beyond recognition. Almost all of these scenarios, whether they occurred or not, *could* have plausibly occurred in a nonprofit organization. I believe that a discussion of these scenarios will improve the ability of our future nonprofit leadership to navigate through many common ethical challenges they could face in the future.

What Is New in the Third Edition

The third edition includes four new chapters: *Transparency and Accountability, Lying and Deception, Codes of Ethics,* and *Ethics Standards in Associations of Nonprofit Organization Professionals.* The chapter on Ethics in Nonprofit Organizations has been substantially revised and expanded. Each of these chapters, in addition to the five chapters added to the Second Edition, includes discussion questions and activities suitable for the classroom.

Some of the material has been drawn from my other books for students and practitioners. Other material is completely new and benefited from the comments and suggestions of some of my colleagues who are university professors, practitioners, or both.

Conclusion

I believe that ethics is the most important element of human behavior we can teach our young children, our college-age population, our future professionals and leaders, and our teachers and professors. We can teach the theory. But as I told my students, we need to communicate our ethics and values by our actions. My intent is that this book will provide a vehicle for students to discuss ethical values that are important to those who will be leading nonprofit organizations. For many of the scenarios included in this book, there is no clear right or wrong answer. And as students consider some of these, I hope they will better appreciate the difficulty of making decisions in the turbulent environment of the nonprofit world, with so many challenges it faces.

What's Next?

I have benefited greatly from feedback I have received about the first two editions, and will continue to seek to improve access to educational materials relating to ethics in nonprofit management education, whether or not I personally developed them. If you have any suggestions, please feel free to share them with me.

Gary M. Grobman

Acknowledgments

Thanks are due to many individuals who inspired me to focus part of my professional life on ethics, including my dissertation adviser, Jeremy Plant, of Penn State University. I would like to acknowledge the contributions made to this book, both directly and indirectly, by many of my students and colleagues. Many of them have read and commented on the material in this textbook that first appeared in other books of mine, such as *The Nonprofit Handbook, Introduction to the Nonprofit Sector,* and *The Nonprofit Management Casebook.*

Gerald Kauffman, a nonprofit consultant from Philadelphia, made many contributions to the material in Chapter 1. I am also grateful for the comments I received from reviewers of the cases that appear in this textbook, including Dr. Salvadore Alaimo of Grand Valley State University; Dr. Paul Grovikar of Northern Ohio University; Dr. Peter Dobkin Hall of the Hauser Center for Nonprofit Organizations at Harvard University and the City University of New York (CUNY); Dr. Leigh Hersey of the University of Memphis; Margery Saunders of SUNY Brockport; Alonzo Villerreal, Jr., of Transformational Strategies; and Dr. Kerri Mollard of Ohio Dominican University.

Thanks are due to Thomas Horn, the author of *Is It Ethical? 101 Ethical Scenarios in Everyday Social Work Practice,* also published by White Hat Communications, who used the format of short ethical scenarios that I've adopted in this book.

I also am grateful to my wife, Linda Grobman, who made many editorial suggestions for this textbook, and was a sounding board throughout its entire development, and to John Hope and Barbara Blank, who proofread much of this material when it was first published in other books.

The second edition benefited from the reviews and comments from the following individuals: Dr. Dyana Mason, University of Oregon; Annette Godissart, doctoral student at Indiana University of Pennsylvania; Daisha M. Merritt, doctoral student at James Madison University; Deborah Smith, Development Director of the Eastport Arts Center; David Brady, Ph.D. student, Administration and Leadership Studies, Indiana University of Pennsylvania; Dr. Putnam Barber; Michael L. Wyland of Sumption & Wyland; Dr. Tim O'Brien, Mutuality Associates; Robert S. Tigner, General Counsel, Association of Direct Response Fundraising Counsel (ADRFCO); Shannon McCracken, Senior Director, Direct Response Marketing, Special Olympics; Ruth Hansen, doctoral student at Indiana University Lilly Family School of Philanthropy; David F. Chapman, Nathan Cummings Foundation; John Jorgensen, Organizational Effectiveness Group; and Joe Geiger, President and CEO, First Nonprofit Foundation.

For this edition, I appreciated the comments and criticisms of the following: Victoria I. Ferrence Ray, Ph.D. Candidate, Administration and Leadership Studies, Indiana University of Pennsylvania, Chief National Programs Officer, Hugh O'Brian Youth Leadership; Ivy Schneider, President, Helix Strategies and an ABD doctoral student at Indiana University of Pennsylvania; Deborah Smith, an independent nonprofit consultant headquartered in Belfast, Maine; Christopher Corbett, an independent nonprofit sector researcher; David Brady, Doctoral Candidate (ABD), ALS Program, Indiana University of Pennsylvania; Audrey Wolf, a student in the Nonprofit Management Master's Program of Adler University; and Ardhandu Shekhar Singh, Symbiosis International University.

Thank you to David Horton Smith, ARNOVA founder and research and emeritus professor, Boston College and an icon in my field of nonprofit management, for providing the Foreword; Ivy Schneider, who edited and proofread the third edition; and most importantly, to Linda May Grobman, my wife, who provided assistance with every aspect of this new edition.

Gary M. Grobman

Chapter 1
Introduction to Ethics

*Note: This chapter is adapted from Chapter 7 of the 4th edition of **An Introduction to the Nonprofit Sector: A Practical Approach for the 21st Century.***

Ethics is a branch of philosophy that refers to "well-based standards of right and wrong that prescribe what humans ought to do, usually in terms of duties, principles, specific virtues, or benefits to society" (Johnson, 2005, p.10). The origin of the word, *ethicos*, is Greek for habit, or customs relating to morals (Guttman, 2006).

Classical Ethical Thought

Humans have wrestled with basic existential questions for as long as they have been able to pose questions: Does God exist? How did I get here and why? What is the meaning and ultimate purpose of life? What happens after I die? Who or what is watching me and judging me? What constitutes a life well-lived? What are the consequences for a life well-lived or one that is not? Does it matter if I act one way when no one is looking and another way when I am being observed?

How one should behave, and why, is one such question that has generated attention by the greatest thinkers of both ancient and modern civilizations.

The Golden Rule, "treat others as you would have them treat you," has evolved in many cultures, and is a basic ethical principle that has its origins in the earliest of writings (Wattles, 1996). Ancient religious writings, such as the Torah, are replete with both Jewish history and hundreds of commandments to follow (exactly 613, according to Jewish tradition), most of which relate directly to ethical behavior toward not only other human beings but animals, as well. Scholars suggest that this document first appeared around 1445 B.C.E. (Slick, n.d.).

"Do not seek revenge or bear a grudge against anyone among your people, but love your neighbor as yourself" appears in Leviticus 19:18, and "So in everything, do to others what you would have them do to you, for this sums up the Law and the Prophets" in Matthew 7:12. "None of you has faith until he loves for his brother or his neighbor what he loves for himself" [Sahih Muslim, Book 1, Number 72] is a passage from the Quran. And, according to the Buddha, (Dhp.130), "All tremble at punishment. Life is dear to all. Put yourself in the place of others and harm none nor have them harmed" (Dhammika, n.d.).

Ancient Greek philosophers were writing about ethical issues even before writing about philosophical issues. Much of our Western ethical tradition can be traced to Socrates (469-399 B.C.E.). In *The Republic,* written about 380 B.C.E. by Plato, one of his students (Socrates) was described as living an extreme moral life. Aristotle (384-322 B.C.E.), a student of Plato, wrote books about ethics—*Nicomachean Ethics, Eudemian Ethics,* and *Magna Moralia,* all of which were influenced by both Socrates and Plato. All three of these books have survived and influenced ethical thought throughout modern history. Virtue ethics is often traced to the writings of Aristotle, who believed that happiness or well-being resulted from having a virtuous character. Among these virtues are prudence, justice, courage, and self-restraint (Johnson, 2005).

Two related approaches to ethics, developed by Zeno of Citrium and Epicurus, also came out of the ancient Greek tradition.

Stoicism, traced to the Greek philosopher Zeno of Citium (333-264 B.C.E.), espoused that living a moral life means avoiding moral judgment and extreme behaviors, such as addictions. The Stoics believed in diminishing the influences of the external world and avoiding the pursuit of worldly pleasures, to achieve serenity of the soul, and to live in harmony with the environment, accepting death as neither avoidable nor frightening (Guttman, 2006). Among the best known Stoics was Seneca (4 B.C.E.-65 A.D.), who lived in Rome and killed himself upon the command of Nero, the Roman Emperor at the time. The Stoics thought that reason was the greatest good that would bring them joy rather than actual pleasure, even if personal pain came from seeking this reason.

Epicurus (341 B.C.E—271 B.C.E.) taught that the greatest good was pleasure and freedom from pain. The Epicureans emphasized the quiet enjoyment of pleasures, especially mental pleasure, free of fear and anxiety. The Epicurians were the first to express the belief that all people everywhere were equal, and that the basic goal of everyone is to seek and obtain joy (Guttman, 2006).

Certainly, writing about ethics and virtues was not restricted to Western culture. In China, Confucius (551-479 B.C.E.), decades before these ancient Greeks, shared ethical lessons that were later written down by his followers, and that in many ways have some parallels to the virtue approach of Aristotle. He espoused the concept of *ren,* compassion for others, which was demonstrated by a form of the Golden Rule, "What you do not wish for yourself, do not do to others," documented in the Lunyu, the ancient text of his teachings (Riegel, 2013).

In the Middle Ages, writers from the religious traditions made major contributions to the literature that influenced modern ethical thought. Thomas Aquinas (1225-1274) was a Dominican friar and priest who developed natural law theory, which stated "good is to be done and pursued, and bad avoided" (Finnis, 2011). He is credited with adding faith, hope, and love to the four Aristotlian virtues. Other virtues have since been added, including empathy, compassion, generosity, hospitality, modesty, and civility (Johnson, 2005), but Aquinas' contribution was a major new paradigm influencing not only Catholics, but those outside of that faith community, and he was honored with Sainthood 50 years after his death.

Maimonides (1135-1204), in his 14-volume *Mishneh Torah,* interpreted the Torah to "provide a framework of guidelines for living a life satisfactory to God" (Guttman, 2006, p. 20). Five centuries later, the Dutch-Jewish philosopher Spinoza (1632-1677) wrote *The Ethics,* which could be viewed as placing the Aristotlian virtues in a non-secular context, and which had a major influence on the Reform Jewish movement (Guttman, 2006).

German philosopher Immanuel Kant (1724-1804) advanced the proposition that all of us should do what is ethically right regardless of the consequences—the "categorical imperative." He said that we have an obligation to follow universal truths, such as behaving so that we do not lie, cheat, or murder, even if doing so may appear to have some benefit (Johnson, 2005).

In 19th century Britain, the writings of Jeremy Bentham (1748-1832) and John Stuart Mill (1806-1873) advanced utilitarianism, an ethical approach that judges the morality of a behavior on its consequences of bringing the most utility to the most people.

Approaches to Ethics

Various approaches to ethics exist. A typology was provided by Dr. Leslie Leip at her presentation at the 2000 Annual Meeting of the American Society for Public Administration (Leip, 2000). Noting that these are not completely inclusive of approaches and that there are subapproaches within them, her list included, among others:

- Utilitarian approach (the most good for the most people)
- Virtue approach (a focus on personal character)
- Divine approach (what "God" commands)
- Ethics of care approach (from the feminist literature)
- Ethical egoism approach (based on "what's good for me")
- Communitarianism approach (based on "what's good for the community")
- Pluralism (a combination of the above, depending on the situation).

Each of these approaches has a distinct frame of reference, although there are common origins to many of them. Among the more general approaches found in the ethics literature are:

Teleological Approach

In short, this approach has been labeled "the ends justify the means" (Fox, 1994). The overarching principle is that decision-making should be governed by creating the most good and the least evil. What matters most are the results that come about once the decision is made, not whether any high moral principles are served. The utilitarian approach is an offshoot of teleological ethics.

Deontological Approach

This approach suggests that there are higher-order principles that are immutable because either "God said so" or because of the equivalent in a secular context. People following this approach will tell the truth even when considerable serious consequences to the individual or society would result by doing so. For example, a person who believes that not lying is a principle that must be upheld at *any* cost may well refuse to tell a lie even when telling the truth might threaten his or her personal safety.

Utilitarian Approach

A derivative of the teleological approach, the utilitarian approach involves measuring and calculating the relative benefits to all members of a group of each act or behavior, and then choosing the act or behavior that creates the greatest good for the aggregate (Pops, 1994). Three types of utilitarianism—act utilitarianism, general utilitarianism, and rule utilitarianism—have been identified.

Act utilitarianism considers the single action of the individual as the level of analysis, and judges what the consequences to society would be if only that individual performed a single act only once. *General utilitarianism* expands that concept to judge what the effect on society would be in the aggregate if everyone acted the same way in a particular case. *Rule utilitarianism* suggests an ethical rule that would likely have the most benefit to society if everyone followed it, even though any single, individual application of the rule might have some negative results to the group occasionally. What binds all three of these types together is the notion that the consequences of following this philosophy are most important, and that, in the aggregate, the act is ethical if society would be better off.

This approach has several shortcomings, according to critics. First, the definition of "society" can change. It is not clear whether the greatest good refers to one's community, one's state, one's nation, one's species, or one's biosphere. Second, it is not always easy to measure and make calculations as to the benefit. Third, this approach can trample basic values that many utilitarianists might still value, such as justice, fairness, and social equity. For example, it may be consistent with utilitarian values to put an innocent man to death if doing so would result in deterring the murder of hundreds of others, a concept that would be anathema to an adherent to liberal ethics (see pages 24-25).

Classic, market-based economic theories, such as transaction cost theory first articulated by Ronald Coase but now associated with Oliver Williamson (Pessali & Fernandez, 1999) and public choice theory (Buchanan & Tullock, 1965), have found their way into the public administration realm. These theories have their roots in utilitarianism. Many of the principles of New Public Management are also consistent with a utilitarian approach to administration, in that they stress efficiency and "most bang for the buck," rather than being sensitive to individual justice and democratic citizenship values (Grobman, 2015). Proponents of public choice theory contend that it is the job of government to do the measurement and calculations and then make public policy decisions based on this calculation. "Efficiency is clearly the preeminent normative force in this baseline view" (Harmon & Mayer, 1986, p. 114). This is a direct utilitarian approach.

Virtue Ethics

This approach was first advanced in the public administration context by George Frederickson and David Hart. Much of the academic literature during the previous decade focused on resolving ethical dilemmas. Virtue ethics shifts the focus toward the personal character of the decision-maker, suggesting that there is a distinct character trait, which they call "benevolence," defined as "the extensive and non-instrumental love of others." (Cooper, 1994, p. 547).

This theme was picked up by Edmund L. Pincoffs in his 1986 book, *Quandaries and Virtues.* The basic idea of this approach is that if a public administrator has the "right" character, he or she will not require a written code of ethics or a set of principles that describes the appropriate behavior.

In *The Six Pillars of Character* (Josephson Institute, 2002), some of these virtues are described. Among them are trustworthiness (honesty, integrity, promise-keeping, loyalty), respect (autonomy, privacy, dignity, courtesy, tolerance, acceptance), responsibility (accountability, pursuit of excellence), caring (compassion, consideration, giving, sharing, kindness, loving), justice and fairness (procedural fairness, impartiality, consistency, equity, equality, due process), and civic virtue and citizenship (law abiding, community service, protection of the environment).

One major difference distinguishing virtue ethics from other approaches is that it suggests that government does much more than serve as the marketplace for reaching a majority consensus.

In the nonprofit world, virtue ethics is often what brings people to the table to do the work that they believe government should be doing but is not. Modern writers in the nonprofit management field, such as Peter Drucker (1990), Stephen Covey (1997), and Margaret Wheatley (1994), have recognized that the personal traits of the nonprofit leader with respect to ethical culture create the climate that bonds the organizational members to a common purpose.

According to Van Hook (1998), the primary role of a nonprofit executive is to set an ethical tone for the organization in its internal and external relationships.

John Carver, whose book *Boards That Make a Difference,* proposes a model of governance in nonprofit organizations that is becoming increasingly attractive (despite being controversial), suggests that the board give the executive director a virtual free hand in achieving its desired outcomes. However, the one area in which the board is permitted to micromanage the executive director under the Carver model is in the area of ethics, in which constraints are explicitly put down in writing and are inviolate (Carver, 1990).

Of course, what is "virtuous" to one nonprofit executive can be unethical to another. Being loyal to the organization is virtuous, and so is whistleblowing. An ethical dilemma often occurs when these two principles conflict. At times, it may be difficult to choose to "do the right thing" when it is impossible to honor both principles. See pages 26-27 for more about ethical dilemmas.

Liberal Ethics

This approach is based on the view that the rights of individuals override the needs of groups and societies. For example, there is currently a public policy debate in state governments concerning whether some innocent inmates on death row are being executed. To those who adhere to the liberal ethical framework and otherwise could support the principle of having the death penalty as an available punishment (of course, many individuals do not support the death penalty regardless of someone's guilt or innocence), executing a single innocent person out of the hundreds executed who are guilty invalidates the death penalty as an appropriate sanction. A traditional teleological approach would argue that it is virtually impossible to eliminate the execution of one innocent person out of hundred. Consistent with this perspective, society is best served in the aggregate by having hundreds of those guilty of first-degree murder executed—with the deterrent effect that this policy ostensibly provides—even if one innocent person happens to fall through the cracks and is executed. The liberal ethics approach emphasizes individual autonomy and a right to privacy.

Kohlberg's Stages of Moral Reasoning

Many ethicists are not only interested in people acting ethically, but they also maintain it is important that they do so for the right reasons. For several millennia, punishment mandated by both religious and civil law has provided a justification for behavior that is socially acceptable, perhaps the best example of an external motivation for good behavior. Other external reasons people might act ethically are to avoid punishment other than legal sanctions (such as that meted out by a parent), to obtain rewards, to have favors returned, to avoid disapproval from others, and to maintain respect from others. The most prevalent internal motivation is to "avoid self-condemnation for failing to live up to the values to which one is committed" (Colby & Kohlberg, 1987). Lawrence Kohlberg devised a 6-part continuum that ethicists find useful in categorizing the different stages of moral development that individuals pass through as they mature. Kohlberg's Stages of Moral Reasoning begins with Punishment and Obedience. Each succeeding stage provides the individual with more intellectual capacity to respond to ethical decision-making. Kohlberg's research in support of these stages consisted of providing subjects with a classical ethical dilemma, asking subjects to provide a justification for their decision on it, and then classifying these individuals within his typology (Kohlberg, 1981).

Kohlberg's typology consists of:

Stage 1. Punishment and obedience. Stimulus/response.
Stage 2. Instrumental relativist. Self-serving good behavior.
Stage 3. "Good boy"; Nice Girl." Meeting the expectations of others with whom one interacts.
Stage 4. Society maintaining/Law and order. Meeting standards imposed by society through law and convention.
Stage 5. Social contract. Seeking to promote rights of all as agreed to by society.
Stage 6. Universal ethical principle. Seeking to act in ethically principled way (Kohlberg, 1981).

According to Kohlberg, most individuals never advance beyond the fourth stage (Svara, 2007).

Ethical Dilemmas

An ethical dilemma is a situation in which there is a conflict between honoring two moral principles, and one cannot act in a way that satisfies one of them without violating the other (see pages 39-40 for ethical dilemmas common to the nonprofit sector).

Over the years, philosophers have crafted some provocative, hypothetical situations in which readers are tasked with making a difficult ethical choice. Depending on one's ethical approach, either choice is justifiable, and these scenarios serve as illustrations of ethical principles that come into conflict. The best known of these has been called the trolley problem, and has been attributed to Phillipa Foote, a granddaughter of President Grover Cleveland. The trolley car problem has many variations, but what follows is a short version:

A trolley is running out of control down a track. In its path are five innocent people tied to the track by a mad philosopher. Fortunately, you can flip a switch, which will lead the trolley down a different track to safety. Unfortunately, there is a single innocent person tied to that track. Should you flip the switch, thus being responsible for killing that innocent person, or do nothing? (Ross, 2017).

In the above scenario, the question "What should you do?" is easy to answer based on whether you take a deontological or teleological approach to ethics (see page 23). Other scenarios are more complex and have been modified with additional information that are designed to delve more deeply into your ethical decision-making principles. Additional classical ethical dilemmas can be accessed at:

https://www.tes.com/teaching-resource/classic-ethical-dilemmas-6259609 and *http://listverse.com/2007/10/21/top-10-moral-dilemmas/*

Rights Based Theories

Utilitarianism (see pages 23-24) has formed the basis of much of the theory justifying government policy for much of American history (Fox, 1994). One can argue that even when this frame of reference is pursued in good faith and policy-makers seek to "create the most good for the most people," there will be many citizens who will fall through the cracks, even with the so-called "safety net" of government programs. One important function of the nonprofit sector is to advocate for the safety net being strong, and to provide essential goods and services when the market is unable to satisfy the essential needs of citizens and government is unwilling or unable to do so.

"Rights-based" theory is an alternative to utilitarianism. It suggests that all people have some basic fundamental rights that ethically cannot be abridged. Among these basic rights are the right to life, liberty, expression, and property. This theory also encompasses protection against oppression, unequal treatment, intolerance, and arbitrary invasion of privacy (Reamer, 2006). One can see the influence of this theory in the First Amendment to the Constitution. An application of this theory comes from the University of Chicago-based philosopher Alan Gewirth who argued that there are three core "goods" that society must value:

Basic goods. These include goods that are required in order to engage in purposeful activity, such as life itself, health, food, shelter, and mental equilibrium.

Nonsubstractive goods. Goods whose loss would diminish a person's capacity to function effectively in society, such as inferior living conditions, harsh labor, being lied to, or being swindled.

Additive goods. These are goods that would enhance an individual's ability to function, such as knowledge, self-esteem, being lifted out of poverty, and education (Reamer, 2006).

John Rawls, a Harvard philosophy professor for four decades, is perhaps the best known proponent of rights-based ethical theory. He recognized that those making decisions about the allocation of resources are more likely to benefit the decision-makers—because of their higher social status—than the rest of the population. So, Rawls suggested a thought experiment whereby decision-makers should pretend that they are unaware of how a decision will affect themselves, a so-called "original position" with a "veil of ignorance." His best known work, *A Theory of Justice*, focused on the concept of distributive justice (see next section).

Professor Rawls recognized that following utilitarian principles in public policy might benefit society as a whole, but might work to the disadvantage of minority populations. So, he argued, two principles of justice should be applied rather than simply identifying the path that creates the most good for the most individuals. These two principles are:

The Liberty Principle. Certain rights must be protected, such as the right to vote and freedom of speech.
The Difference Principle. Everyone should have equal opportunity to reach their goals, and thus marginalized groups, such as the poor, women, immigrants, and minorities, should be free from discrimination (Johnson, 2005).

Distributive Justice

Distributive justice refers to the ethical allocation of rights or goods in society. Without it, it would only be a matter of time until the most powerful used their power to accumulate all of the resources. Under this principle, goods are shared "not by the principle of equality but by the principle of relativity in accordance with the personal contribution of the giver to the welfare of the community" (Guttman, 2006). Thus, under this principle, it is not unethical to pay more to a CEO of an organization than to an able-bodied person who chooses not to work. However, it would be unethical to pay a worker less than a living wage and pay the CEO of the organization hundreds of times more than what is paid to the least paid worker in the organization, who helps create the wealth necessary to pay the CEO. Rawls (see previous section) recognized that is not productive to provide equal resources to everyone (such as by adopting a strictly egalitarian system of distribution) and that it is legitimate to provide more to those whose contribution is more—but only when decisions are made consistent with the Liberty Principle and Difference Principle. Those with disadvantages beyond their reasonable control—such as being disabled, lacking natural talent, possessing substandard knowledge and education, or being in ill health—should be rewarded more with respect to decisions about resource allocation, and everyone should have equal access to opportunity, such as by eliminating discrimination.

Contributive Justice and the "Free Rider" Problem

Contributive justice is the opposite side of the coin of distributive justice. It refers to what individuals are ethically expected to contribute back to society, recognizing that if everyone only took rather than gave, there would be nothing left to take. In the nonprofit sector context, it means that everyone has an obligation to gratuitously provide resources for the common good, whether in the form of donations or volunteer work. It is not sufficient to expect that one's taxes will be all that is necessary to overcome flaws in government's distribution of resources. Contributive justice is a response to the "free rider problem," in which the benefits of certain societal goods and services accrue to everyone, regardless of whether one contributes to those resources.

The nonprofit sector's existence depends on people behaving in ways not necessarily to increase their personal benefit but rather to increase the benefit to society (Grobman, 2015). Contributors to a nonprofit often do so because they perceive a marginal benefit to themselves, such as what they might receive when supporting their local public radio station. But those who contribute to the station do not receive any more benefit than those who do not contribute—the station may be listened to by contributors and noncontributors alike. So, the station, and those organizations in a similar position, make fundraising appeals and call for volunteers that directly or indirectly invoke the principle of contributive justice.

My favorite illustration of the concept of contributive justice is a story posted on the Internet (Marcus, 2010) that has its roots in a portion of the two-millennia-old *Talmud* (Dogele, 2011). The townsfolk decide to present the visiting monarch with a gift of a giant barrel of wine, and they agree that each family will contribute a flask of wine. Each day, families line up to climb the ladder to the top and pour their donations of wine into the barrel. When the king arrives, he is invited to fill his goblet with wine, only to find the barrel is filled with water. Everyone had decided to fill their flasks with water instead of wine, figuring that one flask of water within the giant barrel would not be noticeable.

This story can be a metaphor for how the nonprofit sector is intended to work. No single person is expected to carry the full load of meeting a community need, although the sector is full of heroes who do much more than their fair share. So much can be achieved if everyone recognizes that they have an ethical responsibility to contribute what they reasonably can to the common good, because if everyone takes advantage of becoming a "free rider," no one will be able to ride.

The Platinum Rule and Cultural Competence

Virtually everyone has heard of the "Golden Rule," which in its short form states, "Treat others as you would like to be treated yourself" (see page 21). One limitation of this basic ethical principle, which has become a part of the doctrine of many different religions, is that it assumes that others see it as positive when you follow this rule and treat others as you would like to be treated yourself. This is often not the case, particularly for those who are from different cultures or ethnic backgrounds. An alternative to the Golden Rule is the "Platinum Rule," which addresses this shortcoming (Hall, 2017). It states, "Treat others the way they would like to be treated." A simple example of this is opening doors for another. You may consider this to be a simple courtesy. Your friend who enters behind you may find it paternalistic and objectionable when you hold the door open for her.

The Platinum Rule is particularly relevant in the nonprofit sector with respect to working with multicultural clients and co-workers. In some cultures, it is considered disrespectful to look someone in the eye or, in some situations, have any physical contact. The term "cultural competence" is a term that is used to describe having a skill set that is responsive and respectful to the unique culture of others. It includes actions that respect not only race and ethnicity, but also "sexual orientation, gender identity or expression, and religious identity or spirituality" (NASW, 2015, p. 7).

"Cultural Competency and Diversity" is included among the ten core competencies of the Nonprofit Leadership Alliance (n.d.), which issues the Certified Nonprofit Professional (CNP) credential. Many professions allied with the nonprofit sector, including social work, health care, and education, have recognized the value of skills relating to cultural competence. Inclusion of references to cultural competence in professional degree coursework, professional licensing, ethics codes, and continuing education validate the view that the Platinum Rule is an important ethical value in the nonprofit sector.

Doctrine of Double Effect

The Doctrine of Double Effect, also referred to as the *principle of double effect* or the *law of double effect,* derives from historical Catholic teachings first introduced by Thomas Aquinas. It suggests that it is not moral to perpetrate an immoral act (such as killing someone), even when the intent is to promote some moral end. However, it is ethical to take an action that is in itself moral, even when that action results in collateral harm that is unintended, and action is taken to minimize that unintended consequence to the maximum extent feasible.

As explained in the *Stanford Encyclopedia of Philosophy* (2014), The New Catholic Encyclopedia provides four conditions for the application of the principle of double effect:

1. The act itself must be morally good or at least indifferent.
2. The agent may not positively will the bad effect but may permit it. If he could attain the good effect without the bad effect, he should do so. The bad effect is sometimes said to be indirectly voluntary.
3. The good effect must flow from the action at least as immediately (in the order of causality, though not necessarily in the order of time) as the bad effect. In other words, the good effect must be produced directly by the action, not by the bad effect. Otherwise, the agent would be using a bad means to a good end, which is never allowed.
4. The good effect must be sufficiently desirable to compensate for the allowing of the bad effect (p. 1021).

So, even if one is an individual who believes abortion is murder and abortionists are murderers (and perhaps that women who choose to have an abortion are murderers), in accordance with this principle, it is immoral to kill a doctor who performs abortions, even if the murderer feels that thousands of lives could be saved by such an act.

Philosophers have argued the relevancy and applicability of this concept for centuries, and it has limited direct application to nonprofit organizations with the salient exception of hospitals, nursing homes, and hospices. Policies with respect to end-of-life care are often influenced by this concept. Indirectly, however, there is the possibility that the principle of double effect could have some influence in making decisions when a plan of action might be considered to be immoral, but the outcome expected is, overall, of great benefit. In such a case, one might have no problem with taking such an action using a teleological approach to ethics (see page 23) rather than not taking the action using a deontological approach that relies on a principle, regardless of the expected consequences.

Ethics in Organizations

Writing on the broad topic of ethical behavior is generally attributed to Plato and Aristotle, although the first writing on business ethics per se is traced to Cicero, who wrote *On Duties* (McNamara, 2000). Cicero is considered "one of the great authorities on the necessity of virtue for the good of society" (Hart, 1994).

Once thought to have little relevance to the bottom line in organizations, some of the more recent management strategies, such as TQM and diversity training, are being seen as giving ethical training practical relevance (McNamara, 2000).

Madsen and Shafritz (1990, in McNamara, 2000) divide ethical problems of organizations into two principal types. "Managerial mischief" consists of behavior that reasonable people would recognize as "wrong," such as illegal, unethical, or questionable practices. It can be distinguished from the other type by the lengths to which the perpetrator of the behavior will go in order not to be caught. The other type, "moral mazes," encompasses issues such as potential conflicts of interest, wrongful uses of resources, mismanagement of contracts, and other behaviors with which managers deal on a daily basis.

A description of highly ethical organizations is provided by Pastin (1986):

- They are at ease interacting with diverse internal and external stakeholder groups. The ground rules of these firms make the good of these stakeholder groups part of the organizations' own good.
- They are obsessed with fairness. Their ground rules emphasize that the other persons' interests count as much as their own.
- Responsibility is individual rather than collective, with individuals assuming personal responsibility for the actions of these organizations. The organizations' ground rules mandate that individuals are responsible to themselves.
- They see their activities in terms of purpose—a way of operating that members of these organizations highly value. Purpose ties the organizations to their environments (in McNamara, 2000).

Doug Wallace (in McNamara, 2000) asserts that a high integrity organization has the following characteristics:

- A clear vision and picture of integrity exist throughout the organization.
- Over time, the vision is owned and embodied by top management.
- The reward system is aligned with the vision of integrity.

- Policies and practices of the organization are aligned with the vision; there are no mixed messages.
- It is understood that every significant management decision has ethical value dimensions.
- Everyone is expected to work through conflicting stakeholder value perspectives (McNamara, 2000).

Codes of Ethics

A code of ethics is a systematic effort to define acceptable conduct (Plant, 1994). Ethical behavior in the workplace is enforced through the use of codes of ethics, codes of conduct, ethicists, ethics committees, policies and procedures relating to ethical dilemmas, and ethics training (McNamara, 2000).

Codes of ethics may be general or specific, aspirational or idealistic, coercive or legalistic, and apply to members of a profession, an organization, or an association representing a class of organizations (Plant, 1994). Codes of ethics may be a simple list of ten golden rules (Plant, 1994) or a lengthy, codified system of procedures and ideals such as the one adopted by the National Association of Social Workers (National Association of Social Workers, 1999). It may have the force of law (such as a statutory ethics code for public officials), be a collection of principles that are not law but are morally binding, or simply provide a system of symbolic principles for meaningful communication (Plant, 1994).

Codes of ethics for public officials are fundamentally different from codes for nonprofit organizations (Plant, 1994), and codes for nonprofit organizations differ equally from those for government officials or private business persons. Yet they share many elements.

For more on nonprofit organization ethics codes, see Chapter 10.

Online Resources

Markkula Center for Applied Ethics (Santa Clara University)
https://www.scu.edu/ethics/

Carter McNamara's Ethics Guide
http://managementhelp.org/businessethics/ethics-guide.htm

Ethics entry from the Internet Encyclopedia of Philosophy (peer-reviewed)
http://www.iep.utm.edu/ethics/

The Basics of Philosophy (Ethics pages)
http://www.philosophybasics.com/branch_ethics.html

British Broadcasting Corporation (BBC) Ethics Guide
http://www.bbc.co.uk/ethics/introduction/intro_1.shtml

Discussion Questions

1. Discuss how nonprofit executives who share a virtue ethics approach might have widely divergent responses to dealing with some typical ethical situations. Compare this with those who share a utilitarian approach.

2. Discuss whether the Carver Model (see page 25) is an improvement over traditional governing models, and its advantages and shortcomings.

3. Based on the principle of double effect, would it be morally permissible for a doctor in a Catholic-affiliated nonprofit hospital to purposely act to hasten the death of a terminally ill patient if she knows that doing so would save the lives of several others who would die without that patient's organs?

Activities

1. Compile a collection of newspaper clippings from local and national newspapers of unethical and/or illegal conduct involving nonprofit organizations.

2. Make a collection of junk mail you receive soliciting donations for various charities and causes. Analyze the appeals being made with respect to directly or indirectly referencing the contributive justice concept discussed on page 29.

References

Buchanan, J., & Tullock, G. (1965). *The calculus of consent: Logical foundations of constitutional democracy.* Ann Arbor, MI: University of Michigan Press.

Carver, J. (1990). *Boards that make a difference.* San Francisco, CA: Jossey-Bass.

Colby, A. and Kohlberg, L. (1987). *The measurement of moral judgment.* Vol. 1. New York, NY: Cambridge University Press.

Cooper, T. L. (1994). The emergence of administrative ethics. In T. Cooper (Ed.). *Handbook of administrative ethics.* New York, NY: Marcel Dekker.

Covey, S. R. (1997). *The 7 habits of highly effective people.* Provo, UT: Franklin Covey Co.

Dhammika, B. S. (n.d.) *Guide to Buddhism A-Z.* Retrieved from: *http://www.buddhisma2z. com/content.php?id=154*

Dogele, A. (2011, April 27). Book Review. *The Big Barrel of Wine* by Rabbi Yosef Goldstein. Retrieved from *http://www.thejewisheye.com/zg_barwine.html*

Drucker, P. F. (1990). *Managing the non-profit organization: Practices & principles.* New York, NY: HarperCollins.

Finnis, J. (2011). "Aquinas' moral, political, and legal philosophy," *The Stanford Encyclopedia of Philosophy* (Fall 2011 Edition), Edward N. Zalta (ed.). Retrieved from: *http://plato.stanford.edu/archives/fall2011/entries/aquinas-moral-political/*

Fox, C. J. (1994). The use of philosophy in administrative ethics. In T. Cooper (Ed.). *Handbook of administrative ethics.* New York, NY: Marcel Dekker.

Grobman, G. (2015). *The nonprofit handbook* (7th Edition). Harrisburg, PA: White Hat Communications.

Guttman, D. (2006). *Ethics in social work: A context of caring.* New York, NY: Hayworth.

Hall, G. C. N. (2017, February 7). The platinum rule. *Psychology Today.* Retrieved from *https://www.psychologytoday.com/blog/life-in-the-intersection/201702/the-platinum-rule*

Hall, H. (2009, December 3). Recession prompts watchdog agency to loosen fund-raising standards. *The Chronicle of Philanthropy.* Retrieved from *http://philanthropy.com/article/Recession-Prompts-Watchdog/63201/*

Harmon, M. M., & Mayer, R. T. (1986). *Organization theory for public administration.* Burke, VA: Chatalaine Press.

Hart, D. K. (1994). Administration and the ethics of virtue. In T. Cooper (Ed.). *Handbook of Administrative Ethics* (2nd Ed.) (pp. 107-123). New York: Marcel Dekker.

Johnson, C. (2005). *Meeting the Ethical Challenges of Leadership.* Thousand Oaks, CA: Sage.

Josephson Institute. (2002). *The six pillars of character.* Retrieved from *http://josephson-institute.org/med-introtoc*

Kohlberg, L. (1981). *The philosophy of moral development.* San Francisco, CA: Harper & Row. pp. 411-412. In Svara, J. *Ethics primer for public administrators in government and nonprofit organizations.* Sudbury, MA: Jones and Bartlett Publishers.

Leip, L. (2000, April). *Developing ethical decision-making frameworks: A means for 20/20 vision in the 21st century.* Presentation made at the annual meeting of the American Society for Public Administration, San Diego, CA.

Marcus, Z. (2010). Wine or water. Blog post of November 26, 2016. Retrieved from *https://matt111.wordpress.com/2016/11/28/wine-or-water/*

McNamara, C. (2000). *Complete guide to ethics management.* Retrieved from *http://www.managementhelp.org/ethics/ethxgde.htm*

NASW. (2015). Standards and indicators of cultural competence in social work practice. Author: Washington, D.C.

Nonprofit Leadership Alliance. (n.d.). Alliance competencies. Retrieved from: *https:// www.nonprofitleadershipalliance.org/credential/competency-based/competencies/*

Pastin, M. (1986). *The hard problems of management: Gaining the ethics edge.* San Francisco, CA: Jossey-Bass.

Pessali, H. F., & Fernandez, R. G. (1999). Institutional economics at the micro level? What transaction costs theory could learn from original institutionalism (in the spirit of building bridges). *Journal of Economic Issues, 2,* 265.

Plant, J. (1994). Codes of ethics. In T. Cooper (Ed.). In *Handbook of administrative ethics* (pp. 221-242). New York: Marcel Dekker.

Pops, G. (1994). A teleological approach to administrative ethics. In *Handbook of Administrative Ethics* (2nd Ed.), T. Cooper (Ed.). New York, NY: Marcel Dekker.

Reamer, F. (2006). *Social work values and ethics.* (Third Ed.). New York, NY: Columbia University Press.

Riegel, J. (Summer 2013). "Confucius." *The Stanford Encyclopedia of Philosophy* (Summer 2013 Edition), Edward N. Zalta (ed.). Retrieved from: *http://plato.stanford.edu/archives/ sum2013/entries/confucius/*

Ross, K. (2017). Some moral dilemmas. Retrieved from *http://friesian.com/valley/dilemmas.htm*

Slick, M. (n.d.). *When was the Bible written and who wrote it?* Retrieved from: *http://carm. org/when-was-bible-written-and-who-wrote-it*

Stanford Encyclopedia of Philosophy. (2014, Sept. 23). Doctrine of double effect. Retrieved from *https://plato.stanford.edu/entries/double-effect/*

Van Hook, P. J. (1998). Ethics in non-profit organizations. In *The international encyclopedia of public policy and administration.* Boulder, CO: Westview.

Wattles, J. (1996). *The golden rule.* New York, NY: Oxford University Press.

Wheatley, M. J. (1994). *Leadership and the new science: Learning about organization from an orderly universe.* San Francisco, CA: Berrett-Koehler Publishers.

Chapter 2
Introduction to Nonprofit Ethics

In 2007, the Ethics Resource Center *(http://www.ethics.org)* published *The National Ethics Survey: An Inside View of Nonprofit Sector Ethics.* This study is a followup to three earlier studies of ethics in United States places of work, and the first to focus exclusively on ethics in the nonprofit sector. The study found significant differences among the three sectors in terms of how workers view ethical challenges. First, the study found that nonprofit organization ethical cultures were stronger than their government or for-profit counterparts. Nonprofit employees were more likely than those in the other sectors to report misconduct. However, compared to data collected in previous surveys, organizational misconduct appears to be on the rise, with financial fraud of particular concern. Surprisingly, the survey found that financial fraud, which included alteration of financial records and other documents, lying to external stakeholders and employees, and misreporting hours of work, was more prevalent than in the other two sectors. The study found that mid-sized nonprofits, defined as organizations with 100-9,999 employees, experienced more ethical compliance issues than larger or smaller nonprofit organizations.

One lesson learned from analysis of the data was that ethics programs and the implementation of a strong ethical culture were successful in eliminating misconduct.

Among the report's findings is an "Ethics Risk Index" in which the report ranks various types of misconduct with respect to the risks each poses to the organization:

Severe Risk (happens frequently and usually goes unreported)

- Conflicts of interest
- Lying to employees
- Misreporting hours worked
- Abusive behavior
- Internet abuse

High Risk (happens often and often goes unreported)

- Safety violations
- Lying to stakeholders
- Improper hiring
- Discrimination
- Sexual harassment
- Misuse of confidential organizational information

Guarded Risk (happens less frequently and may go unreported)

- Provision of low quality goods and services
- Stealing

- Alteration of financial records
- Environmental violations
- Alteration of documents
- Bribes
- Using competitors' inside information (Ethics Resource Center, 2007)

Among the general categories of ethical conflicts that are endemic to the nonprofit sector are accountability, conflict of interest, and disclosure (Kaufman & Grobman, 2015). Specific issues of interest are relationships between board members and the staff; relationships between board members and the organization (such as business relationships); self-dealing; charitable solicitation disclosure; the degree to which donations finance fundraising costs rather than programs; the accumulation of surpluses; outside remuneration of staff; the appropriateness of salaries, benefits, and perquisites; and merit pay (Kaufman & Grobman, 2015). For example, pay based on income received rather than mission accomplished is considered unethical. Staff of charities are under more of an obligation not to exploit their position on staff for personal gain (such as charging a fee for outside speaking engagements on their own time) than their for-profit counterparts. Unlike their for-profit or government counterparts, charities generally are under an ethical, if not legal, obligation not to accumulate large surpluses (Kaufman & Grobman, 2015). Salaries, benefits, and perquisites must be "reasonable." Prior to the promulgation by the IRS of temporary regulations on January 10, 2001, relating to this and other "excess benefit" transactions, the legal requirements applying to these issues were in a gray area (Grobman, 2015).

A different set of ethical issues exists around disclosures to foundation and corporate funders. For instance, what is the obligation to disclose changed circumstances after a proposal is submitted and before it is acted upon, such as when key staff have announced plans to leave? If the organization knows that the changed circumstance might affect the decision, is it unethical not to disclose it?

Many of these ethical issues are discussed in more detail in subsequent chapters.

Ethical Dilemmas

There are circumstances that leaders in nonprofit organizations can identify in which there is a clear choice about how to behave. We know it is clearly unethical (and illegal) to embezzle funds that belong to our organizations. We know it is unethical (and usually illegal) to lie to or otherwise deceive potential donors to manipulate them to give. And we know it is unethical (and illegal) to make false statements on our 990 tax returns to make our organizations' performance appear better than it really is. These are just a few examples of situations in which there is little doubt about the choices we can make between doing the right thing and the wrong thing.

Yet, there are often circumstances in which there is some ambiguity about what one's behavior should ethically be, even if the individual has an absolute commitment to behaving ethically. This can occur when there are two or more important ethical principles in conflict, and behaving in a manner that honors one principle may bring about conflict with honoring a different ethical principle that may be equally important.

For example, a co-worker may come to you to discuss a problem and ask you to swear beforehand that you will keep what he says in total confidence, and you agree. And then that co-worker shares information that you feel ethically compelled to share with your board chair, or even law enforcement authorities, to avoid potential harm to the organization or to individuals. In this example, one principle, "preserving confidentiality," might conflict with another, the "duty to report." You have to make a choice not between doing the right thing and doing the wrong thing—as would be the case in deciding whether or not to divert organization resources to one's personal benefit—but, rather, you must make a choice between doing the right thing or doing another right thing when one cannot reasonably do both.

Regardless of which choice one makes, there is at least one ethical principle that would be violated.

This is what is known as an ethical dilemma—a situation in which there is a conflict between honoring two moral principles, and one cannot act in a way that satisfies one of them without violating the other.

Acting with loyalty and in the best interests of one's organization is considered ethical. So is being a whistleblower when that organization is acting unethically itself. It is considered ethical to act in the best interest of your stakeholders (duty of care), and also ethical to let them make decisions for themselves (self-determination). How should you act when you strongly feel that they will not really be acting in their self interest if they make a choice that you strongly feel will harm them? These are common examples of two ethical principles colliding.

Some of the cases and scenarios in this book highlight examples of nonprofit organization leaders facing a choice between being ethical and unethical. Other cases include examples of ethical dilemmas. In these, nonprofit leaders with the best intentions of acting ethically find themselves in situations that are difficult to deal with, because of conflicts among two or more lofty ethical principles that come into conflict.

Resolving Ethical Dilemmas

There are many standard models that ethicists have developed to make decisions about one's behavior when facing an ethical dilemma. One popular model is called RESPECT, developed by Yeo and Moorhouse in 1996 (Guttman, 2006), and is an acrostic for:

- **R**ecognize the moral dimensions of the problem.
- **E**numerate the guiding and evaluative principles.
- **S**pecify the stakeholders and their guiding principles.
- **P**lot various action alternatives.
- **E**valuate alternatives in light of principles and stakeholders.
- **C**onsult and involve stakeholders as appropriate.
- **T**ell stakeholders the reason for the decision.

A model I like just a bit better is attributed to Frederic Reamer (2006), modified slightly for the purpose of this discussion. It is comprised of the following steps:

- Identify the ethical issues that are controversial.
- Identify those who will be affected by the decision.
- Identify the potential courses of action, and the pros and cons of doing each.
- Analyze how each stakeholder might be affected, and how the decision is or is not consistent with one's values, one's organization, and one's profession.
- Consult others who are not affected by the dilemma for some input and advice.
- Make the decision, and document what was decided.
- Follow up and evaluate the result of the decision.

It would not be unusual for a party adversely affected by a decision made by a nonprofit organization leader to contest it in some way. By following a standard model, it is more likely that the decision can be justified. This is certainly welcome if one finds himself or herself on the witness stand in a criminal or civil trial having to defend a decision one has made in response to a situation in which any course of action could be questioned on legal or ethical grounds.

Practical Ethics Issues to Consider in Nonprofit Organizations

The following are some general ethics issues that are appropriate for nonprofit boards and staff to consider to guide organizational behavior:

1. Accountability

Accountability often is overlooked in discussions about ethics. Because of the unique status of 501(c)(3) organizations, they have a special obligation to the public to be accountable for the results of their activities that justify their tax exemptions and other privileges. Organizations should continually challenge themselves by asking if the outcomes produced are worth the public investment.

Nonprofit boards of directors have a special obligation to govern with integrity. Governing with integrity means that the organization recognizes that it is accountable to the public, to the people it serves, and to its funders. Accountability includes the concept that nonprofit organizations exist only to produce worthwhile results in furtherance of their missions.

In addition, accountability encompasses a core system of values and beliefs regarding the treatment of staff, clients, colleagues, and community. Yet, organizational survival needs too often undercut core values. Although everyone in the organization is responsible, it is the board's ultimate responsibility to ensure that its values are not compromised, and that the activities are conducted within acceptable limits.

Staff will sometimes pursue grants and contracts, or engage in direct solicitation campaigns, for the primary purpose of growing. This subtle issue of accountability is seldom discussed. Boards sometimes ask whether the executive director "grew the organization" as the primary criterion for measuring success. Boards have an obligation to ascertain that all activities support the organization's mission.

For more on accountability issues in the nonprofit sector, see Chapter 3.

2. Conflict of Interest

A potential conflict of interest occurs any time organizational resources are directed to the private interests of a person or persons who have an influence over the decision to use those resources. Examples might include the leasing of property owned by a relative of the executive director or a board member, the board awarding itself a salary, the organization hiring a board member to provide legal representation, or the executive director hiring a relative or a board member's relative.

A conflict also can occur when the person (or persons) making a decision expects something in exchange from the person in whose favor the decision is made. One example is the case when an executive director retains a direct mail firm, and the executive director's spouse is hired by that direct mail firm shortly thereafter.

With regard to board members, the cleanest approach is to adopt a policy that does not allow any board member to profit from the organization. It is the duty of every board member to exercise independent judgment solely on behalf of the organization. For example, suppose a board member who owns a public relations business successfully argues that the nonprofit needs a public relations campaign and then is hired to conduct the campaign. The board member's self-interest in arguing for the campaign will always be subject to question.

Suppose, in the above example, the board member offers to do the campaign at cost, and that is the lowest bid. It may be that even "at cost," the board member's firm benefits, because the campaign will pay part of the salary of some staff members or cover other overhead. It may be perfectly appropriate to accept the board member's offer, even though it is a conflict of interest. However, it is absolutely essential that the board have a procedure in place to deal with these types of issues.

Some organizations permit financial arrangements with board members, provided that the member does not vote on the decision. Given the good fellowship and personal relationships that often exist within nonprofit boards, such a rule can be more for show and without substance.

A similar conflict can occur in the awarding of contracts to certain individuals who do not serve on the board. There may be personal reasons for one or more members of the board or the executive director to award contracts to particular persons, such as enhancing their personal or professional relationships with that person.

There are instances in which it is appropriate to have a contract with an insider, such as when a board member offers to sell equipment to the organization at cost, or agrees to sell other goods or services well below market value. Here, too, the organization should assure itself that these same goods or services are not available as donations.

It is essential for the board to confront and grapple with these issues and adopt a written policy to govern potential conflicts of interest, in order to avoid the trap of self-dealing or its appearances. Many potential abuses are not only unethical, but also illegal as a result of the *Taxpayer Bill of Rights 2,* enacted in July 1996 (Public Law 104–168, 110 Stat. 1452).

The *Taxpayer Bill of Rights 2* was signed into law by President Clinton on July 30, 1996. The principal purpose of this law is to punish individuals affiliated with charities and social welfare organizations who are participating in financial abuses, and to provide the government with a sanction other than simply revoking the charity's exemption status. The law expanded public disclosure requirements for annual federal tax returns, including adding information about excess expenditures to influence legislation, any political expenditures, any disqualified lobbying expenditures, and amounts of "excess benefit" transactions.

Both state and federal law have prohibitions against "private inurement"— permitting a charity's income to benefit a private shareholder or individual. Legislation at the federal level was enacted to define what constitutes a prevalent form of private inurement and to refine the definition of a private shareholder. It aims to respond to alleged financial abuses by some organizations perceived as providing unreasonable compensation to organization "insiders."

To curb financial abuses, the law authorizes the IRS to impose an excise tax, 25% in most cases, on certain improper financial transactions by 501(c)(3) and 501(c)(4) organizations. The tax applies on transactions that benefit a "disqualified person," defined as people in positions to exercise substantial influence over the organization, their family members, or other organizations controlled by those persons.

Disqualified persons include voting members of the board, the president or chair, the CEO, the chief operating officer, the chief financial officer, and the treasurer, among potential other officers and staff. The benefit to the disqualified person must exceed the value that the organization receives in order to be subject to the tax. To avoid problems, tax experts are advising organizations to treat every benefit to a director or staff person as compensation, and reflect these benefits in W-2s, 1099s, and their budget documents. Seemingly innocent benefits, such as paying for the travel and lodging expenses for a spouse attending a board retreat or a health club membership for an executive director, may trigger questions about excess benefit. Luxury travel could be considered an excess benefit.

Compensation is considered reasonable if it is in an amount that would ordinarily be paid for similar services by similar organizations in similar circumstances. The term "compensation" is defined broadly, and it includes severance payments, insurance, and deferred compensation.

Most of the provisions relating to intermediate sanctions apply retroactively to September 14, 1995, the date the legislation was first introduced. Steep additional excise tax penalties, up to 200% of the excess benefit plus the initial 25% excise tax, apply for excess benefit transactions that are not corrected in a reasonable amount of time. An excise tax may also be applied to an organization's managers (a term that is meant to include an officer, director, trustee) who approve the excess benefit transaction in an amount of 10% of the excess benefit, up to $10,000 maximum per transaction.

3. Disclosure/transparency

There is much disagreement within the nonprofit sector regarding how much disclosure is required to those who donate to charitable nonprofits. The first obligation of every organization is to obey the laws and regulations governing disclosure. Nonprofits have a legal and ethical obligation to report fundraising costs accurately on their IRS Form 990, to obey the requirement regarding what portion of the cost of attending a fundraising event is deductible, and to comply with state charitable registration laws and regulations.

Nonprofits face a more difficult ethical issue when deciding how much disclosure to make that is not required by law, particularly if the organization believes that some people may not contribute if those disclosures are made. One controversial example of this is Kiva *(http://kiva.org)*, one of the best-known crowdfunding websites, which many feel does excellent work in facilitating micro-loans to deserving entrepreneurs. Its loans in more than 80 countries has approached $1 billion since its founding in 2005. But, among other criticisms, the organization has taken flack for making it appear that potential investors choose to whom to make loans, when in most cases, the entrepreneur any investor chooses to make a micro-loan to has already received a loan, and the investor's funds are channeled to others. (See: *http://www.nytimes.com/2009/11/09/business/global/09kiva. html?_r=0*). As of 2017, the organization earned four out of four stars from the respected charity watchdog group, Charity Navigator.

In the for-profit corporate world, the Securities and Exchange Commission demands full, written disclosure of pertinent information, no matter how negative, when companies are offering stock to the public. There is no comparable agency that regulates charitable solicitations by nonprofits. Nonprofits must be very careful to voluntarily disclose all relevant information and to avoid the kind of hyperbole that misrepresents the organization.

Another difficult issue is whether fundraising costs should be disclosed at the point of solicitation. The costs of telemarketing campaigns or of maintaining development offices are sometimes 80%, or even more, of every dollar collected. Some argue that people would not give if these costs were disclosed. Others argue that if the soliciting organization cannot justify these costs to the public (and in many cases, they are not justifiable), then the organization is not deserving of support.

For more on nonprofit organization transparency, see Chapter 3.

4. *Inappropriate relationships*

Nepotism

Nepotism is the practice of hiring one's relatives. There are clear costs and benefits associated with this practice. On the plus side, an organizational leader will likely know that relative's strengths and weaknesses really well, and can expect a high degree of loyalty to the organization. In the business world, at least for individually owned businesses, nepotism is an acceptable practice in our culture, and it is often celebrated as a way to carry on a family business after the death of the founder. This is not the case for publicly-owned business corporations, many of which choose to implement an anti-nepotism policy.

Federal law against nepotism is codified in Section 3110 of Title 5 of the U.S. Code enacted in 1967 (U.S. Code, 2017). It prevents public officials, including the President and members of Congress, from appointing, employing, promoting, or advancing individuals, or to recommend individuals for appointment, employment, promotion, or advancement in connection with employment in an agency in which they exercise jurisdiction over their relatives. Relatives are defined as the public official's father, mother, son, daughter, brother, sister, uncle, aunt, first cousin, nephew, niece, husband, wife, father-in-law, mother-in-law, son-in-law, daughter-in-law, brother-in-law, sister-in-law, stepfather, stepmother, stepson, stepdaughter, stepbrother, stepsister, half brother, or half sister (Legal Information Institute, n.d.).

Many, if not most, states and numerous local governments also prohibit nepotism.

Among the detriments of nepotism are that hiring relatives discriminates against others who may be more qualified to do the job. Other discrimination may occur because the relative hired is likely to be of the same race or ethnicity as the individual doing the hiring. And it is much more likely that the manager/supervisor, regardless of whether that person is the direct relative who made the hire, will be unable to effectively provide oversight and hold that relative accountable. Furthermore, employees not related to the manager may feel that there is real or perceived favoritism in the treatment of the related employee by managers or leadership. When the relative is supervising the related employee, it is an example of a dual relationship (see page 45).

In the nonprofit organization context, the benefits of nepotism typically accrue to the individual, whereas the costs, if any, accrue to the stakeholders. For example, the son of a CEO may not be able to find a job elsewhere, and a position with her organization may provide a source of income, regardless of whether her son is qualified to perform the duties of that position. So, I would argue that nepotism in some cases is a form of inurement, although one not likely to meet the strict legal threshold that state and federal governments enforce.

Many nonprofit organizations find it useful to adopt an anti-nepotism policy. At a minimum, it makes sense to prohibit employees from hiring, promoting, firing, or supervising their relatives. For an example, see *http://niqca.org/documents/Draft_Nepotism_Policy.pdf*. The federal government has recognized that nepotism, although not illegal, is problematic in the nonprofit sector, both in management and governance. There is a section of the 990 federal tax return (Part VI, Section A) that requires the disclosure of relationships, asking, *Did any officer, director, trustee, or key employee have a family relationship or a business relationship with any other officer, director, trustee, or key employee?*

Many of the disadvantages of nepotism are also at play when family members serve together on a board. Again, decisions are influenced, or give the appearance of being influenced, by the dual relationship. How board members exercise their legal governance duties should not be influenced by any perceived effect on their domestic situation, once the board meeting is over. Maintaining appropriate boundaries under these circumstances is difficult, if not impossible.

No doubt, there are many successful examples of spouses and family members jointly founding and managing nonprofit organizations. But such arrangements are inherently ethically problematic.

Cronyism

Cronyism is the practice of hiring one's friends, regardless of whether they are qualified to perform the work. The advantages and disadvantages of cronyism are virtually identical to those of nepotism—it creates a dual relationship in which professional decisions are often influenced by how they might interfere with a personal relationship. As with nepotism, the hired person is likely to be more loyal to the hirer than someone hired without any previous relationship. Unlike nepotism, the person doing the hiring is not likely to have any direct financial benefit accruing from hiring a friend. Depending on the circumstances, hiring one's friends who are otherwise qualified for the job may be either appropriate or inappropriate (see scenario #11 on page 207). In some cases, even hiring highly qualified friends is not appropriate when it results in discrimination that blocks employment opportunities to those of different genders, races, religions, ethnic groups, or otherwise acts to limit workplace diversity and equal opportunity.

Dual (multiple) relationships

A dual relationship is a situation in which the boundaries are blurred between one's professional relationship to a stakeholder and one's personal relationship. It becomes problematic in a nonprofit organization when there is an impairment of objectivity influenced away from the benefit of the organization and toward one or both of the parties who have a dual relationship, or when one or the other party is at risk of being harmed or exploited.

It is not unusual for dual relationships to begin without any malevolent intentions. Nonprofit staff members often try to help their clients with resources that the organization is unable or unwilling to provide. Some dual relationships begin innocently and inadvertently, such as a nonprofit organization staff member finding himself or herself in a fitness center or house of worship with a client of the organization. Other dual relationships are less benign, when power differences between two individuals, such as a supervisor and a staff member he or she supervises, result in exploitative demands.

There are clear cases when dual relationships are inappropriate. Managers should not pursue sexual or romantic relationships with those they supervise, even when there is the appearance that creating and advancing that relationship is entirely consensual. Creating a business or romantic relationship outside of the organizational relationship is also ethically problematic. Nonprofit staff should not hire clients as their babysitters (or vice-versa), or pursuing romantic/sexual relationships. Neither should lend money to the other.

As a CEO, accepting a lunch invitation from a board member or sharing an evening at a sporting event is likely to be acceptable. Agreeing to a request to meet the Chair's son or daughter on a blind date is something that should be avoided!

Not every situation involving a dual relationship is clear-cut, so it is wise to consider the risks entailed in engaging in one. The best advice I can find is to avoid deliberately entering into a dual relationship whenever possible, and to evaluate what options you may have in order to minimize any conflicts that might result from an inadvertent dual relationship.

Most ethics codes of the helping professions (National Association of Social Workers, 1996; AAMFT, 2015; Benke, 2004) directly address the issue of dual relationships. There is no direct prohibition, but all make it clear that these relationships are ethically problematic and need to be entered with extreme caution to avoid harm to either the professional or the client or reduce objectivity.

Conclusion

There are many other ethical issues that nonprofit organizations may encounter, such as the personal use of office supplies and equipment; time off for volunteering for other nonprofit organizations; personal use of frequent flier mileage; the extent of staff and board diversity; and the use of private discriminatory clubs for fundraisers, board meetings, or other events. The list is endless. Many of these issues are raised in the scenarios section of this book, beginning on page 204.

It is important that nonprofit organizations make a conscientious effort to engage in discussions about ethics and values on a regular basis, recognizing that the charitable nonprofit sector has a special obligation to uphold the very highest standards. Boards of directors of charitable nonprofits have a pivotal role in this regard. Boards cannot play a more important role than ensuring that nonprofits are accountable, and that they operate as mission- and value-driven organizations.

Many who choose to work in the nonprofit sector do so because the stated values of the sector and their personal values are in harmony. It is crucial that such people be vigilant against the erosion of those very principles that initially attracted them to the work.

Only in this way can the public be assured that the charitable nonprofit sector remains worthy of its privileges and continues to occupy its special and unique place in our society.

Online Resources

Independent Sector: Accountability Overview
http://www.independentsector.org/accountability

Independent Sector's Principles Resource Center
http://www.independentsector.org/principles

Carter McNamara's Business Ethics: Managing Ethics in the Workplace and Social Responsibility
http://www.managementhelp.org/ethics/ethics.htm

BBB's Wise Giving Alliance
http://give.org/

Standards for Excellence Institute
http://www.standardsforexcellenceinstitute.org/dnn/

Josephson Institute of Ethics
http://josephsoninstitute.org/

Discussion Questions

1. Should the nonprofit sector be held to a higher ethical standard than its for-profit counterpart? Why or why not? What about compared with the government sector?

2. If a nonprofit executive writes a book about the public policy issues related to his or her work, as the leader of an organization, should the royalties go to the author or to the organization?

3. Can ethical behavior be taught? At what age? Do you think that students in nonprofit management programs will behave more ethically when they lead nonprofit organizations if they have had ethics courses in their educational programs?

Activities

1. Devise an ethical dilemma or ethical challenge that might face a nonprofit executive. Make a table showing actions that the executive might take to address the dilemma consistent with the various ethics approaches described in Chapter 1 and the models to resolve them described on pages 39-40.

2. Visit the websites of the Josephson Institute of Ethics, Independent Sector, the United Way of America, and the Society for Nonprofit Organizations, and review ethics-related articles that are posted on these sites.

Tips for Practitioners

1. Challenge yourself and your organization to hold yourself up to the highest ethical standards, avoiding even gray areas of conflicts of interest and appearances of conflicts of interest.

2. When in doubt, ask yourself, "How would I feel if my family and friends read about this on the front page of the daily newspaper?"

3. Obtain salary surveys published by state associations that represent nonprofit organizations, and determine whether anyone in your organization has an unreasonable salary.

4. Demand that all business relationships with the organization be at "arm's length," and obtain at least three bids on any work that costs at least $1,000, even if a board member claims that he or she will provide the product/service at cost.

5. Consider adopting a formal conflict-of-interest policy. See a model policy developed by the Internal Revenue Service included in its 1023 Form (see: *http://www.irs.gov/instructions/i1023/ar03.html*)

6. Support efforts to improve disclosure and accountability of the voluntary sector. Cooperate with expanded enforcement of laws governing this sector, so that the few nonprofits that are abusing the law do not stain the reputation of the entire sector.

References

AAMFT. (2015). Code of Ethics. American Association of Marriage and Family Therapists. Retrieved from *http://www.aamft.org/iMIS15/AAMFT*

Behnke, S. (2004). Multiple relationships and APA's new ethics code: Values and applications. Ethics Rounds. v35n1, p.66. Retrieved from *http://www.apa.org/monitor/jan04/ethics.aspx*

Ethics Resource Center. (2007). *Ethics Resource Center's national nonprofit ethics survey: An inside view of nonprofit sector ethics.* Arlington, VA: Author.

Grobman, G. (2015). *The nonprofit handbook* (7th Edition). Harrisburg, PA: White Hat Communications.

Guttman, D. (2006). *Ethics in social work: A context of caring.* New York, NY: Haworth.

Independent Sector. (2015). *Principles for Good Governance and Ethical Practice, 2015 Edition.* Washington, DC: Author.

Kaufman, G., & Grobman, G. (2015). Nonprofit organization ethics. In G. Grobman, *The nonprofit handbook,* (7th Ed.). Harrisburg, PA: White Hat Communications.

NASW (2008). Code of ethics. Retrieved from *http://socialworkers.org/pubs/code/default.asp*

National Charities Information Bureau. (2000). *NCIB's standards in philanthropy.* Retrieved from *http://www.bbb.org/*

National Society of Fundraising Executives. (1991). *NSFRE code of ethical principles and standards of professional practice.* Retrieved from *http://www.afpnet.org/Ethics/content.cfm?ItemNumber=3093&navItemNumber=536*

Reamer, F. (2006). *Social work values and ethics.* (3rd Ed.). New York, NY: Columbia University Press.

U.S. Code. (2017). 5 U.S. Code § 3110 - Employment of relatives; restrictions. Retrieved from *https://www.law.cornell.edu/uscode/text/5/3110#*

Chapter 3
Transparency and Accountability

Back in 2012, I received a call from the Indianapolis, Indiana, police department investigating a reported crime. I was asked to verify that I had written a check to my nonprofit professional association, the Association for Research on Nonprofit Organizations and Voluntary Action (ARNOVA).

I was surprised by the call, even though I was familiar with allegations of embezzlement by an ARNOVA staff member. I had received a "Dear Members" email from the organization's president three months earlier.

"We have recently discovered that a trusted individual misappropriated approximately $50,000 from ARNOVA over a period of 28 months, primarily through the misuse of an ARNOVA credit card," the email began. The communication included steps the organization was taking, which included hiring an attorney and a forensic accountant. The email disclosed that the suspected individual was fired and that additional internal financial controls were being put in place.

My recent Google search failed to find any reference to this incident, or what happened to the case and the status of the individual. Apparently, neither the local or national press, nor *The Chronicle of Philanthropy,* the newspaper of record for the nonprofit sector, covered the incident. So, if the leadership of the organization wanted to handle this quietly to avoid embarrassment, it could have done so. Yet, unlike the way many nonprofits in that situation would have handled it—as we know from the *Washington Post*'s exposé about nonprofit organization asset diversions (see pages 89-90)—the ARNOVA leadership chose to be accountable and transparent with its members about the embezzlement.

Why?

Dr. Roseanne Mirabella, Professor of Political Science and Public Affairs at Seton Hall University, who served as the president of the ARNOVA board at the time, remembers the events of 2012 as a difficult time for the Association and not the best time to be the President.

When I asked her about her experience responding to this incident, she told me that she does not remember anyone on the board opposing ARNOVA being completely open and transparent with the membership.

"There was never any doubt in my mind that we needed to be as transparent as we could be with the membership, Obviously, there were issues raised regarding board liability as the fiduciary agents for ARNOVA, and we sought and received legal advice on this. We also received advice on what we could and could not legally share. We also needed to balance this with the need to limit our public discussions in terms of this staff person, given the confidentiality requirements of personnel matters with which nonprofits must comply. The information shared with our mem-

bership had to balance our desire to be fully transparent with our legal and fiduciary requirements as a board."

Now, compare this case with that of the J. Paul Getty Trust, affiliated with the J. Paul Getty Museum. The richest private art museum in the world at the time, its board allegedly covered up from the public its knowledge about lavish staff spending, gifts of art to board members, financial mismanagement, and deals involving stolen art works for months after an exposé in the *Los Angeles Times*. It was only after the California Attorney General's office launched an investigation—eventually leading to the resignation of the CEO of what was, at the time, the nation's wealthiest operating foundation—that the board took any action (Lipman, 2006).

What Is Transparency?

In the context of nonprofit management, *transparency* refers to the degree to which information necessary for stakeholders to make judgments about the nonprofit organization is reasonably accessible.

"With the advent of social media, the sort of information that once would have gotten little press attention even if it were disclosed now gets circulated and discussed widely in what seems like nanoseconds," wrote the late Rick Cohen (2014) in *Nonprofit Quarterly*. "Without expanded disclosure, nonprofits don't get to tell their full stories, denying the public a true understanding of the multiple issues involved in their work."

Many nonprofit leaders resist transparency, seeing it as the enemy. Besides simply deciding that it is the ethical thing to do, there are clear tangible benefits, beyond engendering public trust, illustrated by a story conveyed by Bob Carlson, an Assistant Attorney General in Missouri, who coordinates state oversight of nonprofits. "An organization that tries to follow the best practices of transparency can prevent government investigations," he writes. "On more than one occasion, when I received a nasty complaint about a Missouri charity, I have decided that the allegation might be true. But upon doing a preliminary review online, I found that the nonprofits in question were so transparent that I could verify that the complainers had it wrong, all without leaving my desk. Those nonprofits have no clue how close they came to large and embarrassing investigations" (Carlson, 2011).

What Should and Should Not Be Transparent

Transparency encompasses the accessibility of information relating to audited federal tax returns, IRS determination letters, the names of board members and staff, how donations are being used in support of the organization's mission, minutes of board meetings, public access to board meetings, grant information, budgets, outcome measures, service fee policies, policies about anti-discrimination relating to staff and clients, responding to inquiries from the media, information about loans to officers and staff, and having a website that provides accurate information about the organization (including contact information). Transparent organizations will seek feedback from the public and provide them with convenient ways to offer feedback via telephone, fax, email, and web-based feedback forms. Employees with a grievance are provided with a clear, written policy specifying their rights and procedures of the organization. Board members should have access to all relevant documents and other information they need to do their job, granted by either the board chair or management.

Of course, there are some valid reasons (some of which are legal limitations) to maintain confidentiality and privacy of certain information, such as personnel records, staff performance reviews, salary information, records of clients, and certain donor information. As pointed out by Chen (2010), transparency is not a "one-size-fits-all equation," but should be "guided by an organization's mission, catered to its supporters, and potential supporters, and considerate of the organization's needs, policies, and legal issues."

An example of an organization that takes transparency seriously is the Indianapolis Museum of Art *(http://dashboard.imamuseum .org/).* A visit to its website provides 11 past years of tax returns, 10 annual reports, its mission statement, 10-year strategic plan, the names of its board members and staff, contact information, and even a video of its 2016 annual meeting.

What Is Accountability?

Accountability refers to the degree to which stakeholders and the organization itself take actions to assure that the organization is meeting its legal and ethical obligations and fulfilling its duty to operate in a manner consistent with its stated mission and objectives. As explained by the late Woods Bowman, accountability means acting responsibly and having to answer for the consequences when they do not (Bowman, 2012).

Charity Navigator (n.d.) defines accountability as "an obligation or willingness by a charity to explain its actions to its stakeholders." Accountability in the context of managing and governing nonprofit organizations can be interpreted much more broadly than that. Transparency implies the degree to which an organization is making information public, but that only relates to the communication of factual data in a manner that permits the target of these communications to make judgments and take action. My definition of accountability is that organizations have a mechanism and policies for acting in a responsible manner with complete integrity. They diligently make the best possible efforts to achieve their missions and goals in the most efficient and fair manner that makes the public interest paramount to any private interest. Accountable organizations responsibly address any shortcomings if and when the organization engages in any illegal or unethical practices or fails to achieve reasonable outcomes for its programs.

Accountability includes, among other aspects—

- providing information about evaluations
- publicizing data on how well the organization is accomplishing its mission
- having and enforcing policies that all funds granted or donated to the organization are used solely for the purposes for which they were provided and not diverted for other purposes or expended for private benefit
- ensuring that all decisions are made independently without unreasonable influence by individuals who might have some private interest, financial or otherwise (such as by enforcement of conflict of interest policies)

- seeking input from stakeholders and considering that input before making decisions that affect them
- honoring the legal requirements of duty of loyalty, duty of care, and duty of obedience by sanctioning violators.

Accountability can include internal actions taken by the organization, such as evaluation of how well it is accomplishing its goals by collecting and disseminating outcomes data or by conducting an annual performance review of the executive director. It may include external actions, such as regulators shutting down the organization if it fails to comply with laws and regulations or, as was the case with the Hershey Trust (see pages 79-80), demanding a restructuring and change of culture of its board.

A 1995 statement approved by the Association of Fundraising Professionals (AFP) recognizes that a nonprofit organization has an obligation "to show it is accountable to donors, the people it serves, and the general public." The full statement, which can be found at *http://www.afpnet.org/Ethics/EnforcementDetail.cfm,* provides that "(T)he accountable organization clearly states its mission and purpose, articulates the needs of those being served, explains how its programs work, how much they cost and what benefits they produce."

Accountability Strategies

Examples of accountability strategies include—

- enforcing conflict of interest laws and organization ethics policies
- having a strong whistleblower policy
- complying with the *Sarbanes-Oxley Act* relating to the retention and destruction of records
- honoring limitations enforced by the IRS on compensation
- promulgating, publicizing, and enforcing privacy policies
- conducting annual external financial audits
- evaluations and performance assessments—particularly of the executive director
- membership in organizations that accredit the organization based on transparency and accountability standards (see Chapter 11)
- adopting sector ethics code provisions (see Chapter 10)—with enforcement provisions that sanction those in violation.

In addition, organizations can hire professionals who are loyal to codes of ethics that apply to their profession, such as social workers, attorneys, medical professionals, and fundraisers.

Some nonprofit organizations use public participation as a tool to foster accountability. This might entail publicly disclosing information about planned future activities, scheduling public meetings or hearings, and fostering public involvement in the actual planning process of future activities (Ebrahim, HBS, 2010).

Alnoor Ebrahim (2010) provides a 4-part typology of the components of accountability:

1. *transparency*—collecting data and making them accessible
2. *answerability or justification*—providing clear reasoning for actions and decision
3. *compliance*—monitoring and evaluating procedures and outcomes
4. *enforcement or sanctions*—actions that compel improvements in performance of the other three components

Boards of nonprofit organizations are not true owners of the assets, but rather are deputized to act in trust for that public purpose consistent with their stated missions and are expected to act in the public interest.

Relationship of Transparency to Accountability

Transparency and accountability are two sides of the same "integrity" coin. In fact, many of the academic definitions of accountability incorporate transparency as a salient principle. Without having information available as a first step, stakeholders would be unable to act responsibly and meet their mission obligations. Both are needed to honor the principle that charitable organizations are given special benefits, particularly exemption from federal income taxes and tax deductibility of contributions made by donors, in recognition that they fulfill a public purpose that government is unwilling or unable to fulfill (Grobman, 2015).

For example, disclosing on a website that a board member recused herself from voting on a plan for the organization to hire her public relations firm or that this public relations firm was awarded the contract by the board (rather than not making this public at all) would be an example of transparency. Removing her from the board as a condition of accepting the contract, or requiring that the proposal be offered to the public using an RFP process instead of giving an insider sole access to the business, would be an example of accountability. Even if this situation is completely disclosed (transparency), that has little value unless action is taken that mitigates any damage done to the public. So, simply disclosing a conflict of interest by a board member in benefiting from a board decision by itself does not address the ethical problem—if the end result is that the board member has an unfair advantage over competitors who do not serve on the board.

Transparency and Accountability Promote Trust

Unlike their for-profit counterparts, nonprofit organizations typically rely on the donations of others who do not directly benefit by the services provided by the organization. Thus, there must be a higher level of trust that their donations and public support are being earned by the organization. Few donors, if any, can or do pay much attention to the inner workings of the charities they support. Unless there is a scandal, donors tend to be focused on whether they see results of their donations. A comprehensive website that proactively answers likely questions from stakeholders and the public is a signal that the organization has nothing to hide. Thus, transparency and accountability efforts militate against organization scandals that are often an existential threat to nonprofit organizations.

There are legal and ethical requirements for both transparency and accountability. At the federal level, *The Taxpayer Bill of Rights II* (see page 42) requires all organizations to make their federal 990 tax returns public. The long form of the 990 provides for significant disclosure. Among aspects of the organization that must be reported on this form are the organization's mission and significant activities; the number of employees and volunteers; its total unrelated business income; lobbying expenses; its revenue from contributions, grants, and programs; the names and compensation provided to its top five compensated employees and to other "key" paid employees (those paid more than $150,000); and a list of its officers, directors, and trustees. They are required to disclose information about significant diversions of their assets (see pages 89-90) and other financial information. Most states require charities to register first before soliciting for funds and annually disclose financial information, and there are procedures by which donors and others can access this information. For an example of one state, New York, that provides for online access, see *https://www.charitiesnys.com/RegistrySearch/search_charities.jsp*

Whisteblower Policies

One of the more provocative findings of the 2013 National Business Ethics Survey (Ethics Resource Center, 2014) is that 41% of workers surveyed reported that they had observed wrongdoing in their places of employment. Of the 63% who reported the misconduct that they witnessed, 21% disclosed that they endured retaliation of some kind, about the same as the previous survey (2011), but significantly more alarming compared to the 12% who reported retaliation in the 2007 survey. Many organizations, both for-profit and nonprofit, have included whistleblower policies in their employee handbooks to encourage employees to report wrongdoing internally—and presumably have ethical problems corrected without the damage of a public scandal. However, it is not clear that data indicate the effectiveness of such policies. And in one case, Aspira, Inc., a nonprofit charter school operator, was sued by a whistleblower *(http://www.philly.com/philly/education/ Fired-employee-files-whistle-blower-suit-against-Aspira-says-federal-probe-underway-. html)*, who claimed that she was terminated because she spoke about illegal accounting practices of the organization to the FBI and the U.S. Attorney's Office (Woodall, 2017).

Employees need to feel confident that any report they make about wrongdoing will be confidential, that there will never be retaliation against them for reports made in good faith, and that there is a way to report wrongdoing of superiors. For a sample whistleblower policy, see *https://www.councilofnonprofits.org/tools-resources/whistleblower- protections-nonprofits*

Exit, Voice, and Loyalty. And...

A classic typology of Albert O. Hirschman (1970) provides the framework for three strategies nonprofit stakeholders utilize when they wish to make a nonprofit organization accountable:

1. *Exit.* They can physically or emotionally leave the organization. Although this sends a message to stakeholders, it often results in the organization continuing with its deficiencies.
2. *Voice.* They can complain, pointing out whatever deficiencies they perceive in the organization. Many who go this route take the risk that their communication will result in retaliation.

3. *Loyalty.* In the context of the nonprofit sector, this might entail simply "going along," recognizing that the costs of exit or voice are not worth the benefits.

In many cases of nonprofit organization misconduct, none of these three alternatives is satisfactory. Exit involves costs of finding a new job and moving away, and the voice option may not be effective unless that voice is amplified by like-minded staff members willing to share the risk of retaliation. The physical and emotional costs of loyalty may be unsustainable.

To these three, I would add a fourth strategy: *resistance.* For internal stakeholders, this might entail being an anonymous whistleblower to the media, creating an anonymous social media website to provide "alternative" information, anonymously communicating with members of the board who may not know about unethical behavior in the organization, or anonymously communicating with law enforcement authorities. Note that the 2002 Sarbanes-Oxley *Act* (see pages 115-116) provides whistleblower protection only to those who communicate with law enforcement authorities.

For external stakeholders, resistance might entail creating a competing organization, organizing protests to focus public attention on the situation, writing Op-Ed articles and letters-to-the-editor, or communicating anonymously with board members.

A donor (as well as other stakeholders) may not see firsthand whether the organization is delivering on its promises and needs to make a judgment as to whether to continue support based on information provided by the organization. This compares to the for-profit sector, whereby the public is likely to purchase a service or product and have the ability to immediate judge whether that service or product is worthwhile—and decide whether or not to make future purchases or find another supplier in the marketplace. In contrast, many nonprofit organizations have a de facto monopoly on providing a particular service in any community, and there are barriers to entry for competitors. Many of the clients served by nonprofits are individuals who are unable to find services in the marketplace and are often members of vulnerable groups.

The Montana Nonprofit Association asserts that nonprofits have "a responsibility to establish, achieve, and regularly measure clearly defined levels of performance in their activities and to share those results with the public" (Montana Nonprofit Association, n.d.). Outcome-based management (see below) is one strategy to comply with this responsibility.

Outcome-Based Management

For many larger nonprofits, particularly those that depend on government and foundation grants rather than private donations, the objective of "meeting clients' needs" has become a more formalized process as a strategy to promote accountability. Traditionally, measures of organizational performance for human service organizations were based on a model more appropriate for industrial processes, in which raw materials were turned into finished products. In the language of industrial systems analysis, inputs (the raw material) were processed into outputs (the finished product). In adopting an analogous frame of reference to industry, the conventional thinking was that human service agencies took in unserved clients (input), provided services (process), and changed them into served clients (output). In this way of thinking, organizations improved their output by increasing the number of clients served (Grobman, 1999).

Outcome-based management (OBM) or "results-oriented accountability" (ROA) is a change to this dated paradigm. Results-oriented management and accountability (ROMA) has become the buzzword describing this general tool. OBM focuses on program outcomes rather than simply quantifying services delivered. Program outcomes can be defined as "benefits or changes for participants during or after their involvement with a program" *(from Measuring Program Outcomes: A Practical Approach, United Way of America).*

For example, an organization dedicated to treating people with substance use disorders may have a stellar record of attracting patients through a flashy outreach program. It may be exemplary in convincing doctors in the community to donate thousands of hours of free services to the program, thereby reducing unit costs per patient. It may have few complaints from the patients, who feel the staff are competent and treat them with dignity. An analysis of conventional data might indicate that there is little room for improvement. But, perhaps, no data are collected on whether those treated for substance use disorder by the organization have become independent, avoided interactions with the criminal justice system, and have remained drug-free for an extended period of time—all measurable outcomes for a successful substance use disorder program. If most of the treatment patients were still drug dependent, is that organization providing successful treatment, even if services are being provided? Are funders and taxpayers getting a fair return on their investment?

In the outcome-based management model, the number of patients served is an input. The output is considered to be measurements concerning the change in the condition of the patients after receiving the services. For example, if thousands of patients are served, but the conditions of the patients have not improved, then the outcome is zero, even if the services were provided 100% on time, every patient received a satisfactory number of hours of services, and there were no patient complaints.

It is no longer indicative of the effectiveness and value of an organization to only collect data on how many people sought services, how many were accepted into the program rather than being referred or turned down, how many hours of service were provided, and how much each service cost and was reimbursed. Outcome data together with the above process data are needed to measure the effectiveness and value of an organization. In this way, the organization becomes accountable.

What makes outcome-based management an easy sell to stakeholders is that it is common sense. What is the point of investing thousands, if not millions, of dollars of an agency's resources if the end result is not accomplishing what is intended by the investment—improving the lives of the organization's service users? OBM helps organizations focus on doing what it takes to make people's lives better compared to simply providing services.

In cases in which the data show that an agency is successfully providing services, but those services are not having the intended effect on the clients, then the agency leadership should be the first to recognize that it is wasteful to keep doing business as usual. Outcome-based management is a powerful tool to allow nonprofit organizations to allocate their precious resources to do the most good. If successfully implemented, it can also provide the ammunition to fight the increasing public cynicism about what is often perceived to be a poor return on investment of tax dollars, and increase public accountability. Nonprofit organization funders are increasingly requiring their grantees to adopt it in some form.

Watchdog Groups

Cooperating with watchdog organizations that create sector standards and maintain portals to disseminate information is another strategy utilized by nonprofit organizations to signal to their stakeholders that they are willing to be transparent and accountable. One example is the Standards for Excellence program (see pages 124-125). In addition, there are organizations that collect data on nonprofits for the purpose of sharing it with potential donors and other stakeholders. There are two highly credible charity watchdog organizations, GuideStar and Charity Navigator, that collect and disseminate data on thousands of charities, providing a service to donors and charities alike. Neither has any direct financial relationship with the charities being evaluated. For the most part, the data is self-reported by the charities and both of these organizations have differentiated from its competitor by evolving over the years. Staff and boards of ethical charities routinely look at how these organizations rate their charity, and take steps to address any shortcomings that are identified. Both have their strengths and weaknesses.

GuideStar, founded in 1994 and by far the most comprehensive database of the two, boasts that it provides free access to reports on more than 2.5 million tax-exempt nonprofits, including thousands of faith-based nonprofits that are not required to register with the IRS. Registration is free, although some services are fee-based. This site is the best place to find annual 990 federal tax returns. It has a reputation of being less judgmental than Charity Navigator, allowing consumers to interpret the data without much of a filter.

Charity Navigator was founded in 2001, and claims on its website to be the most utilized charity evaluator. Its database has data on about 8,500 charities. In contrast to GuideStar, Charity Navigator tries to evaluate the efficiency of each charity, assigning star ratings on a 0-4 scale, based on financial data. Only the largest charities are included in the database. In recent years, the evaluations have been expanded to include factors that relate to transparency, outcomes, ethics, and management practices. Data can be accessed without any registration.

Conclusion

The ARNOVA story related at the beginning of this chapter has a marginally happy ending for the organization. The embezzler plea-bargained and pleaded guilty to two felonies. He served 180 days of his 4-year prison sentence, and the remainder was suspended. The court ordered him to make restitution to the organization and its insurance company—although court records show that he paid only a fraction of what was ordered, likely the result of a personal bankruptcy. My recent Google search did not find him working happily for another nonprofit organization, putting it at risk. Justice was served, and who knows how many other organizations were spared because of the willingness of ARNOVA's board and staff to report the crime and not cover it up, rather than simply firing the perpetrator. Transparency and accountability are, at the end of the day, in the best interests of not only the public and the nonprofit sector in general, but the organization's stakeholders.

Online Resources

Introduction to Outcome-Based Management
http://www.socialworker.com/nonprofit/management/improving-quality-chapter-5/

Montana Nonprofit Association's Principles and Practices for Nonprofit Excellence in Montana: Principle of Accountability & Transparency
http://www.mtnonprofit.org/PPNE_Accountability/

United Way Accountability Standards
http://independentsector.org/resource/accountability/

National Council of Nonprofits Transparency Standards
https://www.councilofnonprofits.org/tools-resources/financial-transparency

National Council of Nonprofits Dashboards for Nonprofits
https://www.councilofnonprofits.org/tools-resources/dashboards-nonprofits

Discussion Questions

1. Do you think it is appropriate to list the names of a nonprofit organization's board members on its website? What about their affiliations and other contact information, such as email addresses?

2. Discuss whether having a high degree of organizational transparency makes it more or less likely that the organization's shortcomings will be more visible and subject to public scrutiny.

3. Discuss the limitations of the *Sarbanes-Oxley Act* with respect to whistleblowing, and whether the nonprofit sector's leadership should advocate for changes in that law.

Activities

1. Formulate a list of 10 prominent local charities and create a catalog of the types of information on their websites that relate to transparency and accountability.

2. Research cease and desist orders against charities issued by your state's office that regulates charitable solicitation (if it has one), and see if there are any patterns with respect to the transgressions for which these charities were accused.

3. Identify five local nonprofit organization scandals that you can find from media reports and the Web, and research (through the media or police records and other available resources) what happened to the accused perpetrator with respect to the initial charges, whether any plea-bargaining was involved in the case, the sentence (if convicted), whether restitution was made, and whether the accused, when/if released was still working in the sector at any point following that conviction.

References

Bowman, W. (2012, October 26). Nonprofit accountability and ethics: Rotting from the head down. *Nonprofit Quarterly*. Retrieved from *https://www.nonprofitquarterly. org/2012/10/26/nonprofit-accountability-and-ethics-rotting-from-the-head-down/*

Carlson, B. (2011, March 4). Transparency can keep a nonprofit out of trouble. *The Chronicle of Philanthropy*. Retrieved from: *http://www.philanthropy.com/article/Transparency-Can-Keep-a/227803*

Charity Navigator. (n.d.). How do we rate charities' accountability and transparency? Retrieved from: *https://www.charitynavigator.org/index.cfm?bay=content.view&cpid=1093*

Chen, E. (2010, August 23). Finding the right transparency. Nonprofit law blog.com. Retrieved from *http://www.nonprofitlawblog.com/finding-the-right-transparency*

Ebrahim, A. (2010). The many faces of nonprofit accountability. Draft working paper, Boston, MA: Harvard Business School.

Ethics Resource Center. (2014). Retrieved online from *https://www.ibe.org.uk/userassets/surveys/nbes2013.pdf*

Grobman, G. (2015). *The nonprofit handbook*. Harrisburg, PA: White Hat Communications.

Grobman, G. (1999). *Improving quality and performance in your non-profit organization*. Harrisburg, PA: White Hat Communications.

Hirschman, A. (1970). *Exit, voice, and loyalty: Responses to decline in firms, organizations, and states*. Cambridge, MA: Harvard University Press.

Lipman, H. (2006, February 23). Embattled chief of Getty Trust resigns amid state inquiry. *The Chronicle of Philanthropy*. Retrieved from *http://www.philanthropy.com/article/Embattled-Chief-of-Getty-Trust/171661*

Montana Nonprofit Association. (n.d.). Principle: Accountability and transparency. Retrieved from *http://www.mtnonprofit.org/PPNE_Accountability/*

Woodall, M. (2017, February 9). Fired employee files whistle-blower suit against Aspira, says federal probe underway. *Philly.com*. Retrieved from: *http://www.philly.com/philly/education/Fired-employee-files-whistle-blower-suit-against-Aspira-says-federal-probe-underway-.html*

Chapter 4
Lying and Deception

"Everybody lies."

Fans of the hit television series that ran for eight seasons will recognize this as the mantra of the fictional Princeton Plainsboro Teaching Hospital's misanthropic medical detective, Gregory House, M.D. In many episodes, House would often explain how he was able to make a diagnosis of a patient that eluded every other reasonable explanation by assuming that the patient must be lying about something, because the truth was simply too embarrassing to reveal.

In the context of nonprofit management, even as trust in the nonprofit, government, and private sectors appears to be eroding over time, it is fortunate that lying and deception geared to criminal activity are more the exception than the rule. Perhaps one reason is that many are attracted to the sector particularly because they are altruistic, ethical, and want to work in the public interest. Even as trends suggest a convergence of the three sectors (see Grobman, 2015), polls suggest that the majority of Americans continue to have high confidence in the integrity of America's nonprofits (*The Chronicle of Philanthropy,* 2015), even as high profile scandals within the sector continue to make headlines. In the latest (2015) poll on this issue, conducted by Princeton Survey Research Associates International, 62% of respondents said they had a great deal or a fair amount of confidence in charities compared to 64 percent in the 2008 poll.

"Fifteen percent of those surveyed said they had a 'great deal' of confidence in charitable organizations over all, with 21 percent saying that about charities in their own communities," according to an article in *The Chronicle of Philanthropy,* the sponsor of the survey. This contrasts to a June 2016 Gallup Poll that found less impressive support for other institutions, including Congress (3%), Big Business (6%), newspapers (8%), banks (11%), public schools (14%), and organized labor (8%). According to Gallup (2016), the top scorers in their survey on this question were the military (41%) and small business (30%).

Theological Basis for the Immorality of Lying

The ancients placed a high premium on telling the truth, and both the New and Old Testaments command followers to not lie (see: Leviticus 19:11, Exodus 20:16, Colossians 3:9, and Ephesians 4:24-25). The ninth of the 10 Commandments addresses this directly: "You shall not bear false witness against your neighbor."

A *Washington Post* Fact Checker article gave Ben Carson four Pinocchios for his claim during the 2016 presidential campaign that the Quran encourages Muslims to lie (Kessler, 2015).

Other major religions also expressly address the immorality of lying. The Fourth Buddhist precept, Musavada veramani sikkhapadam samadiyami, means "I undertake the precept to refrain from incorrect speech" (OBrien, 2016).

Hinduism also proscribes lying except under limited circumstances (see *https://hinduism.stackexchange.com/questions/3848/in-hinduism-what-exactly-is-a-lie-and-is-lying-adharma*).

Economic Man

All of the world's major religions are in agreement that lying is wrong under most circumstances. Yet, lying occurs even among the most highly religious, and there is a secular explanation.

Much of the value of our knowledge of theory in the fields of economics, in addition to psychology and other social science theory, is in predicting human behavior. The "why" of human behavior has been a topic of interest for centuries. There are numerous writings about how humans should behave, referred to in Chapter 1. Certainly, religion has played a role in developing a system of principles—some universal, some not—that were intended to govern the "how." A more recent phenomenon is that scientists and philosophers have turned their thoughts and studies to why we behave as we do, other than the often less satisfactory explanation that was available several millennia ago that "because God (or the equivalent of God) said so." One enduring explanation of human behavior is that humans—at least rational humans—act in a way to maximize their self-interest, an observation that some trace to Adam Smith in *The Wealth of Nations:* "It is not from the benevolence of the butcher, the brewer, or the baker that we expect our dinner, but from their regard to their own self interest" (Smith, 2007, p.27).

Of course, this model is much less satisfactory in explaining human behavior with respect to the nonprofit sector than its for-profit counterpart. However, it does serve as a rough approximation to explain why those in the nonprofit sector lie or otherwise deceive.

Leaders of nonprofit organizations often face situations in which it may be of personal benefit, or benefit to their organizations, to lie, exaggerate, obfuscate, prevaricate, distort the fact, misstate, speak disingenuously, or otherwise engage in a purposeful effort to communicate in a way intended to deceive. Among the reasons include—

"To avoid pain or unpleasant consequences; promote self-interest and a particular point of view; protect leaders of the organization; and to perpetuate myths that hold the organization or a point of view together." (Belton, 2005)

In my experience, there are several reasons nonprofit leaders lie or deceive, even when they are otherwise honest.

They need to escape the consequences of being accountable. Even when someone has made a good-faith effort to take actions that have the highest probability of success, an outcome may be negative and/or be embarrassing to the organization. Some organizations have a culture that recognizes that unforeseen or uncontrollable circumstances influence outcomes. They seek to hire decision-makers who make decisions under conditions of uncertainty. There is often an element of risk that a decision will, with hindsight, be the wrong one. Some boards recognize this; others do not. Some chief executive officers (CEOs) recognize this; others do not. A particular staff member may make a reasonable decision based on incomplete information and circumstances beyond his or her control resulting in an unfavorable outcome. Even in that case, that person is vulnerable to disciplinary action, including the possibility of being fired. Moreover, it is not unusual for someone within the organization to be scapegoated for the consequences of a decision in which he or she has had minimal influence, to help others within the organization escape accountability and retain power. At every stage of an internal or external investigation by stakeholders into what occurred resulting in harm to the organization, there may be an incentive for lying to occur. The likelihood of such lying is magnified when the organization has a history of punishing those in the organization who make mistakes, particularly those made with the intent of being in the interest of the organization rather than just in the self-interest of an individual.

They want to influence the outcome of some negotiation. A major part of the job of anyone associated with a nonprofit organization is competing for resources, both with those within the organization and those outside. It is natural to "spin" one's pitch to cast the best light on their ability to accomplish some task; to meet a deadline; to demonstrate they have sufficient influence to motivate others to act for a common purpose; or, as in the case of fundraising, to do whatever might be necessary to manipulate a donor to give more money than she might otherwise give. And it almost goes without saying that many lies would never be told if the person lying expected that the lie would be uncovered and consequences would follow. Telling a lie may never have any consequences, particularly if substantial time has occurred between the telling of the lie and when it is clear to the person receiving the message that a lie was involved. The lie may not be remembered in such a case, and there may not be enough evidence that the lie was intended rather than that circumstances have simply changed.

They want to escape embarrassment. It is natural that most of us feel very uncomfortable admitting mistakes, even in cases when there are no likely adverse consequences. One solution I adopted years ago to mitigate my own reluctance to disclose mistakes was a protocol of communication whenever I made a mistake that disadvantaged a stakeholder. I write an email or letter to the person offended by my transgression that starts, "Oops, I goofed." The communication describes the circumstances of the mistake, includes an apology, and when appropriate, states what I am proposing as a remedy. Almost every time, the recipient of the communication appreciates the honesty and accepts the apology and remedy. And almost every time, I feel better about it, rather than spending valuable time worrying about what I should do about the situation.

Many times, the person who engages in lying is an otherwise honest person but feels, correctly or not, that the benefits of telling the lie outweigh the costs of telling the truth. If one accepts the teleological approach described on page 23, lying is justifiable if it serves the greater good. But, quite often, the benefits of lying are accrued in the short term, and the costs—such as the loss of trust after being found out—accrue in the long term.

Lying in the Nonprofit Sector Violates the Public Trust

Those who govern and manage nonprofit organizations, as with elected and appointed government officials, are placed in a position of trust to deal with public resources. Unlike their for-profit counterparts, they have an obligation to make decisions that are, at a minimum, in the best interest of their organizations (duty of loyalty) rather than in their own personal interest. For-profit leaders certainly can agree that not telling the truth, of course, can have consequences for the public. But, in theory, the market provides an alternative when the public loses trust in a for-profit organization—customers take their business somewhere else, and the for-profit organization may go out of business as a result. The financial consequences accrue to the business owner. This is not the case in either government or the nonprofit sector.

We know from reading the newspapers that lying occurs in all three sectors. In the nonprofit sector, fundraisers may lie to potential donors about how much of the funds they raise are allocated directly toward the mission of the organization compared to the fundraiser. John Bennett, the architect of the New Era Philanthropy Ponzi scheme of the 1980s, crafted a successful lie that convinced many sophisticated and wealthy nonprofit organizations to park large sums of money with him, with the promise he would double their money in a short period of time. Nonprofit CEOs accused of sexually harassing a staff member or embezzling organization funds when that accusation is true would be expected to initially lie about the situation. And when a staff member is fired for misconduct, it is not unusual for the organization's CEO to lie about the reasons, when asked, even when doing so enhances the likelihood the employee will be hired by another organization and engage in the same conduct. A CEO may justify this by judging that the truth may put his organization at risk of a wrongful termination suit, or there may be an agreement between the employee and the organization to not disclose the real reasons for separation, to avoid mutual embarrassment.

Lying is universally considered to be unethical, although it is often tolerated, and in some cases applauded, when the consequences of telling the truth may result in harm compared to lying. How one looks at this is influenced by the ethical approach. A deontological approach suggests that lying is almost always wrong. A teleological approach suggests that lying may be justified when the consequences of telling the truth may be dire. A strict deontological approach (such as that taken by Immanuel Kant (see page 23) suggests that lying for *any* reason is morally wrong.

Tim Muzur (2015) makes the case for telling the truth:

First, lying corrupts the most important quality of my being human: my ability to make free, rational choices. Each lie I tell contradicts the part of me that gives me moral worth. Second, my lie robs others of the freedom to choose rationally. When my lie leads people to decide other than they would have had they known the truth, I have harmed their human dignity and autonomy.

This justification is buttressed by a view of one theologian who adds that telling the truth is not only the right thing to do morally, but contributes to the breakdown in society when not observed:

Truthtelling is essential for authentic communication to occur, and makes genuine interaction between people possible. That is, if truth were not expected, it would not be long before communication would entirely break down. Imagine what it would be like living in a society in which no one expected the truth. How could a person discern what is accurate and what is a falsehood? On what basis could a person make important decisions if there was no expectation of the truth? Life would be chaotic without the norm of honesty (Rae, 2012).

One problem with the teleological approach is that the consequences of lying might be of significant benefit to the person lying (or the organization for which the person is lying), and significant costs to the person being told the lie.

And it makes a difference to some when lying is conducted to benefit the good of the organization and its mission compared to benefitting the individual at the cost of the organization. An ethical dilemma occurs when a nonprofit organization stakeholder faces two competing principles—maintaining loyalty to the organization by lying on its behalf and violating his or her own personal beliefs against lying.

The White Lie

A *white lie* refers to a communication that is known by the communicator to be false, but which is intended to serve a benign purpose. It is quite difficult to function socially in either one's personal or organizational life without telling an occasional white lie to avoid what would otherwise result in a toxic situation. In the nonprofit workplace, telling white lies may be justified as morally acceptable to avoid hurting the feelings of coworkers, donors, or organizational leadership.

Imagine you are the CEO of a charity, and a board member responsible for funding a large percentage of your budget asks you directly about whether you think he is a wonderful person when you (and perhaps every other member of your board) know he is abusive. Providing a truthful answer to such a question, most of us would agree, would be detrimental to your retaining your position. A strict Kantian (see page 23) would tell the truth. I would not expect there are many such individuals successfully running nonprofit organizations.

Deception in Organizations in General

Lying is a form of deception, but not all deception involves lying. Pretending to work without doing so is one example. Appearing to take credit for the work of others without explicitly lying about it is another.

Deceptions in the workplace "are pervasive, and some are actually helpful in carrying out the day's work" (Shulman, 2008). Among the most common examples of deception are deflecting criticism from oneself, shirking work responsibility by either simply avoiding it or finding ways to have others do it, taking a sick day when one is not really sick, and taking actions to curry favor with managers for the purpose of obtaining favorable treatment over one's peers (also referred to as brown-nosing or sucking up).

I find it interesting that there are entire professions that employ deception, either in their entirety or in part. Depending on the context, most would not find this to be immoral. For example, government spies and undercover law enforcement officers routinely take part in elaborate deceptions. Those competing in sports are applauded for their successful deceptions, such as baseball players who pull off a successful hidden ball play. Some take the view that deception in business is quite acceptable under certain circumstances (see Rae, 2012 for an example of a for-profit business founder, Phillippe Kahn, who built a successful business as a result of a clever deception).

And is it lying when a nonprofit executive, trying to haggle over a salary offer to a prospective hire, suggests that "$50,000 is my last and final offer," knowing that if it is rejected, she may indeed make a higher offer? Bluffing is a term that describes one kind of deception, and there are clearly situations in which bluffing is an accepted strategy, that is not considered unethical, particularly when both parties find this to be an acceptable strategy of business negotiation.

Deception in Nonprofits in General

Some low-level deceptions in nonprofit organizations, such as diversion by the organization of money intended by a donor for one purpose to another, may be ethically justifiable using a teleological approach to ethics (see page 23). It is criminal deception, however, that finds its way onto our newspaper front pages and stains the reputation of the sector, adding to public cynicism about the distribution of their donations. Some of the more prominent nonprofit sector scandals are noted in the introduction to this book. And for every one of these, there are perhaps hundreds of cases that do not rise to the level of a national scandal and may merit only a paragraph or two of local media coverage. Of course, there is no way to know how many cases of fraud, embezzlement, conflict of interest, bribery, and exploitation will never be uncovered because of insufficient regulation and enforcement by the government—or because those who might otherwise be willing to disclose criminal wrongdoing are intimidated by a continuing culture that often makes a whistleblower a victim.

Shulman (2008) collected data that indicate more deceptive behavior in nonprofits than their for-profit counterparts. Among his theories to explain this are—

- Nonprofit staff face more pressure to acquire financial resources.
- Nonprofits often utilize the services of volunteers, student interns, and short-term workers who serve in low-paying jobs and who are motivated by having the experience on their résumés rather than monetary reward.
- Nonprofits tend to be smaller than their for-profit counterparts, and thus have less bureaucracy with "more discretionary autonomy" that militates for less oversight and accountability.
- Nonprofit organizations tend to be "driven by a motivating righteous fervor," with the implication that deception is justifiable when it is designed to accomplish a particular public mission.

He developed a typology of nonprofit deception that includes the following:

- Showing favoritism
- Misleading donors
- Withholding information from competitors
- Diverting financial resources to pet causes
- Having conflicts of interest
- Engaging in tax evasion
- Misrepresenting overhead compared to program spending
- Misreporting donation amounts

Note that many other areas of nonprofit organization deception can be found in the scenarios that begin on page 204.

Some Final Thoughts on Lying and Deception

Perhaps a decade ago, the philanthropic community began paying attention to scientific studies that sought to find a genetic explanation for altruism, or the lack thereof.

One German study (Reuther, et al., 2011) found some evidence of such a link, which would have some practical implications for fundraisers and created a stir at the time among the nonprofit sector research community. Perhaps there is a biological basis for lying and deception, as well. Nobel Prize-winning physicist Murray Gell-Mann, writing in his seminal book, *The Quark and the Jaguar* (1994), points out examples of animals engaging in deception to increase their chances of survival—the well-known mimicry of some species of insects, and the lesser known practice of some birds laying their eggs in the nests of other birds. Chameleons are known to change their color to deceive predators, blending into their surroundings.

"But actual lying?" he asks. He relates a story from a biologist friend of his who observed flocks of birds that had a sentinel species (animals that warn other animals of danger, such as from predators) flying symbiotically within the flock that would warn the other species, using a special call, that there was an approaching dangerous raptor. The biologist noticed that the sentinel birds occasionally gave a warning to the flock of an approaching predatory bird when there was no danger, and this occurred with about 15% of its bird calls. The biologist found that "the fake alarm often permitted the sentinel to grab a succulent morsel that another member of the flock might otherwise have eaten." One explanation for the 15% rate of "lying" is that if the rate was higher, the rest of the flock would not find the sentinel bird's lies credible, and if the rate was lower, then the deceptive bird's lying wouldn't be as productive.

What makes this story even more fascinating is the following anecdote Gell-Mann relates (p. 258-259) about one of his colleagues' reactions to his (Gell-Mann's) suggestion that the 15% figure was some basic mathematical constant, perhaps one divided by two pi (15.9%).

When I asked that question of Charles Bennett, he was reminded of something his father had told him about Royal Canadian Air Force units based in England during the Second World War. They found it useful, when sending out a fighter and a bomber together, to attempt occasionally to deceive the Luftwaffe by positioning the fighter below the bomber rather than above. After a good deal of trial and error, they ended up following that practice at random one time in seven (approximately one divided by two pi or 14.3%).

It may be a stretch to draw any firm conclusions from this story. But I would suggest that in cases in which economic man (or woman), following a teleological approach to ethics, might be willing to lie and deceive when the benefits to himself or herself exceed the costs, and there is a reasonable expectation that he/she will not be caught, and that the deception/lie will be credible, this approximate 15% threshold may be hard-wired genetically into our DNA!

And thus lying and deception may also be biologically hard-wired. Some of us are hard-wired to find these to be reprehensible, and others who lack this genetic makeup have a higher propensity to engage in these strategies to obtain some advantage.

Online Resources

The Fundraising Coach: Are you lying to your nonprofit board members?
https://fundraisingcoach.com/2015/01/27/stop-lying-nonprofit-board-recruitment/

Social Velocity's Not Fundraising: 5 Lies to Stop Telling Donors

http://www.socialvelocity.net/2011/10/financing-not-fundraising-5-lies-to-stop-telling-donors/

Discussion Questions

1. Do you think employees of nonprofit organizations are generally more honest and altruistic than their for-profit counterparts? Can any differences between those who choose these sectors be explained by genetic differences in individuals, by culture and upbringing, or a combination of both?

2. After examining the list of institutions included in the Gallup Poll on page 61, how might you expect the current political climate to influence the results of the next poll on this topic?

3. Discuss the hypothesis on page 65 that it would be difficult, if not impossible, for the typical nonprofit organization CEO to get through the workday without telling at least one white lie. What about other types of lies? When might such lies be justified?

Activities

1. Download and share with the class articles you can find in the general and academic press about the relationship of genetics and altruism.

2. Invite a business leader to class to speak about the use of deception in business negotiations and discuss when it is acceptable conduct and when it crosses the line to being unethical conduct.

3. Examine some of the data in the *Washington Post's* database on nonprofit organization asset diversions. Find examples in the database that you suspect are deceptive at best or not truthful at worst, and see if you can verify the information from independent sources.

References

Belton, E. (2005, December 21). Nonprofit truth or consequences: The organizational importance of honesty. *Nonprofit Quarterly.* Retrieved from *http://nonprofitquarterly. org/2005/12/21/nonprofit-organizational-importance-of-honesty*

Eaton, K. (2011, January 26). Is there an altruism gene? Greater Good in Action. Retrieved from *http://greatergood.berkeley.edu/article/item/is_there_an_altruism_gene/*

Gallup. (2016, June). *Confidence in institutions.* Retrieved from *http://www.gallup.com/poll/1597/Confidence-Institutions.aspx*

Gell-Mann, M. (1994). *The quark and the jaguar.* New York, NY: Freeman and Co.

Grobman, G. (2015). The future of the nonprofit sector, in *The Nonprofit Handbook,* G. Grobman; Harrisburg, PA: White Hat Communications.

Kessler, G. (2015, September 22). Ben Carson's claim that 'taqiyya' encourages Muslims 'to lie to achieve your goals.' Retrieved from *http://www.washingtonpost.com/amphtml/news/fact-checker/wp/2015/ben-carsons-claim-that-taqiyya-encourages-muslims-to-lie-to-achieve-your-goals/*

Mazur, T. (2015). Lying. Markkula Center for Applied Ethics. Retrieved from *https://www.scu.edu/ethics/ethics-resources/ethical-decision-making/lying/*

O-Brien, B. (2016). The fourth Buddhist precept. Retrieved from *https://www.thoughtco.com/the-fourth-buddhist-precept-450102*

Rae, S. (2012). Truth, honesty and deception in the workplace: Overview. Theology of Work Project. Retrieved from *http://www.theologyofwork.org/key-topics/truth-deception*

Reuter, M., Frenzel, C., Walter, N., Markett, S., & Montag, C. (2011). Investigating the genetic basis of altruism: The role of the COMT Val158Met polymorphism. *Social Cognitive and Affective Neuroscience, 6*(5): 662-668. Retrieved from *https://academic.oup.com/scan/article/6/5/662/1657142/Investigating-the-genetic-basis-of-altruism-the*

Shulman, D. (2008). More lies than meets the eyes: Organizational realities and deceptions in nonprofit organizations. *International Journal of Not-for-Profit Law, 10(2),* April 2008, pp. 5-14.

Smith, A. (2007). *The wealth of nations.* (An Electronic Classics Series Publication). Meta-libri. Retrieved from *http://www.ibiblio.org/ml/libri/s/SmithA_WealthNations_p.pdf*

The Chronicle of Philanthropy. (2015, October 5). Poll rates public confidence in charities, their programs, and spending. Author. Retrieved from *https://www.philanthropy.com/interactives/confidence*

Chapter 5
Ethics in Fundraising

The roots of our modern system of charitable organizations can be traced to religious writings that are thousands of years old (Levenson, et al., 2013). All of the major religious traditions recognize charity as a path to doing God's work, and both a secular and nonsecular tradition of asking for money and goods to serve the less fortunate remains a thriving and vibrant aspect of American culture. Some of this is attributed to the fact that government in many other Western nations played a much more direct role in meeting the needs of the sick, the poor, the aged, and the infirm. In contrast, the government's role in serving the needy has historically been more indirect in the United States (Grobman, 2015).

Government will, depending on the circumstances and the demand from voters for programs, fund human services, which are provided by nonprofit organizations. Government will avoid providing some services when there is no real voter consensus from the electorate, if they are controversial, but will subsidize private contributions through the tax system. Organizations that provide these services and meet certain accountability and reporting criteria are exempt from paying taxes, and donations to them may be deducted on the donor's federal individual income tax return. If an individual desires to solve some social problem or otherwise promote the public interest in some way, and is unable to convince government to do so, he or she has the option to create a tax-exempt organization, have a committee of like-minded individuals who support that mission to have independent governance and management of the organization, and make efforts to have members of the public provide financial support, subsidized by the government through the tax system (Grobman, 2015).

Individuals, corporations, and foundations donated approximately $390 billion to charities in 2016 (Sandoval, 2017). While it certainly is not unusual that a donor will spontaneously write a check to a nonprofit organization, the vast majority of charitable contributions are the result of solicitations by tax-exempt organizations to individuals, businesses, and foundations. As a result of a history of unethical and fraudulent fundraising, almost every state has enacted laws requiring those that solicit for charitable purposes to register and submit periodic reports about their financial activities. Only Delaware, Idaho, Indiana, Iowa, Montana, Nebraska, South Dakota, Texas, Vermont, and Wyoming do not require registration (Multi-State Filer Project, 2017). The federal government also has placed restrictions on charitable fundraising. It requires charities to document bona fide donations that are eligible for tax-exemptions. It requires reporting on their annual tax returns about the amount of professional fundraising fees, total fundraising expenses, information about very large contributors (using Schedule B) and detailed information about professional fundraising services (using Schedule G). And it limits the exemption and deduction to only those who submit applications and meet certain criteria (IRS, 2015).

In recent years, fundraising has become quite sophisticated. Technology has advanced so that there is much less face-to-face contact with donors. Fundraising has become a profession, with credentialing, training, university courses, and specialized software that makes solicitation more efficient (Grobman, 2015). Ethics codes have been advanced that address many of the issues that relate to fundraising (see Chapter 10). And despite all of this, there is a dark side, as well. High profile cases of fraud and mismanagement have made the public more cynical about whether their donations are really being funneled to charitable purposes. For example, a year-long investigation by CNN investigative reporter Drew Griffin found that 50 U.S. charities "devoted less than 4% of donations raised to direct cash aid. Some charities gave even less. Over a decade, one diabetes charity raised nearly $14 million and gave about $10,000 to patients. Six spent no cash at all on their cause" (Hundley & Taggart, 2013). *The Chicago Tribune* disclosed irregularities within the "Save the Children Federation" child sponsorship program, in which donors who contributed to support individual children were not informed that their sponsored child had died as many as five years before (Anderson, 1998).

Among the ethical issues that are of particular interest in fundraising are:

1. *Fundraisers should obey all laws, rules, and regulations.* The federal government has laws that apply to fundraising disclosure, substantiation, and record-keeping. Thirty-nine states and the District of Columbia require registration and reporting. Some local governments have restrictions relating to solicitation, such as times telephone solicitors may call, door-to-door solicitation, or canning on public streets, or on private property without permission from the owner. Organizations should honor "no solicitation" post-ings. Organizations should train their fundraising staff to know about and comply with these laws, and be scrupulous in insisting that violators will be subject to discipline, even if the intent of the fundraiser was a good-faith effort to benefit the organization. Organization staff members should be encouraged to report violations of law and or-ganization policies, and not look the other way when their colleagues engage in illegal or unethical activities that stain the reputation of the charitable sector in general and the organization in particular.

2. *Privacy and confidentiality must be protected.* Organizations must protect the identity of donors who provide a gift on condition that they remain anonymous. Donor information, including credit card information (see *http://en.wikipedia.org/wiki/Payment_Card_In-dustry_Data_Security_Standard* for information about Payment Card Industry Data Security Standard compliance), Social Security numbers, email addresses, and pros-pect research files must be protected and not disclosed to anyone without a legitimate need to know this information, unless the donor agrees. Donors should be afforded the option to opt out of having their address and/or email address shared with other nonprofit or commercial entities. Organizations that use the services of third-parties for fundraising, gift processing, data management, data analysis, and similar services that require the release of sensitive data outside of the organization must make it clear in their contracts that donor privacy and confidentiality will be protected.

3. *Organizations should meticulously honor gift restrictions of the donor.* From the organi-zation's perspective, it may make perfect sense for there to be some flexibility in how a donor's gift is used, even if it is not quite consistent with the stated purpose of the gift. However, it is unethical to divert the gift for purposes other than those expected by the donor without that donor's express permission. There is certainly nothing wrong with alerting donors about alternative or related uses of their donations when the organization believes it is in their best interest to do so. If the organization solicits donations that are intended to be for unrestricted purposes, that should be clear to donors. Because there is a cost to tracking, managing, and reporting restricted gifts, many organizations will have some minimal threshold in their gift acceptance policy

(see #4 below) that makes it clear small donations are put to use where they are most needed by the organization.

4. *Organizations should have a formal donation acceptance policy.* Organizations should have a written policy governing which gifts (both money and goods) will not be accepted, and the process used to adjudicate disputes. Gifts should not be accepted from those who have values at odds with the organization's gift policy. Included in this policy should be—

- provisions for dealing with contributions from those convicted of major crimes

- when the gift is unlikely to have any value to the organization

- when the donor places restrictions on the gift that are unacceptable (such as requiring it be used for illegal or unethical purposes)

- when the donor's intent is to exploit the brand of the charity to an extent that is unacceptable, and not in the best interests of the charity.

A sample gift policy may be found at:

https://www.gcfdn.org/Giving/Giving-with-GCF/Fund-Policies

5. *Fundraisers should not be compensated based on the amount they raise.* The fundraising profession's leadership has been virtually monolithic in its opposition to paying fundraisers based on the amount they raise, whether through finder's fees (paying a third party who receives a fee based on facilitating a donation, and who gets paid only if the donation is actually made), contingent fees, commissions, or percentage-based compensation (AFP, 2001). One reason is that doing so encourages fundraisers to engage in behavior designed to increase the size of the gift in the short term to the benefit of the fundraiser, even when such techniques are unethical, inappropriate, or otherwise not in the best interests of the organization. Another objection is that such compensation gives the impression that funds being donated for charitable purposes are directly being diverted to private gain *(see: http://www.afpnet.org/Ethics/EthicsArticleDetail.cfm?ItemNumber=734).* Note that bonuses based on fundraising performance are considered acceptable, if not based directly on the amount raised, but rather tied to meeting or exceeding performance goals—particularly when staff members other than fundraisers are also eligible for performance-based bonuses.

6. *Organizations must be transparent in disclosing costs that are related to their fundraising.* They should disclose upon request to prospective donors a good-faith estimate of the amount of their donation that is paying for fundraising. If this is not practical with respect to any particular individual transaction, then the estimate should be based on data for the most recent accounting period. They should be transparent about any use of third-party fundraising professionals. Note that many states require contracts between charities and professional fundraisers to be filed with state regulators, and some make this information publicly available. Also, organizations that spend more than $15,000 annually for professional fundraising services must disclose information about their relationships with these organizations on schedule G of their federal 990 annual tax return.

7. Donors should not have an inappropriate influence or receive inappropriate benefits from the organization in exchange for their donations. The principle behind qualifying for a tax exemption for donations is that the donor is making a gratuitous donation, and is not receiving anything of tangible value in exchange for the donation. But it is not unusual for donors to make unusual and inappropriate requests of the organization that violate this principle. Fundraising solicitations should not be tied to tangible benefits to a donor or potential donor that go beyond what is offered to the general public, with some reasonable exceptions related to reasonable donor recognition. For example, donors and potential donors should not be offered preferential services (e.g., having preferential admission to a college or health care facility) as a quid pro quo for their donations beyond what is permissible under IRS rules). The organization should not be requiring a charitable donation as a condition for receiving preferential treatment. It should be clear that payment in exchange for services is not eligible for tax benefits. One can even make a defensible argument that a donor who makes a sizeable donation as a quid pro quo for having his or her name on a building is not making a gratuitous donation that qualifies for a tax exemption, but rather is simply paying a fee for service in the same way that many corporations spend millions of dollars for naming rights to athletic stadiums and arenas (Drennan, 2012).

8. Organizations should resist undue influence of donors over the organization's programs and activities. It is not unusual for major donors to seek to play a role in influencing programs they fund. Sometimes this influence goes over the line, with the donors micromanaging the program they are funding, stretching the mission of the organization to their personal interests, and having the organization's staff respond to their own needs rather than those of the program's beneficiaries. Organizations should make it clear that donors have limitations on their ability to control the organization's policies and programs. One exception to this might be when the intent of the grant is to provide hands-on management by the grantor, such as what might be the case with some forms of so-called venture philanthropy (Blodget, 2006). If that is the case, then the organization should be clear as to the terms before agreeing to accept such a grant.

9. Fundraisers should have clear boundaries between themselves and donors. It is not unusual for personal friendships to develop between gift officers and donors. There are often opportunities to exploit this relationship in ways that benefit the fundraiser personally and that are unethical and inappropriate. For example, fundraisers should not permit such donors to include the fundraiser in their wills, accept valuable personal gifts, or engage in romantic relationships with their donors.

10. Prospect research must be conducted only for legitimate purposes. Prospect research is a legitimate activity of fundraisers to obtain accurate data about the capacity of a donor to give, their interests, and who from the organization might be the best person to solicit them. Yet, there are techniques that go over the line ethically. Sensitive personal information should not be sought, collected, and catalogued if it is motivated by seeking to have leverage on a donor in a way akin to blackmail or extortion. Fundraisers must not access databases for which they have no authorization or legitimate purpose, pose as others to access sensitive information about donors, or engage in computer hacking to access sensitive files. They should not make threats, overt or veiled, to encourage donors to make or increase donations that are influenced by a desire to keep sensitive information private.

11. *Organizations must be transparent with financial data.* They must meticulously provide breakdowns between program and fundraising costs consistent with accounting rules of regulators and grantors. They should disclose this data to both regulators and donors with good faith. Organizations should resist contracting with third-party fundraisers who will be compensated an unreasonable amount in proportion to their services, even if the organization appears to have some benefit (such as receiving a small amount of money in the arrangement compared to no money in the absence of an arrangement).

12. *Fundraisers should avoid harassment or undue pressure of those being solicited.* They must be completely respectful to the donor and sensitive to the donor's wishes with respect to the donation. They should be willing to terminate the solicitation when the prospect makes it reasonably clear that he or she desires that; to take "no" for an answer when it is reasonably apparent that the prospect does not wish to donate to the organization; and honor contact preference requests of those being solicited, including reduced frequency, contact through certain channels (e.g., do not call, but emailing is fine, or completely to opt out).

13. *Fundraisers should not exploit any decreased mental capacity of those they solicit for the purposes of obtaining or increasing a charitable gift.* They should not knowingly solicit those under 18 without permission from their parents or guardians, or those who are too ill or infirm to understand completely the consequences of their pledges and donations.

14. *All fundraising solicitation materials and communications should be honest, accurate, and up to date.* Solicitors should be willing to disclose the full and correct name and location of the charity for which they are soliciting, identify themselves and the organization that employs them if this is not the charity, explain the mission of the organization and the purpose funds raised will be utilized, say how the individual being solicited can access official financial information about the charity, and provide an opportunity to ask questions about the organization and receive honest answers.

15. *Fundraising costs should not be excessive.* Although the Supreme Court has ruled that statutory limits on fundraising costs are not enforceable, it is unethical for organizations to engage in solicitations whereby the amounts expended for fundraising costs are excessive. It is difficult to determine what reasonably constitutes "excessive," since factors such as the type of organization, its mission, and its lifecycle stage would influence this. There has been much debate over the years about the appropriate minimum threshold for the program costs/fundraising costs ratio. One industry minimum that seems to be a standard suggests that at least 65% of the nonprofit's three-year average annual expenses should be used to directly support programming (Charities Review Council, 2014). Clearly, what CNN found with respect to a veteran's startup "charity" was unethical (Fitzpatrick & Griffin, 2012).

16. *Online solicitations should provide both online and offline contact information for prospective donors.* Contact information should make clear the relationship between the organization, professional fundraisers hired by the organization, and third-party payment processors. It should be clear how much of any donation made by the contributor will be eligible for a tax deduction before a gift is made, if not all of the donation is funneled directly to the charity, but part of it is withheld by any third-party that is not a 501(c)(3) tax-exempt organization itself.

Online Resources

The Association of Fundraising Professionals Ethical Standards

http://www.imaginecanada.ca/sites/default/files/www/en/ethicalcode/ec_hand-book_2011_en.pdf

Canadian Code of Practice for Consumer Protection in Electronic Commerce

http://www.cmcweb.ca/epic/site/cmc-cmc.nsf/vwapj/EcommPrinciples2003_e.pdf/$FILE/EcommPrinciples2003_e.pdf

Activities

1. Research the CNN investigation of fundraising abuses that can be found at: *http://www.cnn.com/2013/06/13/us/worst-charities/index.html*. Then discuss what legislative and regulatory changes might be proposed at the state and federal levels to stop abuses.

2. Research the procedures for charities from outside of Washington, D.C., to comply with charitable solicitation registration laws and regulations of the District of Columbia. Then discuss whether charities are justified in refusing to register and follow these laws and regulations because they believe the requirements are too onerous, are not designed to protect the public from fundraising abuses, and the expense of registration may in some cases exceed the amounts they actually raise from solicitations in D.C.

Discussion Questions

1. The term "charity jacking" has been defined by Beth Kanter as "imitating a successful fundraising campaign theme or idea that has become popular and instead of encouraging donations to the original charity, redirecting donations to another cause" (Kanter, 2014). Discuss the conditions when charity jacking might be acceptable or when it might be unethical.

2. If donors are paying the costs of an entire program, why shouldn't they have the right to make all management decisions relating to that program?

3. If a donor is paying the cost for a new building and conditions the donation on having the building named after her, should she be eligible for a full tax deduction for the donation?

References

AFP. (2001). Position paper: Percentage-based compensation. Retrieved from: *http://www.afpnet.org/Ethics/EthicsArticleDetail.cfm?ItemNumber=734*

Anderson, L. (1998, March 18). Save The Children reacts to probe, plans reforms. *Chicago Tribune*. Retrieved from: *http://articles.chicagotribune.com/1998-03-18/news/9803220001_1_special-report-child-sponsorship-children-federation*

Blodget, H. (2006, November 13). Grant away: Why venture philanthropy is important, even if it sounds ridiculous. *Slate*. Retrieved from: *http://www.slate.com/articles/life/philanthropy/2006/11/grant_away.html*

Charities Review Council. (2014). Accountability Standards. Retrieved from: *http://www.smartgivers.org/wp-content/uploads/2016/12/Accountability-Standards-2014.pdf*

Drennan, W. (2012). Where generosity and pride abide: Charitable naming rights. *University of Cincinnati Law Review*, 80(1). Retrieved from: *https://scholarship.law.uc.edu/cgi/viewcontent.cgi?referer=https://www.bing.com/&httpsredir=1&article=1082&context=uclr*

Fitzpatrick, D., & Griggin, D. (2012). IRS forms show charity's money isn't going to disabled vets. Retrieved from: *http://www.cnn.com/2012/05/07/us/veterans-charity-fraud/index.html*

Grobman, G. (2015). *Introduction to the nonprofit sector (4th Edition)*. Harrisburg, PA: White Hat Communications.

Hundley, K., & Taggart, K. (2013). Above the law: America's worst charities. Retrieved from: *http://www.cnn.com/2013/06/13/us/worst-charities/index.html*

Internal Revenue Service (2015). Charities and nonprofits. Retrieved from: *http://www.irs.gov/Charities-&-Non-Profits*

Kanter, B. (2014 August 28). Has the ice-bucket challenge spawned charity jacking? Retrieved from: *http://www.bethkanter.org/icebucket-challenge3/*

Levenson, J., Rose, D., Cesari, J., & Berlin, C. (2013, December 12). Why give? Religious roots of charity. Retrieved from: *http://hds.harvard.edu/news/2013/12/13/why-give-religious-roots-charity#*

Multi-State Filer Project. (2017, June). The unified registration statement. Retrieved from: *http://www.multistatefiling.org/*

Sandoval, T. (2017, June 13). Donations grew 1.4% to $390 billion in 2016, says 'Giving USA.' *The Chronicle of Philanthropy*. Retrieved from *http://www.philanthropy.com/article/Donations-Grew-14-to-390/240319*

Chapter 6
Ethics in Governance

Allegations of outrageous conduct by the board of the Milton Hershey School Trust splashed across the front pages of many American newspapers in early 2011 (Associated Press, 2011). The picture painted by a disgruntled board member is viewed by many as perhaps the most egregious example of nonprofit board misconduct in recent American history. The Hershey School, a pre-K-12 boarding school with a 2015 endowment that approached $8 billion, was launched in 1909 as a result of the philanthropy of Milton Hershey, the founder of the Hershey Chocolate Company. For perhaps two full decades, the Internal Revenue Service and the Pennsylvania State Attorney General's Office knew of alleged irregularities perpetrated by the board, yet no action was taken. Occasional exposés by the press, particularly *The Philadelphia Inquirer*, chronicled alleged nonfeasance, malfeasance, and in some cases, simple corruption that resulted in board policies designed to personally benefit board members, almost all of whom were politically connected, and who had minimal or no background that would otherwise qualify them for service on the board. Local citizens who read only the local newspaper over the years, the *Harrisburg Patriot-News*, strangely did not read much about the school, other than glowing defenses. What could explain this? The publisher of the newspaper served on the Hershey School's board of directors (Eisenberg, 2011)!

Among the allegations against the board were that—

- Board members received six-figure incomes for service on the board, and did little, if any, work other than attending board meetings.

- The board voted to purchase a golf course partly owned by a board member for $12 million, four times its appraised value. Board members were allowed to golf there for free.

- The board authorized a $70 million unnecessary (according to the hotel's management) upgrade of the Hershey Hotel, where board members could stay for free.

- A trustee hosted a political fundraiser at a property owned by the Trust, and a subsidiary owned by the Trust catered the event without the political party committee having to pay anything.

- The Trust permitted individual retirement accounts into its common funds in a way that personally benefited one of the trustees, even though the trustee was advised that doing this was illegal. Legal costs to the Trust to defend the resulting litigation exceeded $11 million.

Articles in *The Chronicle of Philanthropy* pointed out that the board consisted of self-appointed, politically prominent individuals who had a modus operandi of favoring their own personal interests over those of the children at the school.

The way in which the Pennsylvania Attorney General dealt with enforcing the state laws against conflict of interest is another story (Smith, 2013). Those board members who perpetrated the plundering of the Hershey School may or may not serve prison time, or even be charged and have their day in court to answer for their alleged crimes. Yet there is little doubt that, if these allegations are true, reasonable persons would agree that the board members of the Milton Hershey School Trust were not acting ethically.

The story of the allegations against this board illustrates a worst-case scenario of a board gone rogue, with no accountability for taking actions that are not only unethical, but in almost all states, criminal. Even the most diligent, ethical board members may face situations in which it is unclear what may be appropriate or inappropriate. Board members have an ethical responsibility to assure that the organization's resources are managed faithfully. They must behave to accomplish its stated mission. They must be responsive to the legitimate needs of its stakeholders.

The purpose of this chapter is to raise some typical situations that might arise during nonprofit board service and to discuss some ethical responses to these situations. Reasonable people may disagree on some of these, and it is expected that this chapter will generate spirited discussion in the classroom and around the office water cooler.

Nonprofit Governance Ethical Issues

1. *The board of a nonprofit organization should consist of members who have the ability to make independent judgments to fulfill their governance duties under the law.* Thus, it is inappropriate and unethical for a founder of a nonprofit organization to designate family members and/or personal friends as board members for the purpose of creating a governance structure that will guarantee that the founder will have total effective autocratic control of the organization. Such board members are unlikely to be able or willing to take action if the founder engages in unethical or illegal conduct, or otherwise challenge decisions made by the founder. Having a sham board that will rubber-stamp the decisions made by the individual appointing them subverts the purpose of having a board.

2. *When appropriate, board composition should be diverse demographically, particularly with respect to age, race, gender, religion, political affiliation, and income level.* Diverse representation brings to the table viewpoints that are not likely to be monolithic, so that board decisions are sensitive to a broad range of interests and constituencies. Board operations should be sensitive to the diversity of its members, making all board members comfortable with their service. For example, board meetings should not be scheduled on religious holidays, and food served during board meetings and organization events should not violate religious dietary restrictions of individual members.

3. *Governance should be conducted in good faith, with honesty, integrity, due diligence, and competence.* Board members should recognize that they are serving on the board representing the public interest rather than their own interest. Thus, they are acting unethically when their decisions are influenced by their own personal interests, when they exploit confidential information they obtain as a result of their board service for their personal advantage, when they lie to achieve their objectives, when they have

not done their homework to educate themselves about issues being considered by the board, and when they fail to develop the basic expertise they need to fulfill their duties. For example, they are not fulfilling their duties if they are unable to understand the financial statements and budgets that the management is presenting and fail to ask for clarification. They are also violating their duties if they do not challenge proposed policies that are illegal or unethical.

4. *Board member decision-making must be consistent with laws, and board members must insist that management comply with all laws.* This applies even if there is pressure to skirt them to promote efficiency when the probability of getting caught is low. There are preferential laws that apply to nonprofit organizations, such as exemption from taxes, which are in exchange for particular behavior that is not required of for-profit business organizations. For example, organizations are expected to honor a particular mission that is in the public interest, rather than simply to make a profit. Among these laws are restrictions on fundraising solicitation and requirements to register and disclose financial information, filing and making public tax returns, private inurement restrictions, and conflict-of-interest requirements. In addition, there are many laws that apply to all types of organizations. There are certainly instrumental reasons for complying with all laws, such as the civil and criminal penalties that might apply, as well as the disruption (or the risk of organizational liquidation) and public relations disasters that often are the result of breaking the law. Putting all that aside, it is unethical for board members to break the law, or create a climate or be complicit in a culture within the organization that condones lawlessness.

5. *Board policies should promote an ethical culture throughout the organization.* Perhaps the most important responsibility of a nonprofit board, along with being true to the organization's mission, is to facilitate ethical operations within the organization. This is accomplished through board approval of ethics codes, a conflict of interest policy and accompanying annual disclosure statements for all organizational leadership, a whistleblower policy, hiring of a CEO who will make ethical management paramount and reward ethical decision-making by staff rather than punishing that, and ethics training for board and staff. It is not unusual for "obeying the law" or its equivalent to be the first provision of an organization's or profession's ethics code, and there is good reason for this.

6. *The Board must hold itself and management accountable for misconduct.* Even when it is unlikely that the organization would ever be held accountable if discovered (and the Hershey Trust example above is a salient illustration of this), board members have an obligation to not look the other way or even authorize violations of law even when it appears that the organization would benefit by doing so. Board members have an obligation to actively and strenuously resist proposed board policies that violate the law.

7. *Board members should not share confidential information as a result of their board service with those who have no legitimate reason to have access to that information.* Almost all nonprofit organization board members are volunteers, and they have both professional and personal interests outside of their board service. During the course of one's board work, there are opportunities to have access to information that is of potential pecuniary value to third parties, is politically sensitive, personal, or oth-

erwise gives someone an unfair or inappropriate advantage over others. This sort of information might include marketing plans and strategies, trade secrets, personnel information, and computer passwords. There are explicit laws (the Health Insurance Portability and Accountability Act, HIPAA, comes to mind) that address privacy, and the unauthorized release of private information could subject a board member to actionable litigation. But beyond that, keeping information confidential that is intended by the organization or its leadership to remain confidential, and that is disclosed solely for the purpose of the official duties of the board member, is an important ethical concept. Some organizations require their board members to sign a non-disclosure agreement. A sample can be accessed at: *http://www.scribd.com/doc/52716944/ Sample-Confidentiality-Agreement-for-Non-profits*

In any case, Board members should use the information they learn from their service on the board to further the interests of the organization, and not exploit it for their own personal interest.

8. *Board members should make decisions in the best interest of the organization rather than their own personal interest, i.e., avoid conflicts of interest and fulfill their duty of loyalty to the organization.* Board members are ethically obligated to avoid even the appearance of a conflict of interest. As a basic principle, it is unethical for a board member to be personally enriched financially by service on the board. Every state has laws about this, and even in Pennsylvania where no criminal action was initiated against a board member who served on the Hershey School Trust board, the Attorney General's office has initiated successful criminal actions against state legislators who exploited nonprofit organizations they established for their own benefit. There are federal limitations relating to conflicts of interest for organizations that are federally tax exempt. On a practical level, board members should disclose their conflicts of interest and recuse themselves (i.e., not participate) in decisions by the board when discussing business relationships involving the board member with the conflict.

In practice, disclosing and not participating has minimal practical value. Even without such participation, a board member has a clear unfair advantage in the outcome of any decision of the board compared to someone who does not serve on the board. If the board maintains a policy that no board member will be financially enriched by his or her service, then any "business" relationship between a board member and the organization must be on a pro bono basis. Thus, the board should not contract to have a board member's accounting firm do the financial statements for the organization, or to have an attorney board member represent the organization in court, unless that is done without any fee—as even work performed "at cost" would likely cover overhead.

9. *Board members should not exploit the organization's staff, equipment, facilities, or services for either personal or third-party gain.* The principle is a general one that applies to many others discussed in this chapter: Board members should serve to promote the mission of the organization and not receive any unreasonable benefit from their service. They should not expect staff to run their personal errands. They should not use the organization's offices to conduct their personal or professional activities. They should not use organization vehicles for other than organization business. And they should not divert the organization's resources for other purposes, including to other nonprofit organizations, without express permission from the board.

10. *After fulfilling their duties on the board, board members should return all documents and property connected with their board service that is appropriate to stay with the organization, and that would be inappropriate to be shared with the public.* Just as one would expect staff members to return computers, office keys, computer and paper files, and other property of the organization when they leave, board members have a similar ethical obligation. If there is a good reason to retain some materials, it is entirely appropriate to make a request in writing to the board chair for permission.

11. *The Board speaks with one voice.* Once a board decision on a policy is made, board members should not publicly criticize, undercut, or sabotage that decision. Everyone understands that decisions of a board are often not unanimous, and that board members with diverse backgrounds and who are passionate for their viewpoints are likely to have varying views. There is nothing inappropriate with a board member, when asked, telling the truth and explaining that he or she did not vote for a board policy. And there is nothing wrong with lobbying with one's colleagues on the board to advocate for a re-vote. But this is different from purposely undercutting the decision of the majority, which subverts the process of governance. Those who are in the minority today may find themselves in the majority tomorrow, and may better understand how the governing process is diminished by actions by individual board members, such as publicly denigrating the decisions of the board. It is thus unethical for individual board members to refuse to honor the majority decision of the board, to subvert its policies (such as, for example, writing letters to the editor to advocate for a policy at odds with the board's decision), or to organize an organization's membership to have an insurrection against the board. If a decision (other than one made that is illegal or unethical) is simply too much to bear, resigning is a preferable and honorable option. Board members must support and respect all decisions made by the full board. If a board member disagrees with a board decision, particularly if that board member believes the decision to be either illegal or unethical, he/she should insist that this dissent be officially recorded in the minutes.

12. *Organizations should have a formal, ethical gift policy.* Board members are often called upon to make decisions that generate substantial income (and profits) for third parties. They vote on partnerships with for-profit organizations, mergers, collaborations with other organizations, and contracts for substantial materials and services, such as new buildings, leases, physical plant contractors, and consultants. There is a culture in the business community that acquiesces to providing gifts not out of genuine friendship, but to influence decision-making. Many for-profit corporations have gift policies in place because they know that they pay a substantial cost when their employees' decisions are influenced by a gift. In the nonprofit sector, taking a gift intended to influence a decision, whether by a board member or staff member, is perhaps even more unethical, as the "cost" of the decision influenced by the gift is borne not by the company's stockholders, but by the public. All nonprofit organizations should have a gift policy (see *http://www.giftplanners.com/pdfs/understanding.pdf* for a sample). You and I would likely agree that accepting a pen from a vendor with the vendor's company name on it with a value of perhaps 20 cents is of no consequence, and accepting a vendor's gift of a trip to a conference held at a fancy resort is unethical. The issue that causes difficulty is the gray area between these two extremes. A clear gift policy will spell out exactly what is acceptable and what is not.

13. *Salary and perquisites should be reasonable, and in most cases, board membership should be limited to volunteers.* Every state (and federal law, as well, for federally tax-exempt organizations) prohibits board members of a nonprofit organization from distributing the net revenue of the organization among themselves. This nondistribution constraint is a fundamental distinction between a nonprofit organization and its counterpart for-profit organization. However, accepting a salary for board service is not illegal, if it is reasonable considering the time a board member puts in doing the work of the organization. It may indeed be the case that a salary for board service is essential to attract those with both expertise and the willingness to devote considerable time to govern certain complex nonprofit organizations, such as healthcare systems that may have budgets in the billions of dollars. However, many in the sector, including myself, consider it to be unethical in the absence of such special circumstances. One justification for the special benefits American society provides to organizations is that millions of individuals volunteer to serve, most of them with no expectation they will receive any more benefit (other than psychic benefit) for their service than those who choose not to volunteer. Board members are entitled to receive reasonable compensation for expenses they incur in connection with their official duties, such as travel, food, and lodging related to board meeting attendance, and receive reimbursement for any out-of-pocket expenses they incur on behalf of the organization. Note that there are legal as well as ethical limitations relating to tangible benefits that accrue to organizational insiders (see page 42).

14. *Board members should refrain from engaging in personal conduct that would compromise the reputation of the board/organization.* One need only consider the effect of Bill Cosby's association with Temple University to recognize that the relationship between the venerable actor and comedian and the Philadelphia university harmed the Temple brand. The harm was enough to encourage Mr. Cosby to resign from the board after serving 32 years (Raub, 2014), in the face of the sexual assault allegations that surfaced in 2014. Lance Armstrong suffered through a similar fate. One could argue that it is unfair to remove a board member (or a staff member, for that matter) from the organization when the individual has not been convicted of allegations. On the other hand, board members have the right (and duty) to protect the reputation of their organizations. Removal of a board member when there is credible evidence of misconduct that reflects poorly on the organization is imperative. The ethical response of someone who is accused of misconduct is to resign immediately—and perhaps under the condition that they be reinstated on the board if and when they have proven that the allegations of misconduct are unfounded. Mr. Cosby certainly never admitted any misconduct, but resigning was the honorable thing to do and in the best interests of the university.

15. *Board members acting as staff volunteers are not the "boss."* Board members should not give orders to staff who have not been approved by the full board. When a board member acts as a volunteer in the office, he/she works for the executive director as any other staff volunteer. The staff work for the board, not for individual board members. Generally, the board chair is authorized to interpret the policy of the board when discussing management issues with the executive director.

16. *Unless explicitly authorized in the bylaws, it is unethical for the chairman to overturn formal policy for the organization in the absence of board approval.* Bylaws often delegate authority to an executive committee in the absence of a formal board meeting when it

is not feasible for a board meeting to be held on short notice. But the board chair has no authority to supersede formal board votes that make policy.

17. *Board membership is not honorary.* Board members should insist that new members of the board have integrity, be qualified to serve on the board, and be willing to meet their legal duties, rather than simply being added because of their willingness to make a donation or because they have political clout, among other possible motives. There is an ethical obligation for board composition to further the mission of the organization, so that certain expertise (e.g., financial management, legal, fundraising, personnel relations, public relations, government relations) should be a factor in board recruitment. Some good advice about board recruitment is that a board member should bring to the table at least one of the three W's: wisdom, wealth, or work. And the more of the three, the better. Boards without a good balance of all three are doomed to suffer governance failure. Board members should make reasonable attempts to attend all board meetings, and participate, making decisions that fulfill the legal duties of board service. Board service is not an honorary position, although it may be true that being asked to serve on a prominent nonprofit board brings with it some measure of honor and prestige.

18. *Board members have an obligation to fulfill their duties ethically.* Board members should take whatever steps necessary to assure that the organization does not engage in discrimination or harassment; keep the organization true to its mission; assure that all individuals associated with the organization (including not only board and staff, but outside consultants, contractors, and vendors) maintain the highest ethical standards; and fairly evaluate the executive director (or hire a new one when that becomes necessary).

19. *Board investment policies should promote the organization's values.* Board members should not approve organizational investments that are at odds with the organization's values. It would be obvious that the board of the American Lung Association would not invest in tobacco company stocks. But other investments have more subtle controversial aspects. In addition to tobacco interests, examples of other controversial investments that may be anathema to nonprofits with certain missions include gun manufacturing; medical marijuana; companies that carry out testing on live animals; birth control products; companies implicated in human rights abuses; companies with a history of discrimination against women, minorities, or those from the LGBT community; those that do not pay fair wages, pollute, have policies designed to hurt local communities, or have unsafe working conditions; and alcohol-related interests. Organizations that feel it is unethical to "own" parts of companies that make products or provide services that are not consonant with the organization's mission should make this clear in their formal investment policy. There are often investment funds created that explicitly avoid having components of controversial companies in their list of investments by screening out companies that do not meet minimum social criteria, regardless of their potential for income generation. Socially responsible investing (SRI) is a term used to describe a movement in which both individual and institutional investors are considering social factors in their investment policies rather than simply maximizing their return on investment.

20. *All partnerships and collaborations should be consistent with the organization's mission and values.* Board members should not approve organizational partnerships/collabo-

rations, such as cause-related marketing agreements, or accept donations, that are not consistent with the organization's mission. They should not apply for grants from organizations whose activities are not consistent with that mission. It is quite easy to avoid investing institutional funds in equities inconsistent with the organization's mission. It is a bit more difficult to turn down a sizeable check from a for-profit corporation that seeks to influence the organization's policy with a donation, or to exploit the brand of the organization in a manner that does not serve the organization's mission. If the NAACP did indeed accept a check from the soft-drink industry and then, as a quid pro quo, agree to stand with the company in opposition to public policy designed to improve the health of constituents of that organization, then that decision was unethical (see: *https://nonprofitquarterly.org/policysocial-context/22000-lessons-from-the-naacp-s-public-opposition-to-new-york-city-s-big-soda-ban.html*). See Chapter 3 for more details about the need for organizations to develop a formal donation acceptance policy.

21. *Board members should refrain from hiring themselves.* If being considered for a staff position (particularly executive director), the board member should not participate in any future board meetings and should go through a search process. It is not unusual for a volunteer board chair or other board member to be a candidate for a staff position once it becomes known by the board that a staff member is leaving. But it is not ethical for that board member, particularly the chair, to exploit his or her power to annex the position by a simple vote of the board, without the job being open for a reasonable search, so other qualified candidates might apply and be considered. Otherwise, the board member is exploiting his or her inside information to be hired, and the board has no way of knowing whether it selected the most qualified person for the position. If the chair is participating in the decision-making, it is even more ethically problematic.

Activities

1. Research resources that might be available either online or from state associations to determine whether a salary is reasonable.

2. Research the case of the Hershey Trust board scandal, and then discuss how you would have behaved in that situation as a board member, or as an attorney advising the board.

3. Compile a list of nonprofit organizations that have had a history of scandal, and research what steps were taken by the board to try to restore public trust.

Discussion Questions

1. What are the advantages and disadvantages of having a diverse board?

2. When a board member feels that the board is making decisions in a manner that is either illegal or unethical, is the appropriate response to be a whistleblower or to simply resign from the board? Discuss some examples of situations in which one of these strategies or the other would be the appropriate response.

3. Is it fair to force out a board member who is accused of misconduct before there is some official determination that the person is actually guilty of that misconduct?

4. What might be some strategies a board could pursue to instill an ethical culture in an organization that was previously victimized by unethical management?

References

Associated Press. (2011, February 11). *Hershey charity scandal: Robert Reese, Ex-Hershey official, claims wrongdoing.* Retrieved from: *http://estateofdenial.com/2011/02/18/wrong-doing-alleged-over-hershey-charitable-trust*

Eisenberg, P. (2011, September 14). Hershey School scandal underscores need for watchful governance (PA). *The Chronicle of Philanthropy.* September 14, 2011. Retrieved from: *https://philanthropy.com/article/A-Case-for-Nonprofit/157881*

Raub, L. (2014, December 1). *Bill Cosby resigns from Temple University board of trustees.* Retrieved from: *http://www.latimes.com/entertainment/tv/showtracker/la-st-bill-cosby-resigns-temple-university-trustees-20141201-story.html*

Smith, P. (2013, July 29). Attorney General announces Milton Hershey Trust and Milton Hershey School reforms. Retrieved from: *http://fox43.com/2013/05/08/ag-kane-announces-reform-agreement-with-milton-hershey-trust-and-milton-hershey-school/*

Chapter 7
Ethics in Financial Management

When the transfer of money is involved, there are always ethics and accountability issues. The elimination of waste, fraud, and abuse in nonprofit organizations is not simply a public relations problem. The Madoff financial scandal of 2008 resulted in the crippling or demise of hundreds of nonprofit organizations. High profile scandals involving the Wounded Warrior Project (Tacapino, 2016), Central Asia Institute (Chan & Takagi, 2011), Foundation for New Era Philanthropy (Federal Bureau of Investigation, n.d.), the United Way of America (Charity Watch, n.d.), Hale House (Evans, 2008), Feed the Children (Attkisson, 2010), Asia Institute (CBS News, 2011), Acorn (Strom, 2008), American University (Associated Press, 2005), the United Way of New York City (Strom, 2006), and the Association for Volunteer Administration (Association of Volunteer Administration, 2006) have made national headlines in recent years. But for every such high profile scandal, there may be hundreds of low profile disgraceful incidents of criminal and unethical financial misconduct annually within nonprofit organizations. Many, if not most, will never become public.

Hundreds of major nonprofit organization financial scandals would never have seen the light of day were it not for an obscure question on the federal exempt organization tax return. Tax-exempt nonprofits have been required to report "significant diversions" of their assets on their 990s since 2008. Line 5 of Part VI (Governance, Management, and Disclosure) asks the following question: Did the organization become aware during the year of a significant diversion of the organization's assets? According to the instructions accompanying the form—

A diversion of assets includes any unauthorized conversion or use of the organization's assets other than for the organization's authorized purposes, including but not limited to embezzlement or theft. ...A diversion is considered significant if the gross value of all diversions (not taking into account restitution, insurance, or similar recoveries) discovered during the organization's tax year exceeds the lesser of (1) 5% of the organization's gross receipts for its tax year, (2) 5% of the organization's total assets as of the end of its tax year, or (3) $250,000 (IRS 2015).

Those to whom this applies must provide a written narrative of what happened on Schedule O of the form.

Little notice was made to this either by the general public or by the nonprofit sector until recently. In October 2013, *The Washington Post* published a study of what was reported by organizations that complied with this section of the 990 form. What *Post* investigators found was that more than a thousand nonprofit organizations reported such a diversion, although many, if not most, organizations were somewhat reticent in providing much detail. Included were descriptions of thefts, frauds, and embezzlements totaling more than a half-billion dollars for the top 10 incidents alone, many of which had not been otherwise made public. Among the organizations listed in the database were some of the most recognized charities in America (Stephens & Flaherty, 2013).

The full database is available at: *http://www.washingtonpost.com/wp-srv/special/ local/nonprofit-diversions-database/*

Everyone would agree that putting aside legal issues, embezzling money from a nonprofit is unethical. There are hundreds of other situations in which the ethics of behavior related to financial issues may not be so clear, particularly when that behavior may not necessarily be illegal. Regardless, unethical (and of course, illegal) behavior has consequences that adversely affect not only the organization and its employees, but its leaders, funders, clients, and the community it serves, and it also has consequences for the sector as a whole. As documented by the *Post's* investigation, charity officials apparently are more focused on recovering diverted funds, and perhaps much less on prosecuting the perpetrators. This investigation casts dispersions about their stewardship of funds, and perhaps they feel that donors will be less likely to donate if a scandal becomes widely known. On the other hand, by keeping these incidents quiet and not punishing the perpetrators, they are increasing the opportunities for reoccurrences.

There is a certain degree of trust that society places in nonprofit organization leaders, and the best place to avoid scandals is at the hiring stage. Yet there is an element of the nonprofit culture in which those who have been caught violating the organization's trust relating to the stewardship of funds, and other transgressions, are often quietly permitted to resign after making restitution. They are then able to find similar employment with similar organizations who are unaware of their history, even when these organizations have made a good faith effort to do background checks.

So, even with a need to have some measure of trust in their employees, all nonprofit organizations need to have systems in place to guard against illegal and unethical diversion of their resources. They need to conduct more than simple, pro forma background checks on job applicants, have ethics codes and policies, provide ethics training for their staff and boards, and, perhaps most importantly, create a culture in which ethical behavior is rewarded and unethical behavior is punished.

An organizational culture that condones stealing—whether in the form of allowing office supplies to be requisitioned for personal use, using credit cards to make personal purchases, availing oneself of the office photocopy machine for personal use, or even not penalizing the use of an organization's cell phones for personal texting—may experience a hemorrhage of organizational resources that could be fatal during tough economic times. Buyers who steer purchases to their relatives and friends rather than making arm's-length business decisions that are in the organization's best interest are subjecting the organization to a hidden "tax." Both board and staff leadership have a fiduciary duty to act in the best interests of the organization rather than in their own personal interest, and to manage the financial affairs of the organization prudently. To do otherwise is not only dangerous to the long-term health of the organization, but is both unethical and illegal as well.

Because of the public benefits granted to nonprofit organizations, particularly those with 501(c)(3) tax-exempt status, the degree of accountability for funds is justifiably higher than for for-profit organizations. Nonprofit organizations are entrusted with the care of people, many of whom are vulnerable and who have not voluntarily chosen to receive services from a particular organization. There is an implicit acceptance by the public and government agencies that ethical standards are higher for such organizations than would apply to their for-profit counterparts—although many would argue that all organizations should have high ethical standards, regardless of their sector.

Even with this being the case, there is no federal government regulatory authority over the financial management of nonprofit organizations comparable to the Securities and Exchange Commission (SEC) with respect to publicly-traded organizations. Despite often having very limited investigatory resources, many state attorneys general are authorized to, and do, take action against nonprofit leaders who violate conflict-of-interest laws. It is not unusual to read in local newspapers about the arrest and trials of employees and volunteers who are caught embezzling money from their nonprofit organizations.

Internal Control Systems

An internal control system is an essential component of assuring that the resources of a nonprofit organization are allocated legally and ethically. According to Tom McLaughlin in his 2002 book, *StreetSmart Financial Basics for Nonprofit Managers,* there are six elements of a nonprofit organization's internal control system (Grobman, 2015):

1. *Control Cues.* This involves management and leadership sending signals, both overt and covert, of proper ethical behavior, and training staff in appropriate control policies that promote accountability.

2. *Policy Communication.* This entails having written policies and procedures for accountability and ethics related issues, but in the absence of that, being able to communicate to employees what is acceptable and what is not by email, fax, interoffice memo, or voicemail.

3. *Segregation of Duties.* This involves separating work duties, so one person does not have total dominance over an entire process within the financial system. For example, the tasks of ordering the good or service, filling out the purchase order, writing the check, signing the check, mailing the check, and receiving the ordered goods would be completed by different people within the organization. This becomes a challenge for organizations with only a few employees, but even for a one-person office, a system of checks and balances needs to be developed.

4. *Record-keeping.* This relates to documentation and recording of all financial transactions. Nonprofits can try to minimize their vulnerability to internal fraud and abuse by using a reliable payroll service, contracting out accounts receivable, and taking advantage of financial institutions willing to do cash management for organizations. Of course, doing so increases the organization's vulnerability to external fraud and abuse.

5. *Budgets.* The budget is perhaps the best strategy to control behavior. If there are no funds in the budget, it is difficult for spending to occur that has not been pre-authorized and planned.

6. *Reporting.* McLaughlin's view is that "you only need five financial reports to control the average nonprofit corporation" (p. 207): the balance sheet, revenue and expenses, aged

accounts receivables, cash flow projection, and utilization reporting (which generally refers to how many people are using the organization's services, and to what extent). By looking at these reports periodically, a manager ostensibly can see trouble spots.

Generally, it is considered more efficient if all of the functions described in this financial management cycle are administered by one person. In smaller organizations, the executive director is responsible for all of the tasks described above. Larger organizations, however, will have one person (typically with the title of Chief Operating Officer or Chief Financial Officer) who will have these duties. In the case of the latter, as some high-profile criminal and civil cases have shown with respect to the for-profit sector, it is expected that there will be sufficient communication between the CEO and the CFO or equivalent. The CEO is ultimately responsible for the health of the organization, and simple ethics require that the CEO maintain a close watch over the financial affairs of the organization even if a subordinate staff member maintains day-to-day control over the financial operation of the organization. And, of course, the board and its committees have a role in financial oversight.

Controls for Waste, Fraud, and Abuse

There are two general classifications of systems used to control waste, fraud, and abuse in nonprofit organizations. The first is to discourage these before they occur. The second is to assist in discovering them after they have occurred (Grobman, 2015).

The traditional method of thwarting waste, fraud, and abuse before they occur consists of—

- *The independent auditor's annual audit and the annual management letter.* The management letter is an opportunity for the external auditor(s) to point out to the board any deficiencies seen in the operations of the organization that affect financial accountability and ethical concerns. When you get a management letter that cites chapter and verse with respect to internal control problems, you need to deal with it (and quickly!). This requires a plan of corrective action that is approved by the board and acceptable to the outside auditor before implementation.

- *Internal controls of the organization.* This consists of a system of checks and balances to assure that no one person can control assets without appropriate accountability. This involves the requirement that expenditures be preauthorized by a responsible organization official in accordance with predetermined policies affecting disbursements. All expenditures are recorded by the accountant/bookkeeper, with appropriate documentation for the expenditure becoming part of the file. That financial official has the responsibility to raise any questions about the expenditure. Oversight should include pre-audit checks of all purchase orders and vouchers, and review or approval by someone other than the person making the request before a payment is made, and separating those who order goods and services from those who receive the goods and services and disperse payments. It also can include spot checks of credit card transactions, long distance telephone bills, and cell phone accounts to assure that no personal expenses are charged to the organization.

- *Policies requiring large orders of goods and services to be put out for bid.* This includes related policies that discourage purchasers from dividing up orders into small increments to undermine this policy. This does not necessarily mean that the organization must prepare a formal Request for Proposal (RFP) for every large purchase. It should mean that quotes should be obtained from several qualified vendors and contractors for large purchases.

- *Ethics policies that apply to organization resources.* These policies might apply to credit cards, copying machines, telephones, Internet accounts, cell phones, laptops and tablets, and organization vehicles, for example. Those authorized to make purchases need to have an arms-length relationship to the vendor. These ethics policies would also include what is acceptable with respect to receiving gifts. For example, those who authorize company purchases would be prohibited from accepting gifts from suppliers other than de minimus gifts such as calendars. More substantial gifts, such as a box of cookies, would have to be shared with everyone in the organization. (The free vacation to Las Vegas as a thanks from the vendor to the organization's purchaser would have to be declined.) An ethics policy should also cover the issue of gifts made to staff members from those who receive services. All ethics policies should be reviewed at least annually, updated as appropriate, and communicated to all within the organization.

- *Training all employees on how to deal with the elimination of waste, fraud, and abuse.* The philosophy inherent in this method is that it is difficult to deal with a "bad" behavior when an individual might not have a clear sense as to what that might be in every case. The training should include procedures for staff to report suspected cases of illegal or unethical behavior.

- *Severe penalties for violating the organization's policies.* This involves written policies that require those found to have breached the organization's ethical standards and policies to be fired and referred to criminal authorities when appropriate, or otherwise sanctioned by reprimand or suspension if the violation is in a gray area.

- *Record keeping about all assets and taking a periodic inventory.* This is important, so that when something is missing (such as a laptop computer), an investigation can commence quickly. Many organizations will place bar-coded tags on their assets to facilitate inventory control.

- *Electronic protection of records.* The purpose of maintaining backups is that there remains an electronic trail, if not a paper trail, in the event of a fire or flood that destroys paper records.

Methods used to find occurrences after they have happened include—

- Determining when an employee has suddenly adopted a high lifestyle beyond his/her known income.

- Investigating when it is suspected that purchasers are funneling purchases to personal friends or relatives, or receiving expensive gifts from suppliers.

- Taking swift action when there appears to be missing documentation, "lost" organization checks, or an increased backlog in recording transactions.

- Randomly reviewing credit card transactions and telephone and wireless bills for personal expenses charged to the organization's account.

- Determining which expenses seem too high compared to what they have been historically, particularly when it is difficult to account for that with a reasonable explanation.

Ethical Expense Reimbursement Systems

Organizations incur expenses, many of which can be paid conveniently by check. Many others can be paid by credit card, which is particularly useful for travel expenses. For reasons of good financial management, it is not atypical for newly formed organizations to require two signatures on checks. This is not unreasonable for recurring expenses that can be processed well in advance, such as paychecks, rent, major equipment purchases, and taxes.

Requiring two signatures can occasionally present problems when making small, but reasonable, on-the-spot purchases. An expense reimbursement system should be designed to provide protection against one person making unilateral, capricious decisions on spending, but needs to be flexible enough to keep the organization from being hamstrung when trying to pay $25 for office supplies.

One suggestion is to set up an "imprest account" to pay routine office expenses, requiring only one signature. The authorized person (such as the executive director) has a reasonable sum to disburse from this checking account, which is entirely separate from the "master" checking account. The imprest account is replenished from the master checking account using a check that requires the usual two signatures, only upon a review by the chairperson or treasurer (or both) of what was expended—including supporting documentation, such as receipts. This account should provide an amount needed not only to pay reasonable expenses for the month, but enough to cover expenses for part of the following month, since several days or weeks may elapse during the processing of the expense report.

The organization's leadership should provide general guidelines as to what types of expenses are acceptable for reimbursement and what expenses should be absorbed by the staff. For example, hotel accommodations in any city can range from $60-$300 per night. A dinner can be purchased for $5 or $75. Many organizations refuse to make decisions concerning what is appropriate, and instead provide a per diem allowance—a flat payment that is expected to pay reasonable travel expenses for each one-day period. The staff member then must absorb costs that go beyond this amount.

Many other expense issues arise that require board policies. How much should staff be reimbursed for mileage? What if a spouse attends a conference with a staff member and shares a hotel room, resulting in an incremental cost increase? How will expenses be reimbursed that cannot be directly documented with a receipt, such as tips or parking meter expenses?

All of these issues can be resolved on an ad hoc basis, but it is useful to think about the nature of expense reimbursement before it creates problems. Many organizations have failed because their budgets were depleted by discretionary spending in the absence of an expense policy.

Ethical Financial Management Principles

The following are some of the more common ethical issues that arise in nonprofit organizations related to financial management, and my personal views on these.

1. *Nonprofit organizations must obey the law.* This means that everything relating to financial management should be "on the books," not paying consultants under the table, and not designating staff members as outside consultants when they are legally classified as employees in accordance with IRS rules in Publication 15A (available at: *http://www.irs.gov/publications/p15a/index.html).* They should file all legally required tax returns, charitable solicitation registrations, and reports. If they meet the thresholds for doing so, they should file required unrelated business income tax returns (990T).

2. *Nonprofit organization staff members should not be permitted to exploit organizational resources for their personal gain.* This means that the organization should have policies in place to assure that vehicles, equipment, computers, tablets, and cell phones assigned to staff will remain the property of the organization, and not be transferred knowingly or unknowingly to others or not returned to the organization when the staff member is no longer employed. Policies should make it clear that organizational supplies should not be diverted to purposes other than advancing the mission of the organization and for official duties. This means that the photocopy machine is available only for organization business, unless provisions are made for reimbursement. Organizational leaders should not look the other way when they discover that equipment or organizational funds are missing, and they should take appropriate action to report criminal activity.

3. *Nonprofit organizations should have a gift policy that prohibits staff and board of the organization from accepting gifts of value from those who might benefit from decisions made by them* (See page 83).

4. *Nonprofit organizations should not offer loans to their board members.* Many states, such as Texas, explicitly ban loans to board members and place restrictions on those to staff members (Texas Business Organizations Code, 2006). Although it is difficult to think of a scenario when an organizational loan to a board member is justifiable, there are cases when a loan to a staff member may make some sense. For example, a new employee relocating to take a position with the organization might benefit from a salary advance or loan. Organizations should carefully consider whether a loan truly is to the advantage of the organization and helps advance the mission. And they should make sure that any loans are consistent with "excess benefit transactions" regulations of the IRS, particularly when interest rates are less than what might be available from a private lender. Putting legal considerations aside, loans by nonprofit organizations raise so many ethical concerns that the cleanest approach is simply to not offer them.

5. *Organization management should make a good faith effort to honor the approved budget.* The budget approved by the board is a formal blueprint that, while not legally binding on the organization, is expected to be adhered to with good faith by management. It is unethical for management to consider the budget process to be

simply an exercise to get through, and to consider the budget passed by the board to be advisory only. There are certainly times when it simply does not make sense to honor provisions of the budget. And it may be considered unethical if the budget calls for spending that a reasonable person would consider to be wasteful or unnecessary. A manager should identify any aspects of a board-approved budget that reasonably should be modified, and take steps to have the board consider the reasons management feels this is so, and make formal modifications at a board meeting, rather than unilaterally ignoring the budget. On a related topic, it is unethical for management to spend money that is available in the budget simply because it is available to spend, and because of a fear, real or imagined, that not spending it will result in the budget being cut for future years. This widespread wasteful practice in all three sectors wastes precious resources. There should be incentives to promote spending behavior that rewards managers for eliminating wasteful spending rather than punishing them.

6. *Organizational surpluses should be reasonable.* If the funds of a charitable nonprofit are to be used for charitable purposes, what is a reasonable amount of surplus to accumulate? The Wise Giving Alliance has suggested a ceiling of three times the current year's expenses or three times the next year's budget, whichever is greater (Wise Giving Alliance, n.d.). Organizations should consider the circumstances under which it is appropriate to disclose to prospective donors the amount expected to be used to accumulate a surplus. Clearly, if a major purpose of the solicitation is to build a surplus, that should be disclosed.

7. *Surplus or other unwanted or unneeded property still belongs to the organization.* All assets should be kept track of, and careful records should be kept about the disposition of current assets and the circumstances under which they were removed from control of the organization, either through sale or disposal. It is routine for organizations to purchase up-to-date computers, new furniture, and vehicles. It is clear that the resources that are replaced belong to the organization. If they have any value, they should not simply be thrown out in the trash or given away to staff members. The volunteer race director for the organization's 5K fundraiser should not assume that leftovers of donated granola bars and raisin boxes are his personal property to take home. Some nonprofit organizations have an annual yard sale to sell their inventory of useless supplies, antiquated computers (once they have their hard drives scrubbed), and surplus office furniture.

8. *Resources should not be diverted to uses other than those intended by donors, grantors, or the board.* Management has an ethical (and legal) obligation to assure that resources they receive to perform their vital missions are allocated solely in a way consistent with the organization's mission and that they are used for the programs for which they were obtained. They certainly should not be diverted for personal use. But it is also unethical for these resources to be diverted to other organizations, particularly if there is no reasonable justification for that being done. So, if for example, a staff member is organizing a charity race for another, unrelated organization, it is unethical to use any of the resources of the charity for which she works to support that race, even though the staff member is not personally benefiting and the resources are being diverted for charitable purposes.

9. *Every financial transaction involving a nonprofit organization must be recorded in a manner consistent with legal requirements.* Although it may be "efficient" to sign over a contributor's donation to a staff member to more quickly and conveniently reimburse him for some expenses, the donor's check should be deposited into the organization's account, and then a separate reimbursement check should be written. All financial transactions should be scrupulously recorded appropriately, and there should be sufficient backup of both paper and electronic records to assure that some disaster does not affect the accessibility of the financial management system.

10. *Staff and leadership must avoid conflicts of interest (and the appearance of the same).* Board or staff members (or their relatives) should not serve as the auditor of the organization. Staff members should not steer the organization's business to those who are board or staff members (or their relatives), or who might hire them. They should not make decisions on behalf of the organization that benefit themselves personally. They should recognize that their decisions relating to the organization they serve are tainted by potential conflicts of interest if they involve another organization they serve. The IRS Sample Conflict of Interest policy may be found at: *http://www.irs.gov/instructions/i1023/ar03.html*. Note that there are many cases of a conflict of interest that are not illegal, but they still violate the rules of the IRS against insiders having civil or criminal liability for benefits they receive. However, ethical considerations demand that organizational insiders should not benefit any more than private citizens who are not decision-makers for the organization in trust, even when those insiders recognize that there may be a conflict of interest, disclose it, and recuse themselves from participating in the decision.

11. *No one person should be in control of everything relating to income and disbursements.* The "segregation of duties" described on page 91 minimizes exposure to misconduct, but certainly does not immunize against every possibility. A "checks and balances" system is essential to assure that there are barriers to any single staff person being able to use the organization as his or her personal ATM or to make personal purchases using funds belonging to the organization.

12. *Organizations need to have an ethical investment policy.* Investment policies should be clear in prohibiting investments in businesses that operate against the values or in opposition to the mission of the organization. The investment policy issues that apply to board members (see page 85) apply just as well to staff. An organization's CFO should not choose her husband's financial management company to invest the organization's funds. A CEO who is a baseball card collector should not seek to purchase baseball cards as organizational investments, even if the cards are not intended to ever be in the permanent possession of the CEO. Engaging in this or similar behavior is not necessarily illegal, but it is considered unethical for organizational staff to exploit their position of authority to further their own personal interests, even if there is no intention to "profit" financially from doing so.

13. *Salaries, benefits, and perquisites should be reasonable.* Determining an appropriate salary structure is perhaps the most difficult ethical issue in the nonprofit sector. Ethical considerations arise at both the high and low ends of the salary spectrum. If an organization is funded by grants from foundations and corporations or by

government contracts, the funders can and do provide some restraint on excessive salaries. However, if the nonprofit is funded primarily by individual donations or fees for service, such constraints (other than, perhaps, those relating to the intermediate sanctions regulations of the Internal Revenue Service) are absent. Boards fall into an ethical trap if they reward executive directors based on the amount of income received, rather than on how well the mission is accomplished. A board can consider many criteria when setting the salary of the executive director. These include the size and complexity of the organization, what others in similar organizations are earning, and whether the salary is justifiable to the public. Some nonprofits include proportionality in their salary structures by limiting the highest paid to a factor of the lowest paid (e.g., the highest can be no more than three times the lowest). As a result of enactment of the *Taxpayers Bill of Rights 2* (Internal Revenue Service, 1996), there are now legal as well as ethical restrictions on paying excessive compensation. Ethical management of employees requires that each person be treated with dignity and respect; paid a salary that can provide a decent standard of living; and given a basic level of benefits, including health insurance coverage. A potential critical conflict arises when a charitable organization working to spread its social values treats its staff in a way that conflicts with those organizational values.

14. *Organization credit cards should be provided only to those who have a valid need for them.* Despite their obvious convenience, organization credit cards increase an organization's exposure to fraud and abuse. The paperwork for credit card transactions is typically much less detailed than for conventional invoiced purchases. They can be used to access cash from ATMs, and it may not be clear which employee accessed the account. A best practice is to issue a credit card to a particular staff person with a reasonable credit limit, and prohibit staff members from sharing the card with others. Organizations should be careful in examining all credit card statements for any signs of irregularity. They should have a system in place to require reasonable documentation for all credit card purchases and take action against those who inappropriately use the organization's credit card.

15. *Organizations should act in the public interest, recognizing that they are treated differently than their for-profit counterparts for justifiably good reasons.* Hospitals, nursing homes, colleges and universities, and health clubs may be for-profit or nonprofit. From the outside, they may look the same and offer some of the same services. There are obvious differences in how they are intended to operate. Nonprofit organizations, particularly those that are federally tax-exempt, receive significant benefits because they are expected to behave in a way that achieves some valid mission in the public interest rather than making as much profit as they can. All nonprofits must be aware of their bottom line, as failure to have enough income to support their programs and pay staff means that the organization will not be able to operate for long. Yet it is not unusual for nonprofit organizations to focus on making as much income as possible, sacrificing aspects of their missions that may not be as financially lucrative. It is unethical for organizations to lose sight of being true to their missions and operate to generate as much revenue as they can, even if any net revenue is not distributed to their board members (which would be illegal).

16. *Nonprofit organizations should not sacrifice their long-term needs for short-term gain.* Organizations are intended to remain in stable operation well beyond the time any individual employee or board member might serve. Nonprofit organizations have an ethical obligation to be governed and managed for the long term. They should plan to consider how they would deal with any issues that might interfere with the long-term viability of the organization. Management needs to recognize that it is unethical to make decisions that appear to benefit the organization in the short term, and thus make that manager/CEO look good for the annual evaluation of contract renewal negotiation. That behavior has long-term adverse consequences that will have to be faced by that manager's/CEO's eventual successor. This is consistent with an ethical concept attributed to the Iroquois, who suggest that the current generation should consider how their decisions today will affect those who will live seven generations in the future (Yahoo.com, n.d.).

Online Resources

Carter McNamera's Free Management Library—Financial Management Pages
http://managementhelp.org/nonprofitfinances/index.htm

Blue Avocado on Nonprofit Embezzlement
http://blueavocado.org/content/nonprofit-embezzlement-more-common-and-more-preventable-you-think

National Council of Nonprofits—Financial Transparency Pages
https://www.councilofnonprofits.org/tools-resources/financial-transparency

AZCentral—Top Five Ethical Issues for a Nonprofit Organization

http://yourbusiness.azcentral.com/top-five-ethical-issues-nonprofit-organization-5979.html

Activities

1. Research actual organization whistleblower policies that can be found on the Internet and discuss whether you would feel comfortable being a whistleblower if you discovered widespread embezzlement and other corruption within the nonprofit organization for which you work.

2. Research actual cases of fraud involving nonprofit organizations, and draft policies that might have either prevented the scandals or uncovered them sooner.

3. Read the full text of the *Sarbanes-Oxley Act.* Write a report on which provisions in this law are not mandatory for nonprofit organizations, but might be good public policy if they applied equally to them.

Discussion Questions

1. If a nonprofit organization has only one employee, what controls might be instituted to minimize waste, fraud, and abuse?

2. What dollar amount of abuse should trigger sanctions against an employee with respect

to discovering that such an employee has made personal calls using the organization's telephone account?

3. What control should the board have over the ability of nonprofit executives to spend funds to accomplish organizational objectives? How much flexibility should nonprofit executives have to adjust their budgets in response to new conditions without obtaining board approval?

4. Imagine you are the CFO of the ALS Association in the summer of 2014. What adjustments in financial management might you have considered when you realized your organization was likely to receive more than $100 million in unanticipated contributions in a single month as a result of the "ice bucket challenge"? How might these adjustments have differed if the $100 million came in the form of a one-time contribution from a wealthy donor? What is the ethical response to spend these unanticipated donations in a timely, yet responsible, manner?

References

Attkisson, S. (2010, February 18). Feed the Children scandal: Follow the money. Retrieved from: *http://sharylattkisson.com/feed-the-children-scandal-follow-the-money/*

Associated Press. (2005, October 11). American University trustees oust president amid scandal. Retrieved from: *http://usatoday30.usatoday.com/news/education/2005-10-11-au-president_x.htm*

Association of Volunteer Administration. (2006, February 23). Association for Volunteer Administration February 23, 2006. Retrieved from: *https://www.energizeinc.com/sites/default/files/AVA_Announcement_notices.pdf*

CBS News. (2011, April 19). Questions over Greg Mortenson's stories. Retrieved from: *http://www.cbsnews.com/news/questions-over-greg-mortensons-stories-19-04-2011/*

Chan, E. & Takagi, G. (2011, April 25). 'Three cups of tea' scandal offers lessons for charities and trustees. Retrieved from https://www.philanthropy.com/article/Three-Cups-of-Tea-Scandal/158531

CharityWatch. (n.d.). CharityWatch hall of shame. Retrieved from: *https://www.charitywatch.org/charitywatch-articles/charitywatch-hall-of-shame/63*

Evans, H. (2008, October 8). Hale House shuts doors to orphans. Retrieved from: *http://www.nydailynews.com/new-york/hale-house-shuts-doors-orphans-article-1.303533*

Federal Bureau of Investigation. (n.d.). Foundation for New Era Philanthropy. Retrieved from: *http://www.fbi.gov/philadelphia/about-us/history/famous-cases/famous-cases-foundation-for-new-era-philanthropy*

Grobman, G. (2015). *The nonprofit handbook* (7th Edition). Harrisburg, PA: White Hat Communications.

Internal Revenue Service. (1996). *Taxpayer Bill of Rights II*. Retrieved from: *http://www.irs.gov/pub/irs-utl/doc7394.pdf*

Internal Revenue Service. (2015). 2014 Instructions for Form 990 return of organization exempt from income tax. Retrieved from: *http://www.irs.gov/pub/irs-pdf/i990.pdf*

Stephens, J., & Flaherty, M. (2013, October 26). Inside the hidden world of thefts, scams and phantom purchases at the nation's nonprofits. Retrieved from: *http://www.washington-post.com/investigations/inside-the-hidden-world-of-thefts-scams-and-phantom-purchases-at-the-nations-nonprofits/2013/10/26/825a82ca-0c26-11e3-9941-6711ed662e71_story.html*

Strom, S. (2006, April 14). United Way says ex-leader took assets. Retrieved from: *http://www.nytimes.com/2006/04/14/nyregion/14united.html*

Strom, S. (2008, July 9). Funds misappropriated at 2 nonprofit groups. Retrieved from: *http://www.nytimes.com/2008/07/09/us/09embezzle.html?pagewanted=all&_r=0*

Tacopino, J. (2016, March 11). Wounded Warrior Project execs ousted over spending scandal. *New York Post*. Retrieved from *http://nypost.com/2016/03/11/wounded-warrior-project-execs-ousted-over-spending-scandal/*

Texas Business Organizations Code. (2006). Chapter 22. Retrieved from: *http://www.statutes.legis.state.tx.us/Docs/BO/htm/BO.22.htm*

Wise Giving Alliance. (n.d.). How we accredit charities. Retrieved from: *http://www.give.org/for-charities/How-We-Accredit-Charities/?id=236646*

Yahoo.com (n.d.). What is the great law of the Iroquois? Retrieved from: *https://answers.yahoo.com/question/index?qid=20120119021052AAIKhJq*

Chapter 8
Ethics in Grants Management

Grants play an important role in nonprofit organizations having the ability to make payroll, provide subsidized goods and services consistent with their missions, and otherwise "keep the lights on."

Similarly, fundraising and grants management are inherently ethically problematic. A high level of trust is often assumed by parties to any transaction. There are often large amounts of money involved, with only a cursory accountability for how this money is spent. There are often built-in incentives to be less than honest, even if the individual who is violating this basic ethical principle is doing so with the most selfless of motives, and sincerely feels that he or she is behaving in this way to promote the public good and/or the good of the organization rather than his or her own personal interest. This may actually be the case, or perhaps the person is simply deluding him- or herself with a flimsy rationalization to justify dishonesty.

Many of the ethical issues that arise in relation to grants are similar, if not identical, to those discussed in the chapter on fundraising ethics. Some are unique. What they have in common is the potentially corrupting influence of money. It is not uncommon for people to increase their access to money in a way that society deems to be unacceptable, even resorting to activities that are illegal or unethical.

Everyone would agree that those who apply for grants, find a way to deposit the grant checks into their own personal bank accounts, and divert those funds for personal expenses, are acting both illegally and unethically. However, there are many other behaviors, including some that do not relate directly to money, that are not so clear cut.

The purpose of this chapter is to point out some common ethical issues that relate to grants management, from both the perspective of the grantor and grantee, and discuss the appropriateness of particular behavior. Many of these behaviors fall into a gray area. Particular fact situations may influence whether you might feel that a particular behavior is ethical or unethical, and there is no expectation that any particular behavior is definitely wrong in every case.

There are two national associations that represent those who write grants—the American Grant Writers' Association (AGWA, 2015) and the Grant Professionals Association (Grant Professionals Association, n.d.). Both organizations have ethics codes for their membership, and there are common threads. To some of the issues referred to in these codes, I have added issues that emanate from my own experience as someone who has applied for grants.

1. *Grant writers should not be compensated based on a percentage of the grant total they receive.* Rather, they should be paid a salary, flat fee, or hourly fee for writing the grant, and payment should not be contingent on whether or not the grant is

funded. The rationale for this is similar to that for professional fundraisers (see page 123). For a detailed discussion of this issue, see: *http://grantwriters.org/ethics-and-commissions*

2. *The compensation for the grant writer should not be hidden within other budget line-items in the grant.* When possible, the services of the grant writer should be included in the budget as a separate line-item or included in the organization's own budget under grant-writing or administrative expenses. Otherwise, the organization is being dishonest with the grantor about its budgeting.

3. *Grant writers and/or organizations seeking grants should not pay finders' fees, percentage fees, or commissions to obtain access to donors.*

4. *Grant writers must honor confidentiality.* Data included in a grant may be sensitive. The grant application belongs to the organization once it pays the grant writer for his or her services, and that grant writer has no right to use the material in the application for other purposes without permission. This principle also applies to donor and prospect information.

5. *Grant writers should never pursue grants without the express knowledge and permission of their client organizations.* Organizations may have their own reasons for not pursuing a grant, particularly if it falls outside of the organization's mission, or if it is from a funder with whom the organization chooses not to have a relationship. Regardless, grant writers are acting unethically if they apply for grants without the knowledge of their client organization, unless they have express authorization to do so.

6. *Grant funds applied for and awarded for a particular purpose should never be diverted for another purpose without the express consent of the grantor.* Grantees have an ethical obligation to use funds granted solely for the purpose for which the grant was awarded. There may be cases when it makes sense to use funds for another purpose, but it is unethical to do this without the knowledge and consent of the grantor.

7. *Grant writers should disclose any conflicts of interest they may have with pursuing a grant, and always make the philanthropic purpose paramount to their own personal gain.* There may be cases in which the grant funds could be used to benefit financial interests (such as a private company) controlled by the grant writer. This should never happen, but at a minimum, any such conflict of interest should be disclosed.

8. *All information and data included in a grant application, including information about principal staff, their competence and experience, data used to support the application, and the purposes for which awarded funds will be used, must be truthful and accurate.* There is certainly an incentive to exaggerate information in a grant application to make the application appear more attractive with respect to community need, outcomes, budget information, support from community leaders, expertise and education of organization management and staff, and other aspects of the application. Embellishing information for any reason is not only unethical, but could adversely affect the reputation of the organization if and when it is determined that information provided was not fully accurate and truthful.

9. *If circumstances change with respect to information in the application, either before any grant is approved or after one is approved, the grantor needs to be expeditiously notified.* For example, an organization is obligated to notify the grantor when a key staff member who is responsible for activities related to the grant leaves the organization.

10. *Grant writers should never submit "cloned" applications.* These are grant applications that are basically templates with identical or similar language that are not custom-written to serve the organization. See: *https://grantresults.wordpress.com/tag/ethics* for more on why cloned grant applications are unethical.

11. *Organization staff should not initiate inappropriate personal relationships with grantors that create a dual relationship and influence what should be a completely professional relationship between the grantor and the grantee.* For the same reasons, grantmaking staff should also avoid creating dual relationships that may color their decisions relating to grants.

12. *Grant writers, grantors, and grant evaluators should never engage in activities that do not fall within their individual boundaries of professional competence.* In addition, they should keep current with developments in the field (e.g., through continuing education, attending conferences, networking with colleagues, and participating in the activities of professional associations) to improve their skills. As stated more succinctly in the ethics code of the Grant Professionals Association, its member should "continually strive to improve their professional competence."

13. *Organizations receiving grants should maintain complete custody of funds from any grant they receive rather than permitting a third party grant writer or consulting organization to receive the funds for later transfer.* As a related principle, the organization seeking the funding should always be the formal grant applicant rather than a grant-writing organization, individual, or other entity that is simply providing a grant-writing service.

14. *Grantors should maintain appropriate boundaries between themselves and the organizations they fund.* It is important for grantmakers to recognize that their grant does not give them the right to abuse their power to influence or otherwise manage the governance, mission, and policies beyond what is necessary to reasonably manage the grant. Grantors should be grateful to grantmaking organizations, but they should recognize that they are participating in an equal partnership in which the grantor is providing funding and the grant recipient is also providing resources—time, creativity, expertise, and hard work for a common objective.

15. *Grantors should not engage in holding false competitions for grants when they have already determined that they are awarding a grant to a particular grantee.* Otherwise, organizations with reason to feel that they are both eligible and potential awardees may invest substantial time and money developing a grant application for which they have no chance of being successful.

16. *Grantors should provide reasonable notice to their grantees that a grant will not be renewed.* They should provide the organization with as much time as possible to

take steps to plan for the cessation of funds and, if possible, suggest replacement funds to keep the program funded by that grant operating.

Online Resources

American Grant Writers' Association
http://agwa.us

Grant Professionals Association
http://www.grantprofessionals.org

Grant Whisperer's Ethics in Grantwriting
http://grantwhisperer.com/grant-proposal/grantwriting-and-ethics/

Grant Writer Ethics in Compensation

blog.ecivis.com/bid/110602/Grant-Writing-The-Ethics-of-Compensation%3fhs_amp=true

Discussion Questions

1. Is there too much pressure on nonprofit organizations to apply for grants based on the availability of the funding, rather than by sticking to the mission and purpose of the organization? What are the ethical implications of this?

2. What are the dangers of an organization paying a grant writer based on how much money the grant writer raises, rather than an hourly or fixed-fee rate? Can you make an argument that for organizations that have no budget to pay a grant writer, it may be appropriate to pay only for successful grants?

Activities

1. Download five foundation fundraising applications. What features do they have in common? Find a common grant application form that can be used to apply for grants from a range of funders that have agreed to accept this form. How do any of the questions asked relate to ethical issues?

2. Invite a grant writer to speak to your class about the ethical implications of writing grants.

3. Invite an official from a foundation to speak to your class about the ethical implications of making grants.

References

AGWA. (2015). American Grant Writers' Association. Retrieved from: *http://www.agwa.us/*

Grant Professionals Association. (n.d.). *About.* Retrieved from: *http://www.grantprofessionals.org/about*

Chapter 9
Ethics in Personnel Management

Few can argue with the view that a nonprofit's human capital is its most important resource.

The board hires the executive director (or CEO), who influences the ethical culture, direction, morale, image, and financial stability of an organization. Yet, even the least senior employee can have a significant impact, negative or positive, on the organization. Employees can be creative, nurturing, versatile, ingenious, inspiring, and team-building. Or they can be disruptive and destructive—infecting morale and creating scandal that can ruin the reputation of a charity that took decades to foster.

The shock waves from the Penn State child sexual abuse and Bernie Madoff scandals are continuing to be felt. The forced resignation of the American Red Cross's chief executive in 2001, blamed in part on an alleged policy of deceptive fundraising, made front page news. One of her successors also was forced to resign after just six months on the job following disclosure that he had an inappropriate "personal relationship" with a subordinate (Crary, 2007). Millions of viewers have become skeptical that their charitable donations are reaching intended needy recipients after a CNN investigation discovered that little, if any, of the money from contributions to The Disabled Veterans National Foundation were doing anything more than lining the private bank accounts of fundraisers (Fitzpatrick & Griffin, 2012).

As our society becomes more litigious, unethical behavior by a board member, employee, volunteer, financial advisor, or accountant can have disastrous consequences. Many human services nonprofits that work closely with aging populations, children, and people with disabilities have had experience defending the actions of their employees in court, and they are at risk for damage suits that run in the millions of dollars. In some cases, unethical staff performance is a matter of life and death for at-risk clients. The responsibility for governing a nonprofit ethically or choosing staff wisely should not be taken lightly.

Each hired employee is an investment by a nonprofit beyond the salary paid to him or her. The chemistry of an organization is changed by a new hire, and bad hiring decisions, such as the result of a failure to perform a valid background check or assuring that he or she will be a good fit, can haunt an organization for many years or destroy it completely.

Qualified and trained personnel who advance the mission of the organization in a legal and ethical manner are an organization's most prized assets. Staff members need to feel that the organization is flexible enough to respond to their individual needs. Conversely, the organization must have the ability to operate efficiently, effectively, and economically, and to treat all employees fairly and equally. It is not unusual for some employees in any sector, even when they are inherently honest, to engage in unethical behavior to "even the score" when they feel that they are being exploited in some way (Gerstner & Day, 1997). An organization's management must treat its staff fairly and ethically, instill an ethical culture, reward ethical behavior, and punish behavior that is not ethical. When it does, employees are most likely to do their work in a legal or ethical manner.

Ethical Personnel Policies

A nonprofit organization may have one salaried employee or hundreds. Regardless, a written personnel policy that embraces the organization's standards of ethical behavior can prevent disputes that, in some cases, can destroy an organization even before it gets off the ground. Obviously, a personnel policy for a small organization will be less complex than that of a large one. It is advisable to review personnel policies of several organizations of similar scope and choose among the provisions that are most sensitive to your organization's needs. It is not necessary to reinvent the wheel, but having a wheel is important (Grobman, 2015).

The personnel policy should be revisited periodically, if only to consider the changes that may need to be made because of the advance of technology. The policy should be clear on what is permitted with respect to using the computer and Internet service provided by the organization, both on organization time and personal time while in the office. For example, use of the computer to retrieve, store, or disseminate pornography should be expressly prohibited. Other policies should address other prohibited uses, such as visits to gambling sites, playing games, looking for other jobs, forwarding copyrighted material, hacking into the system, or using the organization hardware and/or software for other illegal purposes. Once a policy is adopted or revisions are made, a signed acknowledgment should be obtained from every employee indicating they have received the document and understand it.

If the organization expects to enforce limitations on an employee's own personal use of the Internet, that needs to be explicit in the personnel policy. Provisions relating to confidentiality of organizational information, how one's personal illegal or unethical activities might reflect poorly on the organization, or how the staff member posts publicly about the organization on blogs or social media should be included in the policy.

Ethics Issues in Personnel Management

Some of the issues of interest relating to ethical personnel management are the following:

1. *Organizations should train their employees and require them to honor intellectual property laws.* Organizations should not condone copyright violations or computer piracy for organizational purposes, or otherwise promote the violation of intellectual property rights of others. This means not pirating computer software, and not posting copyrighted materials on their Web sites without express written permission from the copyright holder and paying royalties when required. They should not make copies of this book chapter (or any other copyrighted material) and provide it to each of their board members without first obtaining permission from the publisher. Doing so is not only a violation of federal law, but it is also unethical.

2. *Employees should be entitled to retain outside remuneration that is not related to their employment.* Income directly related to the employee's employment with the organization

should belong to the organization. Executive directors and other staff often are offered honoraria or consulting fees for speeches, teaching, providing technical assistance, or other work. The ethical issue is whether the staff person should turn the fees over to the nonprofit employer or be able to retain them. Potential conflicts can be avoided if the policy is based on the principle that all reasonably related outside income belongs to the organization. Thus, an executive director's honorarium for speaking to a national conference as a representative of the organization or an expert in his or her field would revert to the employer, but his or her fee for playing in a rock band on weekends could be individual income. The argument for this policy is that the line between the employer's and the employee's personal time is not so easy to draw. An argument against this principle is that employees' usage of their spare time should be of no concern to the employer. Is it ethical for an employee to exploit the knowledge and experience gained on the job for personal gain? Are we buying only time from our employees, or do we expect that we are getting the undivided professional attention of that person? If the board or executive director is silent on this issue, the assumption is that earning outside income is a private matter. If the organization expects that moonlighting is not appropriate for salaried employees, then it should make that clear in either the personnel policy or in the employee's contract.

3. *Salaries, Benefits, and Perquisites should be reasonable.* Determining an appropriate salary structure is a sensitive, yet important, ethical issue. There is a comprehensive discussion on this issue on pages 97-98.

4. *Inappropriate personal relationships should be prohibited.* Nonprofit organization executives and board members must not engage in sexual harassment, or behavior that makes an employee feel uncomfortable, at best, or threatened and intimidated, at worst. Employees should be treated fairly, which among other things, means that no favoritism should be permitted with respect to work assignments. Nepotism—the hiring of family members—should be prohibited, as this is a conflict of interest and creates a dual relationship. Nonprofit executives and board members should seek to keep personal friendships from influencing professional judgment. It is a conflict of interest for supervisors to have romantic/sexual relationships with those they supervise. Many organizations feel it is problematic to permit such relationships even when there is no supervisory relationship, and do not permit it.

5. *Organizations should strive to help employees maintain an appropriate work-personal life balance.* While there are logical reasons to respond to work-related emergencies during non-business hours, employees should be afforded time to take vacations, deal with personal and family health-related issues, sleep, exercise, eat, spend time with their families, and otherwise not be expected to be on the job 24/7. Managers should not make it difficult for employees to meet family caregiver obligations.

6. *Inappropriate dual relationships should be avoided.* Staff members should not be asked to "volunteer" to run personal errands for their supervisor because he or she is too busy with organizational matters to manage his or her own private tasks. Employees and their supervisors should not have business relationships other than those related to their official organization duties. Such dual relationships can poison or otherwise have a counterproductive influence on the professional relationship that is appropriate between managers and those they supervise.

7. *Organizations should seek to have a diverse workforce, commit to nondiscrimination in policies and programs, and instill a culture of respect for cultural differences.* Discrimination should not be permitted in hiring and promotions, even if it does not meet the threshold required for legal violations. Efforts should be made to build a diverse workforce, including for leadership positions. Cultural differences among staff should be respected to the maximum extent possible. The organization should not tolerate bullying; hazing; or jokes targeting the race, color, sex, age, sexual orientation, national origin, disability, or religion of individuals. It should create a working environment where all employees feel safe and are treated with dignity and fairness. This also means that employees are expected not to impose their religious or political views on other workers or organization stakeholders when it is clear that such communication is unwelcome or is likely to be.

8. *Organizations and employees must honor confidentiality and privacy to protect sensitive information that should not be publicly disclosed.* This means that employee records should not be shared with those who do not have a legitimate business reason to have access. It means that supervisors should not share with others information they learn from the employees that is expected to remain in confidence. And it means that workers should not share information that should be private and confidential, particularly on social media sites, but also in public areas, such as restaurants and elevators.

9. *Organization employees should not be coerced to make donations to the organization.* Organizations should not pressure or otherwise require their employees to make charitable contributions to the organization as a condition for keeping their jobs. Employees should not feel that there may be work-related consequences for refusing to donate, such as by harassment, public humiliation, or threats for those who do not pledge to give their "fair share." There is nothing wrong with soliciting staff members and other organization stakeholders to support the organization. But there is something unsavory when the solicitation is tied to factors that would make any donation less than gratuitous (and thus eligible for a tax deduction) in the best case, or simple extortion in the worst case. For example, employees may feel pressure, whether intended or not, if they are solicited by the person who makes decisions about their work assignments, discipline, or salary. Some organizations have been known to require donations, and even for a particular amount based on the employee's salary. In some organizations, both nonprofit and for-profit, a manager's evaluation may include the degree to which charitable goals have been met. Donations from employees can be encouraged, but there should never be any retaliation if an employee does not choose to donate for whatever reason.

10. *Managers should not give "good" recommendations to employees who are fired for misconduct, and illegal conduct should be reported to appropriate authorities.* It is not unusual in the nonprofit sector, or in the corporate culture in general, for an employee dismissed for misconduct to not have the reasons for dismissal shared with future prospective employees. There are some reasons why this is so. Organizations are fearful of wrongful termination suits or other retaliation from the employee, such as divulging confidential information to others. There is some benefit to keeping things as quiet as possible and making the fired employees as "happy" as possible. The problem occurs when an unethical employee applies for another job, and the successor organization is making a good-faith effort to determine what they can about that job seeker's perfor-

mance. Ethically, that prospective employer is entitled to be told the full truth—or at least not lied to. Perhaps the organization that dismissed this employee itself performed a background check on the employee, and was not told the truth, and as a result, the cycle of unethical (or illegal) conduct was again perpetrated. So, while it may be difficult, organizations should be upfront with those who have a legitimate need for information about the employment history of these dismissed employees. Organizations should report theft and embezzlement to law enforcement officials. These wrongdoers should be figuratively and literally taken off the streets, rather than simply moving down the road and plying their misconduct for others with impunity.

11. Organizations should be accountable for allegations of misconduct of their leadership and staff. They should act appropriately and ethically to investigate accusations of illegal and unethical conduct, and take reasonable disciplinary action against those who engage in illegal or unethical conduct. It may not be unusual for organizations to fire the victim or the messenger and take actions to protect the perpetrator of organizational misconduct. Disturbing accounts of the treatment of college students who alleged that they were victims of sexual assaults illustrate what may or may not be an isolated example of conduct inconsistent with this principle (Kingkade, 2014). The recent sexual abuse scandals involving The Catholic Church and Penn State University have provided evidence that engaging in these behaviors is not only illegal and unethical, but results in more long-term damage to the institutions than might otherwise occur had the organizational leadership acted appropriately once abuses were discovered. It is a national (and international) scandal when victims of abuse are afraid to make reports, but there is some justification for that, considering how both institutions and legal authorities often act in a way to discourage reporting (See: *http://www1.umn. edu/humanrts/svaw/harassment/explore/6reporting.htm*).

Online Resources

Carter McNamera's Personnel Policy Advice
http://managementhelp.org/personnelpolicies/index.htm

Markkula Center for Applied Ethics: Ethics in Human Resources

https://www.scu.edu/ethics/focus-areas/business-ethics/resources/ethical-challenges-in-human-resources/

Activities

1. Contact your state Human Relations Commission and determine if there is any literature available about laws that affect hiring and interview questions. Why is it considered unethical to ask certain questions even in the absence of any legal requirement not to do so?

2. Download a sample of nonprofit organization personnel policies from the Internet and note which provisions relate to ethical behavior.

Discussion Questions

1. Should nonprofit organizations have a special obligation to pay living wages to their employees, or should there be a recognition that if employees are willing to work for less than livable wages, this is appropriate because of the limited resources of many organizations?

2. Is it unethical for an executive director to simply hire a personal friend who has the ability to do a job with the organization, rather than opening the job up to candidates from the public?

3. If an organization's personnel database is hacked, what is the ethical obligation for the organization's management to notify affected employees?

4. What are the pros and cons of building a diverse staff in a nonprofit organization? Are these different in a for-profit organization?

5. Is it appropriate or inappropriate for an organization to place restrictions on personal relationships among staff? Does it make a difference if the employees have a supervisory relationship? Does it make a difference if they do not have a supervisory relationship, but work in the same department?

References

Crary, D. (2007, November 27). Scandal forces U.S. Red Cross to ask its new leader to resign. Associated Press. Retrieved from: *http://www.startribune.com/nation/11922081.html*

Fitzpatrick, D., & Griffin, D. (2012, May 8). IRS forms show charity's money isn't going to disabled vets. CNN Special Investigations Unit. Retrieved from: *http://www.cnn.com/2012/05/07/us/veterans-charity-fraud/index.html*

Gerstner, C. R., & Day, D. V. (1997). Meta-analytic review of leader–member exchange theory: Correlates and construct issues. *Journal of Applied Psychology*, 82(6), 827–844.

Grobman, G. (2015). *The nonprofit handbook.* Harrisburg, PA: White Hat Communications.

Kingkade, T. (2014, November 18). Why it really matters when college officials say terrible things about rape. *Huffington Post.* Retrieved from: *http://www.huffingtonpost.com/2014/11/18/college-officials-rape-things-they-say_n_6173254.html*

Chapter 10
Codes of Ethics

Whether called a Code of Ethics, Code of Conduct, Standards of Practice, or something similar, it is important for every nonprofit organization to have a document addressing what behavior is acceptable for organization leadership and staff. These documents may be quite general and consist of provisions that express values that provide not much beyond a *spirit* of behavior. Or they may be quite detailed, addressing specific situations that may be plausible for stakeholders to experience, and provide concrete guidance on what is acceptable and unacceptable. They can have explicit provisions relating to sanctions against those who violate their contents, including referral to criminal authorities, suspension, or firing. Or they can simply be a set of aspirational platitudes that provide only broad guidance to those facing actual work situations within the organization.

Written ethics codes have a long history. The first documented case of one is Hammurabi's Code, which dates from the 18th century B.C.E. The historian Willa Marie Bruce (1998a, 1998b) notes that the Athenian Code 11 centuries later provided that its citizens would "never bring disgrace to this our city by any act of dishonesty or cowardice...," and that the first code in the United States was spoken as part of a sermon in 1630 by John Winthrop, the first Governor of the Massachusetts Bay Colony. Whereas most of us have heard of the Hippocratic Oath that dates from the 5th century B.C.E., the first modern written code of ethics was proposed in 1794 by Thomas Percival, applicable to physicians and surgeons as a reaction to the hospital where he worked turning away patients in need. Today, almost every recognized profession has its own ethics code, and it has become popular in the last 50 years or so for individual business organizations and nonprofits to have their own ethics codes, supplementing those of their trade and professional associations (Grobman, 2002).

Ethics Codes Are the First Step to Building an Ethical Organization

It is certainly clear to me that simply having such a document is only the first step toward creating an ethical climate and culture within an organization. From my experience, the most valued aspect of building an ethical organization is for leadership to set an example by behaving ethically, and making it clear that unethical behavior is punished and ethical behavior is rewarded. Many organizations have a formal written policy expressing the value of ethical treatment of customers and clients. Yet, some of them take punitive action against individuals within the organization who choose not participate in unethical behavior, and who report the unethical behavior of others. The recent case of Wells Fargo Bank comes to mind as I write these words in December 2016. In this case, bank employees who called the corporation's ethics hotline to report unethical behavior were fired (Egan, 2016). According to one press report, employees received ethics training that encouraged them to report ethics violations (Cowley, 2016).

Having an ethics code, ensuring that stakeholders know it exists and understand it, having an ethics hotline or other mechanism to report violations, and having training in how one should behave consistent with the code will not guarantee having an ethical organization—particularly when management condones retaliation against those who are trying to behave ethically. One needs only to say the name "Enron" to conjure up the image of a corporation with a reported $63.4 billion in assets that went belly up as 2001 came to a close because of the unethical behavior of its employees—despite the fact that Enron had a comprehensive, 64-page ethics code. This scandal, which also destroyed a previously respected accounting firm, Arthur Andersen, was a prime motivation for enactment of the *Sarbanes-Oxley Act* (see pages 115-116).

So while having an ethics code is not a panacea to avoid unethical behavior within organizations, having an effective ethics code is a good first step in building an ethical organization.

Why Nonprofits Need Ethics Codes

One could argue that having an ethics code is valuable in nonprofit organizations for altruistic reasons alone. The sector is committed to a mission that serves the public rather than for private, personal gain. An ethics code serves to make it clear that this principle deserves to be preserved, particularly when many nonprofits serve individuals who are old, infirm, indigent, or otherwise are vulnerable and do not have access to private markets to meet their needs. Nonprofits rely on private fundraising and have transactions that annually reach $390 billion (Sandoval, 2017), relying on a high degree of trust between donors and the organizations to spend money as intended.

Yet there are some selfish reasons for having an ethics code beyond it being simply "the right thing to do." When and if organization stakeholders are caught doing something unethical, the effect on the organization, as a result of reduced public trust and bad publicity, can be catastrophic. Having a comprehensive ethics code provides tangible guidance to all stakeholders about what is not acceptable conduct—and some associated with the organization may not be completely clear on what is considered unethical behavior without that guidance. A strong ethics code can serve as a signal to clients that the organization can be trusted, and that those who act unethically on behalf of the organization will be held accountable. Thus, it serves as a warranty for the organization's services.

When ethics codes become widespread and are enforced, it can often forestall action by government to provide statutory regulation as an alternative to self-policing. Ethics codes make sure everyone in the organization is on the same page with respect to enforcing common values, such as when there are provisions relating to anti-discrimination of staff and clients. With employees of organizations being much more culturally and educationally diverse than they might have been a few decades ago, an ethics code can serve as a template for shared values expected from the staff.

Perhaps the most important purpose of having an ethics code is to influence behavior of stakeholders. Without an ethics code, it is often not clear whether actions by a stakeholder are inconsistent with what is deemed acceptable by the organization's governors and top management. Thus, it may seem like "common sense" that there is nothing wrong with a fundraiser receiving a percentage of funds he or she raises. But there is a consensus among the professional associations that serve the fundraising sector (see page 123) that there are unintended consequences of compensating fundraisers based on the amount they raise that often result in unethical behavior. If an ethical code exists and this particular behavior is included as being unethical and unacceptable, then fundraising managers will know to avoid compensating their staff in this manner. While it may be true that "you can't legislate morality," it is equally valid that you cannot avoid bad behavior if you do not know what that encompasses.

Creating an Ethics Code

Although it may be the case that certain generic provisions can be included in virtually any nonprofit ethics code, it makes sense to consider the organization's mission, values, vision, culture, and expectations from the public and create a custom-made ethics code.

Putting that aside, certain provisions belong in every nonprofit ethics code. The Internal Revenue Service (IRS) itself has encouraged organizations to have formal ethics policies with respect to conflicts of interest, advocacy, and lobbying not only for ethical reasons, but to ensure compliance with tax laws that apply to federally-exempt nonprofit organizations. A sample conflict of interest policy suggested by the IRS can be found at: *https://www.irs. gov/instructions/i1023/ar03.html*

The Internal Revenue Service (2016) recommends that nonprofit organizations adopt this sample policy when filing the documents required to qualify as federally tax-exempt. The IRS's 1023 Form Instruction Book notes that—

A "conflict of interest" arises when a person in a position of authority over an organization, such as a director, officer, or manager, may benefit personally from a decision he or she could make.... Adoption of a conflict of interest policy is not required to obtain tax-exempt status. However, by adopting the sample or similar policy, you will be choosing to put in place procedures that will help you avoid the possibility that those in positions of authority over you may receive an inappropriate benefit.

Whistleblowing Policies

Another generic provision of value is a whistleblower policy. The federal *Sarbanes-Oxley Act,* enacted in 2002, is a comprehensive accountability, transparency, and anti-corruption law that applies mostly to for-profit corporations. However, there are two provisions that apply to nonprofit corporations, as well, relating to destruction of documents and prohibiting retaliation against whistleblowers. The latter provision provides that—

Sec. 1107. RETALIATION AGAINST INFORMANTS.

(a) IN GENERAL- Section 1513 of title 18, United States Code, is amended by adding at the end the following:

(e) Whoever knowingly, with the intent to retaliate, takes any action harmful to any person, including interference with the lawful employment or livelihood of any person, for providing to a law enforcement officer any truthful information relating to the commission or possible commission of any Federal offense, shall be fined under this title or imprisoned not more than 10 years, or both.

The federal protection afforded to whistleblowers by this law only applies when the misconduct is reported to a law enforcement officer and does not apply when it is reported within the organization or to the public via the media. This law provides limited protection to whistleblowers, and as I write this, it is not apparent that this section has ever been invoked to protect a whistleblower who was retaliated against in the nonprofit sector.

Ethical organizations should be encouraging their employees to make good-faith reports of misconduct internally without fear of retaliation so it can be addressed by the leadership appropriately. The alternative is risking a public scandal that could result in unnecessary and irreversible damage to the organization's reputation. A whistleblower policy provides the infrastructure to reinforce a culture that supports employees who know the importance of maintaining an ethical environment in their organizations.

A sample of a reasonable whistleblower protection policy published by the National Council of Nonprofits (2010) may be found at: *https://www.councilofnonprofits.org/sites/ default/files/Sample%20WhistleblowerPolicy%202.2010.pdf*

Common Provisions in Nonprofit Organization Ethics Codes

The following are among the most common generic provisions that are found in the ethics codes of nonprofit organizations, with some samples taken from an actual code where noted:

1. *Supremacy of the public interest.* "Promote the interests of the public and put service to the public above service to oneself." Code of Ethics, American Society for Public Administration (ASPA).

2. *Client interest over profit motive.* "Conduct oneself in a professional manner and represent a client's best interests within the limits of one's professional responsibilities." American Society of Media Photographers.

3. *Respect and comply with all federal, state, and local laws.* "*Respect and support government constitutions and laws, while seeking to improve laws and policies to promote the public good.*" American Society for Public Administration (ASPA).

4. *Respect and honor confidentiality.* "Certified Records Managers shall be prudent in the use of information acquired in the course of their duties. They should protect confidential, proprietary, and trade secret information...." Institute of Certified Records Managers.

5. *Fairness.* "*Be fair and reasonable in all professional relationships....*" Certified Financial Planner Board of Standards.

6. *Anti-discrimination.* "The organization shall not on the basis of race, color, creed, sex, national origin, marital status, or religious beliefs, family, social or cultural background, or sexual orientation, unfairly: exclude any student from participation in any program...." Code of Ethics, Nebraska State Education Association.

7. *Corruption.* "The enterprise shall prohibit bribery in any form." Asia-Pacific Economic Cooperation Anti-corruption Code of Conduct for Business.

8. *Truthfulness.* "Seek truth and report it." Society of Professional Journalists.

9. *Professional competence.* "Social workers should provide services and represent themselves as competent only within the boundaries of their education, training, license, certification, consultation received, supervised experience, or other relevant professional experience." National Association of Social Workers.

10. *Responsibility/taking credit for work.* "A health information management professional shall... take responsibility and credit, including authorship credit, only for work they actually perform or to which they contribute. Honestly acknowledge the work of and the contributions made by others verbally or written, such as in publication." American Health Information Management Association Code of Ethics.

11. *Enforcement.* "If the Commission on Standards and Ethics determines that unethical conduct has occurred, it may impose sanctions, including reprimand, censure, probation, suspension, or permanent revocation of membership...." The American Occupational Therapy Association.

12. *Promoting the profession.* "The Logistician will strive to enhance the public awareness and knowledge of logistics...." SOLE, The International Society of Logistics.

13. *Sexual harassment.* "...it is unprofessional behavior to condone sexual harassment or to disregard complaints of sexual harassment from students, staff or colleagues. Such actions allow a climate of sexual harassment to exist and seriously undermine the atmosphere of trust essential to the academic enterprise...." Organization of American Historians.

14. *Equality and impartiality in decision-making.* "A mediator shall decline a mediation if the mediator cannot conduct it in an impartial manner. Impartiality means freedom from favoritism, bias or prejudice." American Bar Association, American Arbitration Association, & Association for Conflict Resolution—Model Standards of Conduct.

15. *Accuracy and truthfulness of marketing.* "...Marketing communications must be clear and truthful. Marketers must not knowingly make a representation to a consumer or business that is false or misleading...." Canadian Marketing Association Code of Ethics and Standards of Practice.

16. *Quality.* "We will strive constantly to provide high quality and educationally valuable programs and services. We regularly will evaluate and review our work in order to improve those programs and services and will seek out and adopt exemplary practices." NAFSA: Association of International Educators.

17. *Substance abuse.* "It is unethical for a dentist to practice while abusing controlled substances, alcohol or other chemical agents which impair the ability to practice. All dentists have an ethical obligation to urge impaired colleagues to seek treatment. Dentists with first-hand knowledge that a colleague is practicing dentistry when so impaired have an ethical responsibility to report such evidence to the professional assistance committee of a dental society." American Dental Association.

18. *Personal integrity.* "All employees and leadership are expected to conduct their personal and professional life in a manner which "inspire(s) the confidence of the public." Code of Ethics, Association of Arson Investigators.

19. *Information transparency and accountability.* "Truthfulness and transparency are essential to ethical education abroad practices. The fundamental premise is that education abroad practices should be open and clear, and that decision-making processes should be appropriately disclosed and periodically reviewed." Forum on Ethics Abroad Code of Ethics.

20. *Misrepresentation of professional/academic credentials.* Members shall not "claim that an IAAO professional designation unless authorized, whether the claim is verbal or written, or to claim qualifications that are not factual or may be misleading." Code of Ethics, International Association of Assessing Officers.

21. *Objectivity.* "The financial analyst, in relationships and contacts with an issuer of securities, whether individually or as a member of a group, shall use particular care and good judgment to achieve and maintain independence and objectivity." Chartered Financial Analysts Institute (formerly known as the Association for Investment Management and Research).

22. *Reporting violations of the ethics code or laws to the appropriate authorities.* Members are expected to "immediately report to the ethics committee any known or suspected violation of this code of ethics." American Institute of Parliamentarians.

23. *Conflicts of interest.* "Marriage and family therapists do not provide services that create a conflict of interest that may impair work performance or clinical judgment." American Association for Marriage and Family Therapy.

24. *Gifts.* "A member should not directly or indirectly solicit any gift, or accept or receive any gift whether in the form of money, services, loan, travel, entertainment, hospitality, promise, or any other form, under circumstances in which it could reasonably be inferred that the gift was intended to influence him, or could reasonably be expected to influence him, in the performance of his official duties or was intended as a reward for any official action on his part." International City/County Management Association.

25. *Respect for client dignity and self-determination.* "AOM members respect the dignity and worth of all people and the rights of individuals to privacy, confidentiality, and self-determination. AOM members are aware of and respect cultural, individual, and role differences, including those based on age, gender identity, race, ethnicity, culture, national origin, religion, sexual orientation, disability, language, and socioeconomic status, and they consider these factors when working with all people." Academy of Management Code of Ethics.

26. *Respect for pluralism and diversity.* "Members (shall) demonstrate concern for the legal, social codes and moral expectations of the communities in which they live and work even when the dictates of one's conscience may require behavior as a private citizen which is not in keeping with these codes/expectations." Code of Ethics, Student Affairs Administrators in Higher Education.

27. *Macro advocacy.* (Members shall) "work to improve and change laws and policies that are counterproductive or obsolete." Code of Ethics, American Society for Public Administration.

As a matter of preference, some organizations with ethics codes choose to have separate documents that deal with conflict of interest policy, whistleblowing, conduct of employees, and computer/Internet use (including social media)—each of which directly or indirectly have an ethics component. As with ethics codes, it is essential that all board and staff know these policies exist and will be enforced, and have sufficient knowledge and training relating to their content.

Online Resources

Illinois Institute of Technology Ethics Code Collection
http://ethics.iit.edu/ecodes/

Independent Sector's Statement of Values and Code of Ethics
https://www.independentsector.org/resource/is-code-of-ethics/

Michigan Nonprofit Association's Code of Ethics
http://www.c4npr.org/clientuploads/Board%20Governance%20Resources/NCNA%20Sample.Board%20Code%20of%20Ethics.Michigan%20Nonprofit%20Association.pdf

National Council of Nonprofits' Ethics Code Pages
https://www.councilofnonprofits.org/tools-resources/code-of-ethics-nonprofits

Sample Ethics Code for Nonprofit Board Members
http://www.adelphi.edu/wp-content/blogs.dir/91/files/2012/09/codeofethics.pdf?t=1347913001-77806

Illinois Institute of Technology Searchable Ethics Codes Collection
http://ethics.iit.edu/ecodes/about

Andrew Olson: How to Create an Ethics Code
http://ethics.iit.edu/ecodes/authoring-code

Discussion Questions

1. Discuss the advantages and disadvantages of having a formal organizational ethics code.

2. Discuss the advantages and disadvantages of having specific sanctions mandated within an ethics code.

3. Discuss the pros and cons of having policies that regulate romantic relationships between managers and those they supervise, and between co-workers without such a direct relationship.

Activities

1. Download a sample of nonprofit organization ethics codes that you find on the Internet. Make a list of ethics codes provisions that tend to be featured in these codes.

2. Obtain any ethics codes or codes of conduct of your school/institution, and analyze it in the context of what you have learned from reading this textbook.

3. Analyze the ethics code of the professional association that you are likely to join or have already joined. Considering what you have read in this book, what modifications might you suggest to this code that would promote more ethical conduct by your professional colleagues in that field?

References

Bruce, W. M. (1998a). *Codes of conduct.* In *The international encyclopedia of public policy and administration* (Shafritz, J., Ed.), Boulder, CO: WestView Press.

Bruce, W. M. (1998b). *Codes of ethics.* In *The international encyclopedia of public policy and administration* (Shafritz, J., Ed.), Boulder, CO: WestView Press.

Cowley, S. (2016, September 27). *Wells Fargo employees claim retaliation.* ArchyNewsy. com. Retrieved from: *http://archynewsy.com/wells-fargo-workers-claim-retaliation-for-playing-by-the-rules-new-york-times*

Egan, M. (2016, September 21). *I called the Wells Fargo ethics line and was fired.* CNN Money USA. Retrieved from: *http://money.cnn.com/2016/09/21/investing/wells-fargo-fired-workers-retaliation-fake-accounts/*

Grobman, G. (2015). *The nonprofit handbook (7th Ed.).* Harrisburg, PA: White Hat Communications.

Grobman, G. (2002). *An analysis of codes of ethics of nonprofit, tax-exempt, membership organizations: Does principal constituency make a difference?* Doctoral Dissertation. The Pennsylvania State University.

Internal Revenue Service. (2006). *Instructions for Form 1023.* Retrieved from: *https://www. irs.gov/pub/irs-pdf/i1023.pdf*

National Association of Social Workers. (1999). *Code of ethics.* Retrieved from *http://www. naswdc.org/pubs/code/default.asp*

National Council of Nonprofits (2010). *Sample whistleblower protection policy.* Retrieved from: *https://www.councilofnonprofits.org/sites/default/files/Sample%20Whistleblower-Policy%202.2010.pdf*

Sandoval, T. (2017, June 13). Donations grew 1.4% to $390 billion in 2016, says 'Giving USA.' *The Chronicle of Philanthropy.* Retrieved from *http://www.philanthropy.com/article/Donations-Grew-14-to-390/240319*

Chapter 11

Ethics Standards in Associations of Nonprofit Organization Professionals

In recent years, there has been a trend toward turning nonprofit management into a recognized profession, with credentialing becoming available for fundraising executives, association managers, and nonprofit organization managers. Organizations such as the Association of Fundraising Professionals (AFP), the American Society of Association Executives (ASAE), the Grant Professionals Association (GPA), the American Grant Writers' Association (AGWA), and the National Council of Nonprofit Associations—and the state and local chapters of these organizations—have sought to professionalize their memberships.

Government at all levels has the taxing power backed by the force of law to compel its citizens to finance the services it provides. For-profit businesses generate their revenue through market transactions, in which there is a quid pro quo—money exchanged by a consumer for goods and services that will benefit that consumer. Charities, in contrast, generate much of their revenue through nonmarket mechanisms such as seeking donations—in the form of voluntary contributions from the public and grants from foundations and government. This form of revenue generation offers a ripe area for fraudulent practices, and many of the ethics-related principles that differentiate nonprofit organizations from their government and private sector counterparts focus on this area.

A Historical Perspective—Fundraising Ethics

Until 2003, there were two major ethical codes focusing on fundraising standards for charitable organizations. The first, which was developed during the late 1980s and went into effect in 1992, is the National Charities Information Bureau's (NCIB) Standards in Philanthropy (2000). The standards were not enforceable by law, but served as a guide to both donors and those who run the charities. The standards were grouped into nine areas:

1. Board Governance

2. Purpose

3. Programs

4. Information

5. Financial Support and Related Activities

6. Use of Funds

7. Annual Reporting

8. Accountability

9. Budget

Another code, the Council of Better Business Bureaus' (BBB) Standards for Charitable Solicitations, was first published in 1974.

In 2001, NCIB merged with the Better Business Bureau Foundation and its Philanthropic Advisory Service (PAS). The new organization, the Better Business Bureau's Wise Giving Alliance, developed an updated code, published in March 2003. In 2007, the BBB rebranded its charity resources with a "Start With Trust" campaign. Charities that meet its standards are now referred to as "BBB accredited charities." The 20 standards that comprise this influential ethics code can be found at: *http://give.org/for-charities/How-We-Accredit-Charities/*

Among the most controversial aspects of this code is the provision that calls on charities to allocate at least 65% of their donations for program expenses, spending no more than 35% of related contributions on fundraising. This is a higher standard than either the NCIB (60%) or the BBB's Philanthropic Advisory Service (50%) had enforced prior to the merger.

In December 2009, the Wise Giving Alliance announced it was temporarily loosening its standards because of the severe recession. For the fiscal years ending in June 2008-2010, organizations still qualified for the Wise Giving Alliance stamp of approval if the organization spent at least 55% of donations on program expenses and no more than 45% on fundraising. In 2013, the standard was restored to a minimum of 65% for program expenses and a maximum of 35% for fundraising expenses.

Other standards in this code provide for regular assessment of the CEO's performance, establishment of a conflict-of-interest policy, the completion of a written assessment of the charity's performance at least every two years, and standards protecting donor privacy. The new standard frowns upon accumulating unrestricted net assets available for use that exceed either three times the amount of the past year's expenses or three times the current budget, whichever is higher.

The national professional association of fundraisers also has an ethics code. The Statement of Ethical Principles of the Association of Fundraising Professionals (AFP) was adopted in 1991 when that organization was known as the National Society of Fund Raising Executives (NSFRE, 1991). AFP "exists to foster the development and growth of fund-raising professionals and the profession, to promote high ethical standards in the fund-raising profession and to preserve and enhance philanthropy and volunteerism." This code was amended in 2007 and expanded to 25 principles.

AFP's ethics code consists of a set of general ethical principles, introduced by a preamble that recognizes the stewardship of fundraisers and the rights of donors to have their funds used for the intent they expect.

Many of these principles are deontological, and would be appropriate for any type of organization, such as to "foster cultural diversity and pluralistic values, and treat all people with dignity and respect" and "value the privacy, freedom of choice and interests of all those affected by their actions." Some of the principles are appropriate for public organizations, such as having an obligation to "safeguard the public trust." Others are parochial to the profession, such as to "put philanthropic mission above personal gain" and "affirm, through personal giving, a commitment to philanthropy and its role in society."

One year after the adoption of the AFP principles, the organization adopted its "Standards of Professional Practice" and incorporated them into its ethics code. Its 25 principles are mostly in the form of "members shall" and "members shall not."

A statement within the Code notes that violations "may subject the member to disciplinary sanctions, including expulsion, as provided by the (AFP's) Ethics Enforcement Procedures."

Some of these standards are perfunctory, such as "members shall comply with all applicable local, state, provincial, federal, civil and criminal laws." Others are general and broad, with implications that are not easily subject to interpretation, such as "members shall not exploit any relationship with a donor, prospect, volunteer or employee to the benefit of the member or the member's organization." Among issues raised by the standards are conflicts of interest, truthfulness, privacy, and financial accountability.

Another issue raised in the principles is the standard that "members shall not accept compensation that is based on the percentage of charitable contributions...."

With regard to performance-based compensation, some states have expressly prohibited lobbyists from signing contingency fee contracts in which they are paid only when they are successful in getting a bill or amendment passed by the legislature. The theory is that such contracts encourage lobbyists to engage in efforts that go beyond the boundaries of acceptable behavior. On the other hand, contingency fees are routine for attorneys in civil cases. It is also not unusual for professional fundraisers to be paid a percentage of the amount they raise. Many in the field find that this practice promotes unethical solicitations (e.g., presentations that exaggerate facts, minimize disclosure, and other behavior to intimidate and harass potential donors), and it is interesting that a major professional organization such as the AFP has taken an unequivocal position in opposition to compensation based on the amount a fundraiser raises. This is an example of a teleological approach to ethics (see page 16), in that there is nothing inherently unethical about basing compensation on "performance."

A 2001 White Paper published by the Association of Fundraising Professionals (AFP) with an excellent discussion about this issue can be found at: *http://www.afpnet.org/Ethics/EthicsArticleDetail.cfm?itemnumber=734*

Independent Sector's Statement of Values and Code of Ethics

In February 2004, Independent Sector (2015) adopted a *Statement of Values and Code of Ethics for Nonprofit and Philanthropic Organizations,* and recommended that it serve as a model. The statement identifies a set of values to which nonprofits may subscribe, including commitment to the public good, accountability to the public, and commitment beyond the law. It also outlines broad ethical principles in the areas of personal and professional integrity, mission, governance, legal compliance, responsible stewardship, openness and disclosure, program evaluation, inclusiveness and diversity, and fundraising. The full text can be accessed at: *https://www.independentsector.org/resource/is-code-of-ethics/*

A related document, *Principles for Good Governance and Ethical Practice,* was published in 2007 and updated in 2015. The latest edition provides a discussion about 33 ethics-related issues of interest to the nonprofit sector, divided into the four categories of legal compliance and public disclosure, effective governance, strong financial oversight, and responsible fundraising. Adoption of the *Principles* is entirely voluntary, and there is no enforcement mechanism for organizations that violate any of its provisions.

Standards for Excellence

In 1998, the Maryland Association of Nonprofit Organizations initiated an ethics and accountability code for the nonprofit sector entitled *Standards for Excellence*®. Along with the code, the program includes educational components, a voluntary accreditation process, and a basic legal and regulatory review. As a result of several major grants, the program has been expanded beyond Maryland to include nonprofit support organizations in the District of Columbia and six other states— Alabama, Delaware, Ohio, Oklahoma, Pennsylvania, and Virginia. These are known as "Replication Partners." There are three national Replication Partners—The Arc of the United States, the American Nurses Association, and the National Leadership Roundtable on Church Management. The Santa Clara University Markkula Center for Applied Ethics is a Regional Replication Partner. The National Standards for Excellence Institute administers the program for all partners and for nonprofits in states that do not have a licensed partner.

The 67 performance standards for both research best practices and legal and regulatory requirements are grouped in six areas:

1. Mission, Strategy, and Evaluation

2. Leadership: Board, Staff, and Volunteers

3. Legal Compliance and Ethics

4. Finance and Operations

5. Resource Development

6. Public Awareness, Engagement, and Advocacy

The focus of the program is to provide education and resources to encourage nonprofits to adopt ethical and legal practices. Organizations choosing to become accredited demonstrate that they adhere to the standards by participating in a 3-phase review process, which includes peer reviewers examining all practices. The process includes submitting an application documenting their compliance with the standards, as well as paying a fee and moving through the 3-phase review process. Once the peer-review panel affirms that the organization meets the standards, the statewide Standards for Excellence Committee does a final review and approves the organization. The organization receives a Seal of Excellence, with the expectation that having the Seal will provide the organization with increased credibility with donors and grantmakers. Organizations desiring to ensure that all legal and regulatory components are in place may apply for the Basic Legal and Regulatory Review and become recognized as "Standards Basics" approved organizations. Organizations achieving approval under Accreditation or "Standards Basics" receive national recognition on GuideStar.org. Organizations are accredited for an initial 3-year period, must reapply for a 3-year renewal, and then may renew for 5-year periods. There is a process for accredited organizations to have that accreditation revoked if they are found to have violated standards after an investigation by the program.

The full set of standards for national certification can be found at:

http://www.standardsforexcellenceinstitute.org

Among the standards are:

- The board should have stated performance expectations and hold board members accountable for attendance at meetings, participation in fundraising activities, committee service, and awareness of program activities.

- On average, over a 5-year period, a charity should assure that the fundraising revenues as compared with expenses have a greater than 3:1 ratio.

- Fundraisers, whether or not they are employees or independent consultants, should not be compensated based on a percentage of the amount raised or some other commission formula.

- Nonprofits must be aware of and comply with all applicable federal, state, and local laws. This may include, but is not limited to, complying with laws and regulations related to IRS filing requirements, governance, human resources, licensing, financial accountability, taxation, valuation of in-kind gifts, unrelated business income, document retention and destruction, related entities, data security, accessibility, fundraising, lobbying, and advocacy.

Ethical Standards for Grant Writers

The Grant Professionals Association (GPA), based in Overland, Kansas, was formed in 1998 and was initially named the American Association of Grant Professionals. It is incorporated as a 501(c)(6) tax-exempt professional association and has more than 2,000 members. It bills itself as "the first organization focused solely on the advancement of grantsmanship as a profession and the support of its practitioners" (Grant Professionals Association, n.d.). The organization conducts an annual conference and annually publishes the *GPA Journal.* It is a leading organization in establishing a formal credentialing process for grant professionals, forming the Grant Professional Certification Institute (GPCI), which has as its core purpose "overseeing the development of critical standards within an ethical framework that will help define the future of grantsmanship."

The first set of ethical principles, a Code of Ethical Conduct, was adopted by the organization in 1999. The latest version of the Association's Code of Ethics was adopted in October 2011. It consists of 10 general ethical principles it expects its members to honor and 20 specific professional obligations. A copy of this Code can be found at: *http://www.grantprofessionals.org/ethics*

According to the organization, "The GPA Code of Ethics reflects only the highest standards in professional behavior and incorporates the standards promulgated by American Fundraising Professionals and other professions dedicated to serving the greater public good." A review of the code validates this claim.

For example, the code makes it clear that members should work for a salary or fee rather than percentage compensation based on grants, and should not accept a finder's fee or commission. Their compensation should not be written into the grant without the approval of the grantor. There are provisions relating to confidentiality, plagiarism, accurate accounting and solicitation materials, conflicts of interest disclosure, lawful behavior, professional competence, and not diverting funds for purposes other than those provided for by the grant. Included are general, aspirational provisions relating to honesty, integrity, privacy, cultural diversity, and treating all individuals with dignity and respect.

There is an enforcement provision in the Standards of Professional Practice within the Code that subjects violators of the standards to disciplinary sanctions by an elected committee of the membership, including the possibility of expulsion from the organization.

The American Grant Writers' Association (AGWA), founded in 2002, is based in Largo, Florida, is also a 501(c)(6) professional trade association (AGWA, 2015). The organization has about 1,000 active members and offers its own professional credentialing program—Certified Grant Writer®.

Its latest Professional Standards and Code of Ethics was adopted in July 2016. The provisions of the AGWA code are similar to, if not identical to, those of the GPA and have common themes.

This Code consists of 10 general principles (e.g., "members bring credit to their profession by their demeanor") and 23 professional standards. As with the code of the GPA, the AGWA also prohibits compensation that is not salary-based, specifically, that the member "may not accept compensation that is a retainer, bonus, commission-based, or contingency-based." Compensation may not be accepted on a percentage of contributions or contingent on the awarding of the grant. This code does not permit members to receive or handle any of the funds from a grant award, and it requires that the client be the grant applicant rather than the grant writer. As with the GPA, the code does not permit members to pay finders' fees to obtain access to donors.

Many grant writers are members of the Association of Fundraising Professionals (AFP), founded in 1960, formerly known as the National Society of Fund Raising Executives (NSFRE) (Association of Fundraising Professionals, n.d.). Based in Arlington, Virginia, AFP serves more than 30,000 members with 233 local chapters around the world (Association of Fundraising Professionals, 2017). It is a 501(c)(3) public charity. AFP has a comprehensive ethics code (see: *http://www.afpnet.org/Ethics/content.cfm?ItemNumber=3093&navI*

temNumber=536), professional credentialing program (see: http://www.afpnet.org/Professional/CertificationList.cfm?navItemNumber=554), extensive opportunities for professional development/continuing education (see: http://www.afpnet.org/Professional/?navItemNumber=504), and a website page devoted to general fundraising ethics (see: http://www.afpnet.org/Ethics/EthicsArticleList.cfm?navItemNumber=538).

Online Resources

American Grant Writers' Association
http://www.agwa.us/

Association of Fundraising Professionals
http://www.afpnet.org

BBB's Wise Giving Alliance
http://give.org/

Carter McNamara's Business Ethics: Managing Ethics in the Workplace and Social Responsibility
http://www.managementhelp.org/ethics/ethics.htm

Grant Professionals Association
http://www.grantprofessionals.org/

Independent Sector: Accountability Overview
http://www.independentsector.org/accountability

Independent Sector's Principles Resource Center
http://www.independentsector.org/principles

Standards for Excellence Institute
https://standardsforexcellence.org/

Josephson Institute of Ethics
http://josephsoninstitute.org/

Discussion Questions

1. Discuss the roles of government, watchdog groups, the media, and national associations in keeping nonprofit organizations transparent and accountable. How effective do you think each of these is? Are there cases in which it may not be unethical for a nonprofit organization to spend substantially more on fundraising than it does on programming?

2. Are there cases in which it may be ethical for a nonprofit organization to spend substantially more on fundraising than it does on programming?

3. Can a good case be made that it is ethical for fundraisers and grant writers to be paid a percentage of the amounts they raise?

Activities

1. Compare and contrast the three fundraising ethics codes of Independent Sector (*http://www.independentsector.org/code_of_ethics*), the Wise Giving Alliance (*http://give.org/for-charities/How-We-Accredit-Charities/?id=236646*), and the Standards for Excellence (*http://www.standardsforexcellenceinstitute.org/dnn/*). Consider who developed them, to whom they apply, how strict the standards are, what they cover, and any consequences to organizations that violate the standards. Create a table to compare provisions relating to common topics covered by these codes.

2. Compare and contrast the two ethics codes for grant writers mentioned in this chapter.

3. Invite a certified fundraising professional to speak to your class on the topic of whether such certifications are really effective in training those in the field and protecting the public, or are simply a strategy to increase their value by differentiating themselves from those who lack such certification.

References

AGWA. (2015). *American Grant Writers' Association.* Retrieved from: *http://www.agwa.us/*

Association of Fundraising Professionals. (n.d.) *History of the Association of Fundraising Professionals.* Retrieved from: *http://www.afpnet.org/About/content.cfm?ItemNumber=727*

Association of Fundraising Professionals. (2017). *AFP Fact Sheet.* Retrieved from: *http://www.afpnet.org/About/content.cfm?ItemNumber=1069*

Better Business Bureau. (2010). *Start with trust.* Retrieved from *http://www.bbb.org/*

Grant Professionals Association. (n.d.). *About.* Retrieved from: *http://www.grantprofessionals.org/about*

Independent Sector. (2015). *Principles for good governance and ethical practice,* 2015 Edition. Washington, DC: Author.

National Charities Information Bureau. (2000). *NCIB's standards in philanthropy.* Retrieved from *http://www.give.org/for-charities/How-We-Accredit-Charities/*

National Society of Fund Raising Executives. (1991). *NSFRE code of ethical principles and standards of professional practice.* Retrieved from *http://www.afpnet.org/Ethics/content.cfm?ItemNumber=3093&navItemNumber=536*

Case 1
Jane's Dilemma—Hiring the Development Director

"Thank you, and I appreciated our meeting," Jane said, rising to shake Bernie Plotkoff's hand. She would have preferred to avoid this customary gesture at the end of such a meeting, but she knew it would have been rude to do so. "I'll be in touch soon, perhaps next week, about whether you were the successful candidate for this position," she added stiffly, trying to conjure up a smile—which was a struggle, considering the circumstances.

Jane's stomach knotted up, and she began to sweat profusely as she considered her options, none of which were attractive.

For fifteen years, Jane Doesky had devoted herself to making the A. K. Schwarzkin Charitable Foundation the best charity it could be. She was well-paid as the executive director of the organization, and the income was now much more necessary than when she was first hired, because her mother was in a nursing home, and she was making payments of $6,000 each month to the home. Mom showed increasing signs of developing Alzheimer's, and Jane feared that this would necessitate having her moved to a unit that provided services to these patients, with a substantially higher monthly charge.

Jane had sacrificed her personal life, making herself available to the organization 24/7. She had the usual number of crises during her tenure, but had always come through with solutions that were creative. Her colleagues in the general nonprofit community held her in high esteem for her integrity and leadership.

Now, it appeared that not only was her job on the line, but the continued existence of the charity was at risk. It was a perfect storm that had put her in this unenviable situation—a flagging economy, the trust of a friend and colleague that was violated, and the resignation of the organization's dependable, long-time Director of Development and de facto chief financial officer, Myron Cohn, for "personal reasons." Almost everyone knew what those "personal reasons" were by now, as the newspapers had had a field day documenting the financial scandal that had rocked the Jewish charitable community in general and the Schwarzkin charity in particular.

Cohn had fallen hook, line, and sinker for the Madoff Ponzi scheme, investing most of the foundation's assets, lured by a promise of returns that were substantially better than the market. Doesky had trusted Cohn's judgment, providing only cursory oversight over his financial management, recognizing that he had an exemplary track record and almost 20 years more experience than she had. Once it became evident that $30 million in Foundation assets were gone with virtually no chance of any recovery, Myron had submitted his resignation, content to retire to a comfy condo in Florida. Leaving Jane and the Foundation holding the bag. An empty bag.

Jane thought back to her meeting a month before with her board chair, Goldie Sharaf-sky, who had been livid after hearing about how much the Foundation had lost. She had summoned Jane to her own office, located in a posh, downtown office building adjacent to Rittenhouse Square in Philadelphia. Once there, she had provided Jane with a deftly-delivered ultimatum.

"I'll be frank," Goldie had begun, closing the door for privacy, her tone of voice masking any cordiality that had usually been there whenever Jane was asked, infrequently, to meet in Goldie's office. More often, meetings between the two were held over a casual lunch in one of the trendy cafés along Broad Street. Jane did not expect this meeting to be pleasant, but she felt blindsided by what followed.

"I've exchanged some telephone calls with the Foundation leadership, and we have come to a consensus on how to handle this unpleasant situation with the financial scandal," Goldie began, her words measured. Jane did not take this as a good sign for what was to come.

"Your job is on the line here. Since the Foundation has taken such an unexpected hit from both the scandal and poor fundraising brought on by the tanking of the economy, everyone's job is on the line, including mine as chair. One of our board members, I won't tell you which *mumser* that was but you could probably guess, even suggested liquidating the Foundation. Others wanted to simply fire you and rebuild. Even your supporters are *kvetching.*"

Jane felt the blood rush to her head. But she said nothing. Maintain some control, she thought.

"I fought to keep you. I can't find any justification for simply giving up," Goldie continued. "So many people depend on our programs. And you have considerable talent that I think can work to our advantage as we try to recover from this debacle. I know Myron let you down, and God knows, I can understand why you let him have free rein over investment policy. But when push comes to shove, you are responsible and accountable for the results of all of the Foundation's employees."

Jane took a deep breath, waiting for the shoe to drop. It did.

"So, here's what we decided. You have two years to rebuild the Foundation's assets to a level that we feel comfortable funding our commitments, and you will be evaluated in a year and must demonstrate that you are making significant progress toward achieving that goal. If you can agree to do that, you can stay; otherwise, we will provide you with two months of severance pay, shake hands, thank you for your service over the years, and launch a search for your successor."

Jane, speechless, shaken, simply nodded her head and left after exchanging the bare minimum of parting pleasantries.

Now back in her office, contemplating what was told to her in confidence by the third candidate she had interviewed that day for the vacant Director of Development position, her anxiety heightened as she considered what he had offered to her.

Bernie Plotkoff was a name well known to her. She was intrigued that he had applied for the vacant position although she granted him an interview more out of curiosity than any realistic expectation that she would actually hire him. He was the current Director of Development for the S.D. Leibman Foundation, the Swartzkin Foundation's principal competitor for charitable donations directed to serving Jewish adolescent runaways and missing children. Both foundations had been established at about the same time, inspired by the disappearance of Chandra Levy in Washington, D.C. during the summer of 2001. At one time, the boards of both foundations had considered merging, but relations between the two organizations had soured during negotiations and both had gone their separate ways. The board chairs of both organizations at that time had once been personal friends, bonded by the shared trauma of separate, but similar, family tragedies involving young family members.

Yet following the breakup of the proposed merger, they were no longer on speaking terms. While this breakup appeared to be irreconcilable at the time, most board members and staff leadership, including Jane, judged that an eventual merger would be inevitable, particularly when economic times necessitated an end to competition for funds and programs that served essentially the same clients.

Jane had to admit that the Leibman Foundation was the more successful of the two, attributed for the most part to the aggressive fundraising tactics of the development director whom she had just finished interviewing as part of her process to find a successor to Cohn. "Aggressive" was perhaps too polite a word to describe Bernie's fundraising reputation. The Leibman Foundation raised millions of dollars, including from some folks who contributed to both foundations.

The Leibman Foundation's fundraising tactics were anything but low-key. It was among the first to enclose a check in its direct mailings that recipients could cash regardless of whether they made a contribution, instilling an additional level of guilt to make one. It was one of the few Jewish charities that enclosed a small prayer book or religious article such as a yamulke (a skull cap), which would make recipients who were religiously observant to be violative of Jewish law if they simply tossed the mail piece into the trash rather than having it undergo a ritual burial.

It was rumored that Leibman's annual development budget included a line-item for the hiring of a private detective, and that Plotkoff utilized the services of shady Internet database businesses that sold information to anyone for a fee—information that most of us would assume would not be available publicly to anyone. This was part of what is called "prospect research," what otherwise was a legitimate technique of fundraisers to learn about the capacity of donors and potential donors. As "refined" by Plotkoff, it was more akin to "spying."

In short, the Leibman Foundation sanctioned whatever worked, kept constant pressure on giving, and held over-the-top lavish fundraisers that attracted giving that only minimally was provided because of the organization's mission. And the grand conductor of the fundraising strategy was Bernie Plotkoff, looked upon with undisguised disdain by many of his colleagues, most of whom were secretly envious of the results he recorded for his employer.

Prior to the interview, Jane had no evidence to think that he did anything overtly illegal, although it would not have come as a surprise to her if he routinely crossed the line of ethical conduct without a second thought. If he did so, she would have attributed it to being a zealot for the cause, and she wouldn't have expected that he violated professional ethics for his own personal gain. Now that she had finished her interview with him and heard his pitch, she had second thoughts about her judgment about both his ethics and his allegiance to following the letter of the law in pursuing his craft.

What Bernie had offered her was communicated quite directly, and he didn't make any effort to veil his proposal in euphemistic references to make it appear less distasteful to her. She was shocked by his brazen *chutzpah,* and she felt even a bit insulted that he would trust her to keep his offer in confidence.

He offered to leave the Leibman Foundation for Cohn's position, giving two weeks' notice. He would want his current salary that he received from Leibman, plus a 10% raise. He would want an unvouchered expense account of $20,000 annually and a company car. On top of that, he would expect an annual incentive bonus of 2% of the amount he raised. He would guarantee that he could increase the Foundation's fundraising income by 100% in the first year, and make up most of the losses from the Madoff financial scandal by focusing particularly on donors who had the capacity to participate in planned giving.

What gave Jane even more pause was what he told her would be his strategy for achieving these lofty goals, and when he disclosed that, Jane didn't doubt his ability to come through and save her own job as well as keep the foundation viable for many years to come.

Bernie intimated that he had on disk all of the fundraising records of the Leibman Foundation, including all of the prospect research files and history of giving for 10,000 donors, about four times the number of donors that were in the Schwarzkin fundraising database. Hire him, and he would integrate that disk into the fundraising operations of the Schwarzkin Foundation. Even without this database, his contacts alone would result in millions of dollars in additional donations to the Foundation. And with this database and the files that came with it, the Schwarzkin Foundation's future would be cemented, and its major competitor for donations, the Leibman Foundation, would be crippled. Within a year or two, the Leibman Foundation leadership would be begging for a merger, so the integration of the database files and the end to destructive competition between the two organizations would come to an end. So, while his plan might be somewhat on the shady side, all of the money raised would be going to a cause both organizations support, so in the long run, what would be the harm?

As Jane contemplated how difficult it might be to find another job in this economic environment, she considered the pros and cons of Bernie's proposal.

Discussion Questions:

1. What are Jane's options, and what are the pros and cons of each option?

2. Should Jane report the offer she received from Bernie to anyone within or outside of her organization?

3. How much should the fact that Jane needs to maintain her income to support her mother's nursing home costs factor into her decision? Discuss any conflict between Jane's ethical responsibility to act in the best interests of the organization and the need to serve her own interests, and how such a conflict should be resolved.

4. How much does the fact that these two organizations are likely to merge sometime in the near future factor into her decision?

5. Discuss the ethics of each of the fundraising strategies used by Bernie Plotkoff.

6. Discuss what is appropriate with respect to prospect research and what are some of the prospect research techniques that might cross the line of acceptability, even if they are effective.

7. Discuss the pros and cons of paying fundraisers based on the amount they raise. Why do almost all organizations that represent fundraisers have ethics codes that consider compensation based on the amount a fundraiser raises to be unethical?

Note: This case originally appeared in *The Nonprofit Management Casebook: Scenes From the Frontlines.*

Case 2
Evaluating Dr. Luddite, Harristown Asperger's Syndrome Foundation Executive Director

Tempers were beginning to flare at the mid-August board meeting of the Harristown Asperger's Syndrome Foundation, and the atmosphere was hot enough as it was. The air conditioner had been turned down in the conference room to save on cooling expenses and satisfy a "green agenda" advanced by a coalition of nonprofits of which the Foundation was a member. The board was split right down the middle on whether to fire its long-time executive director, an action that the chair of the Foundation and convener of the meeting, Stephen Huddleston III, had considered to be inconceivable only hours ago.

"Dr. Luddite should retire gracefully," brusquely accused Ryan Powers, a 30-something investment banker with an MBA who had little patience for beating around the bush. He had been the one a half-hour previously to offer the motion not to renew Dr. Luddite's contract, effectively firing him on December 31.

"Absolutely," agreed Tom Davies, the only "Generation Z" member of the board and only a few years out of college himself. "He should step aside and let a younger person with fresh ideas and experience in running a modern nonprofit bring the Foundation into the 21st century. Or at least the 20th century," he added pointedly, thinking he was being funny.

Powers and Davies had been a tag team, taking turns at battering the executive director without any indication that they would ever run out of ammunition against him. It might take some fancy footwork along with some parliamentary maneuvering for the CEO's defenders to deflect their frontal attack and provide enough acknowledgment of their complaints to placate them and other disgruntled board members. What would it take to convince them to withdraw their motion and substitute something more constructive and more in the interests of the Foundation? Even if their motion carried, Huddleston was confident that he could muster a re-vote on the action by having another meeting before December 31 with the attendance of some of the board members who were absent today. But it would take a major effort to smooth ruffled feathers, and who knows how Dr. Luddite would interpret the board's current debate once it leaked out to him what was occurring, as it inevitably would.

"I don't think either of you appreciates how much Dr. Luddite means to this organization," parried Ruth Winnett. She was one of the original board members of the organization and among the legions of individuals who worshipped Dr. Luddite and raved about his accomplishments on behalf of those like her who had a child with Asperger's Syndrome.

"This organization would never be able to replace him if he decided to leave voluntarily, and it would be a disaster to fire him, not to mention how unfair it would be to him.

He has devoted his entire professional life to our cause, and we should be judging him on the results of his efforts, not the specific management techniques that he uses. I think we would be better served if both of you left the board if you're not happy, rather than having Dr. Luddite leave."

"Okay, let's get back to focusing on the Personnel Committee's executive director evaluation recommendations and the motion on the floor," implored Mr. Huddleston.

Mr. Huddleston surveyed the conference room one more time, looking for any sign that the 16 members of the Harristown Asperger's Syndrome Foundation board before him would reach a consensus on the future of its long-time executive director and organizational co-founder. *We should have found some way to throw at least three of these folks off the board last year before it got to this, and perhaps I deserve some of the blame for letting things deteriorate to the point they have,* he admitted to himself.

The main agenda item was what was expected to be a perfunctory approval of the formal annual executive director evaluation report of the Personnel Committee. The committee, which was appointed by the chair, had generally agreed that Dr. Luddite's performance was exemplary, but he could improve the management of the Foundation by infusing some technological innovation into its operations.

But things were getting out of control at this meeting. Some renegade members of the board were using the discussion of the report to express their dissatisfaction with the organization's leadership in general, and the quality of the leadership of Dr. Michael Luddite, in particular. Chair Huddleston was irritated; this was the type of situation that needed to be diffused before it reached the board meeting stage. As a courtesy, Mr. Powers, the apparent leader of the cabal engaged in trashing Luddite, could have at least given the chair a heads-up that there was going to be a challenge of some kind. The debate did not appear to be spontaneous with Powers, Davies, and two others speaking out against retaining Dr. Luddite.

Now in the last year of his two-year term as chair, Mr. Huddleston had accepted the position by unanimous vote, and he had helped guide the organization through some turbulent economic times. He had forged a good relationship with Michael Luddite, Ph.D., the CEO and an icon in the social service community for nearly a half-century, who worked tirelessly for children with Asperger's and the families who cared for them. Putting aside the substantial discomfort that would accrue to the organization by firing Dr. Luddite, Huddleston knew that a search for a replacement executive director would consume significant time and resources of the Foundation (and those of himself, personally), and that it would be unlikely for the organization to find someone of Dr. Luddite's experience and national stature.

In 1995, the Luddites' eight-year-old grandson had been diagnosed with Asperger's Syndrome after a frustrating three-year search for the cause of his often baffling behavior. At the time, Dr. Luddite had been the long-serving director of the State's Medicaid program, serving a succession of Republican and Democratic Governors and their politically appointed Secretaries of Health and Human Services. For almost three decades, none had given even a thought to replacing Dr. Luddite, as was routinely the case with all other deputy secretaries in the department. He was a nationally respected expert on many aspects of the program, and his résumé documented his vast experience over the years advising presidential commissions, the National Governors Association, and others who were influential in shaping public policy in that area.

That same year, Dr. Luddite had been abruptly fired over his unwillingness to implement certain cost containment policies demanded by the Governor's Office. Rather than retiring on his substantial state pension, as many in his position might have done, Luddite instead engaged in a Herculean effort to organize a coalition of parents and health care providers focused on Asperger's. Both he and his wife, a registered nurse, had devoted the next 15 years to advocacy at the state and federal levels to find effective treatments if not an outright cure, provide government support for providing services to families with the syndrome, and educate the professional health community and the public about it.

Asperger's Syndrome (a.k.a. Asperger's Disorder, or Asperger's) is a behavioral syndrome associated with autism that affects approximately one in every 5,000 children in the United States and around the globe—although epidemiological studies to gauge its prevalence have varied widely. Its name derives from Hans Asperger, the Austrian medical doctor who in 1944 was the first to catalog its symptoms—an impairment in non-verbal communication, physical clumsiness, and limitations empathizing with others. It had taken another half-century before Asperger's had become a standard diagnosis, a delay that had caused immense grief and suffering to the families of children with the syndrome, who often suffered through the frustrations of misdiagnoses. There is no known single cause, although a genetic link has been established. There is also no reliable treatment; rather, the symptoms are managed by behavioral therapy. Those who also suffer from depression and anxiety—which are not unusual to accompany Asperger's—receive medications targeted to relieving those particular symptoms. In recent years, autism, ADD, and ADHD had become well known nationally as a result of extensive media interest. Asperger's Disorder was less well-known, though certainly more known as a result of the work of Dr. Luddite and the Foundation.

As with other behavioral disorders in children, such as ADHD, Asperger's is both over-diagnosed and under-diagnosed, partly attributable to the fact that there is a wide spectrum of the syndrome's degree of severity. The Foundation had dedicated much of its efforts to assuring that the health care community received the education it needed to appropriately diagnose the syndrome, and had been one of the leading organizations to assist in the development of screening instruments.

As it was, Dr. Luddite was not present, as he was traveling across the country to help organize a parallel foundation in another state. He would not have been in the room while his evaluation was being discussed, but it might have helped if he had been accessible to answer questions. For most nonprofit executive directors, being on the opposite coast would not be a major obstacle. The fact that Dr. Luddite was unreachable during this crisis only underscored the point his detractors were making.

The Foundation was Luddite's vision from the beginning. He and a small group of parents and grandparents had incorporated the Foundation, and they seeded its operations from their personal funds. At first, there had been no paid staff, and Dr. Luddite had chaired the board and voluntarily, with the assistance of his wife, managed the Foundation. After only two years, a well-heeled member had bankrolled the organization with a six-figure contribution with promises to renew the gift annually. At that point, Dr. Luddite decided to become the organization's executive director and continue to serve on the board in a non-voting, *ex officio* capacity. Mrs. Luddite had continued to serve on the board and served as its chair until her death in 2002.

Initially, Dr. Luddite suffered through a severe case of founder's syndrome. This term has been used to describe situations in which the founder of an organization dominates decisionmaking through his or her commitment, passion, or personal charisma. This dominance eventually becomes inappropriate behavior as the organization matures and governance and management become more decentralized through a group of diverse stakeholders. But in time, he became more comfortable with the more restricted role of CEO. Helping him through this often painful process was an outside consultant hired to develop a five-year strategic plan for the foundation. Eventually, Dr. Luddite and the board recognized that it was Dr. Luddite's job to manage, and the board's job to govern. In time, Dr. Luddite had accepted this division of responsibility.

Dr. Luddite was always respectful of board members, but it was not unusual for him to ignore the board's directions on occasion, particularly when he perceived that the board had overstepped its authority and was inappropriately micromanaging. For example, back in 2007, the board had passed a resolution, offered by the organization's treasurer, directing Dr. Luddite to invest the Foundation's entire available bank account with Bernie Madoff, a former chairman of the Nasdaq Stock Exchange. Madoff had formed a private investment company that seemed to offer good returns on investments that far exceeded the conservative investing Dr. Luddite arranged on behalf of the Foundation. Despite occasional nagging telephone calls from the treasurer, Dr. Luddite continued to place the Foundation's investments in less risky, and less lucrative, investments. When the Madoff scandal broke in 2008, the board recognized that had Dr. Luddite followed its directive, the Foundation's assets would have been completely wiped out.

In almost every case when he had ignored the direction of the board, Dr. Luddite's instincts were prescient, and it was rare that anyone on the board ever pointed out his occasional lapses of blatant insubordination. In almost every case, a reasonable person would have concluded in retrospect that it would have been disastrous for some of the board's direction to have been followed. For years, board chairs had given Dr. Luddite some slack to use his judgment, even if he might have to violate a board resolution in spirit, if not the letter.

Clearly, his experience and his commitment to the welfare of the families the organization served were evident, and his paramount concern during his tenure as the CEO was never himself. The board was grateful that he had been willing to accept a 10% pay cut during last year's budget shortfall, and the organization's revenues were enhanced by book royalties from a primer on Asperger's Syndrome he had authored and that he had designated to be paid to the organization rather than to himself.

Board members and chairs came and went. Dr. Luddite was the public face and voice of the organization, and most would concede that even with his limitations, replacing Dr. Luddite when he chose to retire would be traumatic for the organization and the cause it advanced.

Yet, at least three members of the board were actively seeking to have Dr. Luddite removed from his position and were clamoring for his head on a platter. And they were finding increasing support from a cadre of relatively newly-elected board members who were sympathetic to a change in direction for the organization and were jockeying for either a change in staff leadership or a change in marching orders provided to the current leadership. These two factions of board members were in an alliance against the executive director, but it was clear to Mr. Huddleston that if they succeeded, they would be in opposition to themselves if and when the axe fell on Dr. Luddite. And if they succeeded, the continued viability of the organization might well be threatened, as several major funders remained under the spell Dr. Luddite was able to cast on them and provided grants on the basis of Dr. Luddite's star power. If Dr. Luddite went down, the generous funding from these donors would likely be history. And Mr. Huddleston was in the middle of it all.

For his part, despite imploring from Mr. Huddleston, Dr. Luddite refused to help his own case, which Huddleston attributed to simple stubborn arrogance. He ran the organization virtually the same way he had when he first established the organization. The good news was that he ran the organization with energy and vigor, bristling with integrity that was communicated to the Foundation's ten employees through both deed and word. Even now, approaching 75, he could be seen bounding up three flights of steps to the organization's offices rather than taking the elevator. Although health might become an issue in future years, none of his detractors on the board dared to make the case that he no longer had the mental or physical capacity to lead the organization. Rather, the problem, admittedly becoming a more serious problem with the passage of time, was that Dr. Luddite was technophobic.

This had been amusing at times during the 1980s, as the business world had embraced the productivity increases spurred on by the personal computer. Dr. Luddite would still be seen at his state office into the late hours hunching over at his desk banging out letters and reports on the trusty old Remington typewriter he had used to type his doctoral dissertation in the late '60s. During the 1990s, this was becoming less amusing to observers and more inconvenient. And entering the 21st century, some members of the board recognized that this was becoming a real problem that needed to be addressed. The world had changed almost overnight.

Nonprofit organizations were clearly always several years behind their for-profit counterparts in adopting new technology. But at some point, every nonprofit organization came to understand the role technology had in improving the way they delivered goods and services, and in communicating with their stakeholders. And, more and more, stakeholders of nonprofits had come to expect the organizations to use these new technologies.

Dr. Luddite spurned offers of training, and Huddleston's predecessor as chair once had given an ultimatum that Dr. Luddite needed to learn some new skills or face some sanctions. But that chair had rotated off the board to an amorphous "advisory committee" before achieving any change in the executive director's behavior. The situation today was different; the board's new policy to evaluate the executive director provided an ill-timed forum to discuss Dr. Luddite's glaring weaknesses, which in previous years were simply ignored.

Looking around the room, Mr. Huddleston estimated that at least 14 of the 16 board members present had used either their cell phones or Blackberries to check their email during the meeting. Perhaps half of them had sent a text message—Mr. Huddleston had received three of these texts himself within just the last 30 minutes. The last one was from one board member sitting not more than three feet away across the table, John Winters, a balding, corpulent man in his mid-50s who texted.

"Time 2 fir tht old dinasr."

Mr. Huddleston shuddered to think who else in the room had received the same direct message from Winters. But one thing was for certain; it wouldn't have been Dr. Luddite, who refused to even carry a cell phone.

The organization had a working Web site, but it was something that Dr. Luddite had managed, totally by outsourcing, simply to assuage the board. He did not participate in making the site interactive, such as by posting a blog, or by providing electronic newsletters. While his colleagues in the nonprofit community were using the Internet to recruit employees and volunteers, raise funds through online charitable auctions, fundraise and friendraise using Facebook and MySpace pages, and forge revenue-generating affiliation agreements with online retailers, Dr. Luddite turned up his nose at almost any suggestion that related to harnessing the power of the Internet. He refused to even have an email address and would not have had any idea how to access any email he received had he had one. He was a master at one-on-one meetings and radiated a personal charisma that won over many a person who might have been oppositional.

But today, Dr. Luddite was besieged by a phalanx of board members intent to can him and, perhaps, replace him with a younger person who had not even been born when personal computers had been invented.

Despite this disdain for technology, Huddleston was a strong supporter of Dr. Luddite, but recognized that this aspect of his personality could well be the Achilles Heel that resulted in his dismissal, if not at this meeting, at a future one. And the seeds of a potential firing had been sown two years earlier when the board, under the urging of a new organization funder, agreed to institute an annual evaluation of the executive director. At the time, no one was questioning Dr. Luddite's leadership of the organization, and this was considered to be a *pro forma* initiative. Most thought it made sense anyway, as eventually, the reins of leadership would change. Whoever led the organization should be subject to a periodic board evaluation, certainly one of the management controls that are expected to be under the purview of the board. Unfortunately, the addition of three new board members, each of them sporting the latest model of iPhone that appeared to be in constant use, were feeding calls for the board to fire Dr. Luddite.

Mr. Huddleston suspected that in front of him, there was a meeting within a meeting, as the three primary conspirators plotted to fire the executive director, texting among themselves, exchanging strategy.

Joining these three insurgents were several board members who felt that the mission of the organization was too narrowly focused, and that the concentration on Asperger's should be broadened to include all Autism Spectrum Disorders (ASD). They did not feel that Dr. Luddite was willing to extend the reach of the services provided by the organization to serve the growing number of families with a family member having an ASD diagnosis. And perhaps two other board members felt that Dr. Luddite was getting too old and should retire, and that the board should hire someone who would provide fresh leadership. Each had felt some sense of being betrayed by Dr. Luddite whenever he had ignored a board resolution.

Mr. Huddleston estimated that if anyone made a motion to remove Dr. Luddite, perhaps eight of the 16 in the room would join together to force him out, despite having disparate reasons for doing so. The board consisted of 21 members, and five of them were absent. All five were long-time board members, and would likely support Dr. Luddite if they were present. He considered whether to invite them to participate in the meeting by conference call for a reconsideration of the vote if the motion to fire received a majority, but he hoped to avoid a showdown.

Discussion Questions

1. Is it ever appropriate for an executive director to ignore the express directive of the board or chair of the board?

2. When is it appropriate for a board chair to take actions to remove members of the board for other than missing board meetings or not participating in working on behalf of the organization?

3. Was it appropriate for Dr. Luddite's wife to serve on the board at the time he was the executive director?

4. How much loyalty does a nonprofit organization owe to a long-time executive director whom it judges, for reasons beyond that staff member's control, to be underperforming?

5. How much additional power does the chair of the board typically have compared to any other member of the board? Discuss how this power can be abused.

6. What are ways members of the board can deal with a chair who has Founders Syndrome?

7. What does it mean that "It was Dr. Luddite's job to manage and the board's job to govern"? What are the differences between these two tasks?

Note: This case originally appeared in *The Nonprofit Management Casebook: Scenes From the Frontlines.*

Case 3
Navigating a Dual Relationship at the Public Interest Policy Center

With only a single item on the agenda and to the consternation of the chair, the board meeting was starting to deteriorate into a free-for-all of shouting, recriminations, accusations, and name calling.

Denise Willow, the besieged executive director of the Public Interest Policy Center, was the general target of the verbal arrows slung by individual board members who felt betrayed upon learning even more salacious details of Denise's behavior relating to the William A. Ivystone Foundation, the Center's newest and at the moment, largest funder. She did have some defenders among her board, mostly among the handful of female members who were more sympathetic about Denise's assertion that there was a de facto double standard that applied to men and women in her position.

Certainly, no one on the board had ever complained when Denise had used her charm and more than ample physical attractiveness to schmooze up potential donors and entice them into supporting the Center. However, there had to be some reasonable limits to how far a staff member could appropriately play that game without risking serious damage to the Center's respected reputation. It was clear to everyone in the room, including Denise, that someone needed to put on the brakes on this runaway train—thus the call by the chair of the board of the Center for this emergency board meeting to decide what steps to take. None of the apparent options was attractive. *We are in damage control mode here,* thought David Payton, Esq., the chair.

The meeting was in its third hour of contentious wrangling. Denise had been granted all the time she asked for to relate her side of the story, providing even more details about her relationship with William Ivystone, the Foundation President, than some board members present felt were necessary. She explained to the board that she recognized the seriousness of the situation, and the board deserved to know what had happened, as she sat next to the chair at the long, polished oak table in the conference room of Payton & Payton, P.C.

Several board members had calmly asserted that Denise clearly had crossed the line of what was acceptable and should be fired. Others had done so without being calm. And some other board members were willing to overlook this major indiscretion, recognizing that Denise had otherwise been a model manager and leader, and she had acknowledged her failures in dealing with this situation, showed remorse, and was willing to make things right and move on with that potentially Herculean task.

Her recent travails accommodating this particular major donor had begun innocently, and then had incrementally snowballed into a surreal soap opera that threatened the integrity of the Center and perhaps its continued existence as an independent public policy think tank. Some on the board, despite conceding that she had committed a major *faux pas,* felt uncomfortable firing the Harvard Law School graduate, and both the first African American and first woman executive director in the Center's seventy-year history.

Denise's hiring had been no accident, coming within a few months after the local daily newspaper had concluded a five-part investigation into the diversity, or lack thereof, of some of the most prominent nonprofit organizations in the area. The lack of diversity of the Public Interest Policy Center was particularly egregious, considering its mission to advocate on behalf of the disenfranchised and victims of discrimination, including women and minorities.

Almost the entire board of the Center had consisted of white males. The Center's professional staff of four had consisted entirely of white males, and the low-salaried support staff were virtually all female. Everyone affiliated with the organization was embarrassed by the disclosures, particularly since the Center made a major focus of its efforts addressing public policy issues relating to the poor, the sick, women, and minorities. The word "hypocritical" had been used in the newspaper editorial following up on its investigative exposé. The state's wire services had picked up the story and disseminated it to the rest of the state.

Spurred to act quickly by some key stakeholders outside of the organization, the board had made a major effort to recruit qualified minority candidates for the executive director's position. That position had become open after the Center's long-time executive director had been recruited as an Assistant Secretary in the Department of Health and Human Services by the Obama Administration. The board had also recognized that it needed itself to become more diverse, and had recruited three new board members—a white female, an Hispanic male, and an African-American female.

Well, that diversity goal certainly wasn't achieved in full just yet, Denise thought wryly, looking at the group around the table that was serving as the inquisition. Of the 16 present, 12 were white males, three were white women, and one was the African-American female. The average age of the board members was perhaps 65, more than twice Denise's age.

Denise felt that those judging her now around the room were unable to empathize with the situation in which she had found herself. She conceded that she had chiefly herself to blame for these circumstances. But she felt that she was the scapegoat for the shortcomings of the board. After all, it was the board that had failed to follow the very parts of the organization's strategic plan to stop the hemorrhage of unnecessary expenditures. That plan, with substantial input from Denise, had proposed creative ways to increase the income of the respected state-based public policy think tank so it would not have to rely on the continued largesse of any single source of funding.

The timing of her current troubled relationship with the board couldn't have been worse. The Ivystone Foundation had appeared out of nowhere almost exactly one year ago. Its President, a knight in shining armor, had offered his substantial resources to the fair maiden to keep the Center afloat during trying economic times. She had certainly done nothing illegal. In her mind, she was the *victim* of this sordid situation, and it was quite possible that she would suffer the consequences of being victimized while the perpetrator would not only escape with impunity but be able to continue as a stalker and sexual predator until someone took a public stand. Not likely that her spineless board of mostly old white men would do any such thing, she judged, as it had a lot to lose.

"Did you sleep with Ivystone?" Manfred Wishnick asked, more of an interrogation than a question, his penetrating icy stare indicating to Denise that he wouldn't believe her answer no matter how she answered. He was a 70-ish board member, the chair of the Resources Committee, who she suspected would not hesitate to offer a motion to summarily fire her if she had nodded her head affirmatively. Mr. Wishnick had been livid when learning that Denise had applied for a grant from the Foundation without first consulting the board. He had been adamant that the board of directors should be consulted about all potential major grants as part of its governance responsibilities, and that the executive director did not have carte blanche authority to submit grant proposals to funders without prior approval by the Resources Committee. The checks and balances inherent in board review were necessary, he asserted, to assure that the terms of the grant didn't violate any board policy, and that any project funded by the grant was consistent with the organization's mission and values. Not everyone on the board, however, shared that view.

"That question is out of order," ruled David Payton, the chair of the board, who had had a good relationship with Denise, at least up until it had leaked out several months ago that there was something going on between her and the Ivystone Foundation President that was more than a professional relationship. Since that time, Denise perceived a more frosty relationship from him that at times bordered on hostility. She knew that if she totally lost his support, she and the Center would part, perhaps today. If it did come to that, it might be difficult to even get a good recommendation to use for her job hunting, let alone the severance pay she would need to pay the bills in the interim. She also knew that if she were fired for misconduct, she would not be eligible for unemployment compensation.

"I think it is quite relevant to our discussion," responded Wishnick, heatedly. "If she is sleeping with a funder, that is a major conflict of interest and colors how she deals with the demands this funder is placing on our organization."

"No, I'm not sleeping with him, and did not sleep with him," she answered truthfully, without waiting for her chair to respond to Wishnick. But it was quite true that they had engaged in almost every kind of inappropriate behavior short of that threshold during the first six months she and the President of the William A. Ivystone Foundation had known each other, and she certainly wasn't planning on sharing any of the sordid details. What had begun as "harmless" flirting had slowly escalated into something more until it had reached a threshold that had made Denise not only uncomfortable but fearful about her personal security. Ivystone had turned into a stalker, once Denise had made it clear that any personal relationship they had was over.

As the board continued its venomous debate, Denise reflected back on how she got here.

When she had first met Ivystone at a public policy conference, sitting next to him quite by accident (or so she thought at the time), she had found him quite attractive and engaging. He was wearing an obviously expensive, custom-tailored suit with an ostentatiously large diamond encrusted wedding band. He had a warm smile and a laugh that had captivated her. She found him, at least initially, to be charming. Denise found the attention he was giving her to be flattering, and they had had a stimulating, spirited conversation about the luncheon speaker's views on "The Future of the Nonprofit Sector."

He had also been a good listener.

Denise had shared with him her frustration with the financial distress of the Center caused by the withdrawal of support of two key individual funders and the decline of individual memberships brought on by the worsening economy. He had been sympathetic, and mentioned that he might be able to help in some way. They had exchanged business cards. She hadn't known at the time that he was the scion and sole heir of a steel industry magnate who had entrusted his son with managing the philanthropic trust fund the elder Ivystone had established more than 30 years previously, now with assets approaching $160 million. He hadn't mentioned at the time that he was affiliated with any foundation. His card simply had his name and a home telephone number. When she got home, she had Googled him and found immediately that he was the President of a major family foundation. This fact had piqued her interest in following up with him soon for one purpose or another. For a fleeting moment, she imagined herself as Mrs. Ivystone, living a lavish lifestyle of summer homes in the Hamptons, the Caribbean, and London, eating at the best restaurants, flying into New York on a private jet simply to see the latest Broadway Show, and perhaps controlling millions of dollars to dole out to various philanthropic causes. That fantasy didn't last very long once Denise recognized that Ivystone had very little else going for him other than good looks, money to burn, and charm. And one obvious complication—he was married to a socialite from another prominent family. Her Google search had also yielded a substantial trove of less flattering hard information as well as gossip, including media accounts of convictions for illegal drug possession and a statutory rape charge that had been dropped after the victim had refused to testify.

Denise had called him first. Over lunch, at a secluded table in a fancy French restaurant, he had offered to provide the Center with Foundation funds. There was no hint of any *quid pro quo* beyond commissioning the Center to simply expand its mission of developing public policy papers.

The initial $5,000 contract he had offered required the Center to provide the Foundation with ten White Papers on public policy issues, along with a political analysis. The issues were clearly within the range of interests of the Center, which might have welcomed doing the papers without any compensation at all had they come from a board member, staff member, or member of the State Legislature. Denise considered this grant to be a windfall, and the Center certainly needed the money. She did not consult with the board before signing the contract.

But then, the relationship with Ivystone started to change into a *Fatal Attraction*-like nightmare involving the intertwining of two individuals and two organizations with polar opposite agendas.

Denise had had no warning that the first, subtle requests to compromise the Center's integrity would escalate into demands that would place the organization in turmoil and threaten its existence. A combination of a poor economy and the loss of several funders had eroded Center revenues. Without his Foundation's money, Denise realized that the Center would be in danger of not making payroll for the first time in its history. Several other policy think tanks in the state capital, both liberal and conservative, had recently folded, victim of some of the factors that were threatening the fiscal health of the Center.

During those first six months after the initial contract, she had negotiated a new series of contracts with the Foundation to prepare various policy papers. Each contract was for a higher amount of funding, certainly welcome to the Center, which was starved for revenues. Yet with each new contract, more lucrative than the one before, the deliverables were policy papers with a focus farther away from the Center's interests of generating public policy recommendations geared to protecting the interests of those with little voice in the State Capitol. What Ivystone was asking for at first, and later demanding to a greater extent, was material that could advance the Ivystone Steel business interests, often directly in conflict with the interests of the disenfranchised the Center was committed to serve, pursuant to its charter and mission statement.

Ivystone's insatiable demands on the organization had escalated with each contract. He had first requested, then demanded, that drafts of each policy paper be submitted to him for review. Denise had complied because of what she felt was a blossoming personal friendship. At first, these drafts came back with only minimal editing. More recently, they had been returned with substantive edits that conflicted with the supporting data and the Center's ideological slant. Denise had felt violated.

Several times, Ivystone had "suggested" that Denise consider hiring various Ivystone cousins for clerical positions. Considering that the Foundation was providing substantial funding, she had complied. At the time, it had seemed a good idea, and she saw it as a way to justify the continued increases in financial support of the Foundation. Now she regretted surrendering to this infiltration of her organization with sycophants without any real talent or motivation to advance the mission of the Center, and who were clearly more loyal to her organization's benefactor than to her and the Center.

Denise also had shepherded through board approval Ivystone's suggestion that the Center honor Senator John Wingnut, a.k.a. "Senator Steel," as its Legislator of the Year, the first Republican state legislator to be so honored in the 20 years the Center had bestowed such an award. During his entire 30-year Senate career, Sen. Wingnut had voted against almost every position advocated by the Center. However, Wingnut was a staunch opponent of the death penalty, not because it was administered unfairly and disproportionately carried out against those who couldn't afford decent legal representation (as the Center had pointed out in various policy papers over the years), but rather because it simply cost the state too much in legal fees to carry out an execution from its initial court decision through all of the appeals process. Denise had rationalized to her board that having Senator Wingnut as a friend of the Center might pay some dividends down the road. Comments from some board members such as "you sleep with dogs you wake up with fleas" still echoed in her head, and more than a few dues-paying Center members had protested the award by refusing to renew their $35 memberships. The grants from Ivystone dwarfed the loss of a few thousand dollars in membership fees. However, Denise mourned the loss of these loyal supporters whose trust had been violated and who were now actively disparaging her organization.

So far, the board had deflected by postponements Ivystone's request to add three of his nominees to the Center's board by explaining the objectives to increase board diversity. Ivystone had accepted the delay in responding to that request, but he was clearly miffed by the constant rebuff of his effort to expand his influence over the Center's governance.

However, his persistent and relentless efforts to slowly invade and conquer the Center were the least of Ivystone's actions that caused Denise substantial personal grief.

Once Denise discovered his past indiscretions—at least those that were transparent through a routine Internet search, she did not find him to be as attractive as she had during their initial times together. She was becoming more adroit at deflecting his almost constant invitations to be alone with him, but felt the relentless pressure. When he called her at home in the evenings, which was often, she always found an excuse to politely terminate the conversation as soon as she could. She briefly considered calling the police when she found him following her one day. But she did not want to alienate him totally, as the contracts to the Center were a lifeline to get it across the bridge to healthier financial times. He had hinted that increasing the annual grants provided by the Foundation from $200,000 to $500,000 would not be unreasonable if the Center's work continued to please him.

Denise had engaged in an elaborate kabuki dance of resistance to the Foundation President's advances. He was constantly plying her with elaborate and expensive gifts, accompanied by incessant entreaties to fly away with him on his private plane to "discuss the Center's future grants." His real intentions were transparent. The only thing that held her back was a feeling of discomfort with getting involved with someone who could hold so much sway over her professional life. And, of course, putting aside the fact that he was married, there were rumors about him that his intentions with respect to those of the opposite sex were, to use a euphemism, less than honorable. When she had recently found evidence that other female staff members of organizations receiving grants from the Foundation were also receiving the same level of attention from its President, she had abruptly stopped seeing him for any reason and informed her board chair about the situation.

As she sat through this board meeting, Denise felt like her head was in a vise. More accurately, it was her organization that was being squeezed. At the time she participated with her board chair in hammering out a formal memorandum of understanding with the Foundation to provide $200,000 annually in funding in exchange for preparing a new series of public policy white papers, the arrangement had sounded almost too good to be true. Now Denise regretted the day she had even heard of the Foundation or its President, who had been making both her personal and professional life miserable.

William A. Ivystone, IV, a. k. a. "Four," as the Foundation's President was called behind his back by his friends and enemies alike (and certainly he had less flattering names ascribed to him by his enemies), acted as if he was royalty, and everyone else, particularly the beneficiaries of the Foundation's millions of grant dollars, was a peon. Those who weren't deemed to be loyal subjects were banished from his Kingdom. Although the chief staff person for the Foundation, he also completely controlled his board of directors, mostly thirty-something blood relatives of William Ivystone, without having a vote himself, or any need to have one.

Those few in the Ivystone clan who had shown any real acumen or talent for business were funneled up the corporate ladder running businesses spun off by the senior Ivystone. The underachievers and slackers, and there were many, were relegated to serving on the philanthropic board, with their modest salary supplemented by the proceeds from the trust fund the elder Ivystone had established for each of his young nieces, nephews, and cousins at birth.

Four had consolidated his power by finding a way to remove those on the board who wouldn't give him a free rein to both manage and govern the Foundation. He ran into little resistance from the board, many of whom were grateful for the $25,000 annual salaries they received for doing absolutely no tasks other than attending the four board meetings each year and perfunctorily voting in favor of making the grants on the list provided to them by their King, William the 4th. Achieving a quorum at these meetings was never in doubt. The saturnalia that followed each board meeting, held in a private suite at the Ritz Carlton, made it worthy to show up. No one on the board cared to inquire whether the cocaine that was available at these parties came from the Foundation's substantial entertainment budget or from the monthly payments from Four's personal trust fund.

It has been said many times that power corrupts and absolute power corrupts absolutely. In all Foundation matters, Four held absolute power and wielded it with impunity. He was a legend for using the resources of the Foundation to advance not only his professional, but also his personal agenda. He acted as if the money doled out by the Foundation was his own, a criticism often leveled at even the most reputable and professional foundation CEOs. He was also alleged to consider female individuals within the organizations benefiting from the Foundation's largesse to be members of his personal harem. It was understood that payments had been made by the Foundation to maintain the silence of several staff members of grantee organizations and others with respect to Four's often inappropriate behavior.

It was also well known throughout the foundation community that Four adroitly steered Foundation grants to his personal friends, and to those with whom he either had personal relationships or to those he desired to pursue for such a purpose.

The day in and day out demands of the Foundation on not only her time but on the soul of the Center had affected Denise not only emotionally, but physically, as well. At her latest meeting with Four, she had felt breathing problems severe enough that an ambulance had to be called. Although a heart attack had not been diagnosed, the cardiologist had found enough abnormalities to admit her for observation. Her blood pressure was high, and the symptoms, which were attributable to a panic attack, had made her realize that she couldn't continue with this relationship, personal or professional.

But cutting the cord and ending the relationship was not quite so simple. Ivystone could, with one stroke of the pen, threaten to end her means of livelihood, as well as the good work the Center did for the poor, needy, ill, aged, and others who had minimal voice on public policy issues at the state level.

Finding a comparable job was out of the question, with unemployment at its highest level in more than a quarter century and growing every day.

She had made the decision to beg and grovel at this board meeting to keep her job, and agree to do whatever it took to return to the time when she had never heard of William Ivystone or his Foundation, even if she had to take a substantial pay cut.

The board continued its bickering, and Denise thought back to things she had learned about the foundation sector in general and the Ivystone Foundation in particular during her ordeal.

The abuses Denise saw within the Ivystone Foundation were far from being an anomaly. Of course, most of the thousands of private foundations authorized under Section 509 of the Internal Revenue Code followed the rules. But there were constant calls for reforming those rules, which many observers, including those within the foundations themselves, conceded did not serve the public interest.

For example, the IRS requires foundations to give out a minimal amount in grants in order to maintain their tax-exempt status, currently just 5% of their net investment returns, a scandalously low amount. What is not generally understood is that these foundations are permitted to include all administrative and operating costs, which may include salaries and fees paid to the foundations' trustees, within that threshold. So in practice, many foundations are able to shelter enormous wealth from taxes, with only minimal amounts of that wealth being allocated for charitable purposes. There are few effective oversight mechanisms to assure that the philanthropy that is intended to benefit the public is not diverted to the personal benefit of those who serve on the foundation boards.

But as Denise came to understand firsthand, being the object of Ivystone's attention was not his only objective. It was not inconceivable that his intention was to convert the Center into a de facto wholly-owned subsidiary of the steel industry's propaganda machine, and thus show to his father that he was capable of taking over the entire family business when the time came for Dad to retire.

Denise, with some relief, heard indications that the meeting was reaching a conclusion and her ordeal would soon be over.

"Well, we have some options here, but none of them are attractive," summarized the board chair. "First, we can cut our losses, do the honorable thing, and sever all contact we have with the Foundation. Going with this option will obviously be traumatic and painfully expensive. We would all have to work together to find a new source of funding to replace this loss of income. We will have to have a major restructuring of our staff to accommodate the cuts to balance a budget." He looked around the room, and half of those present were nodding their heads, and the other half were showing signs of distress about this option.

"A second option might be to salvage the relationship with the Foundation for future contributions by making it clear that the Center must maintain its independence and intellectual integrity, but make sure, by board resolution, that Denise is to have no further direct contact with Mr. Ivystone."

"Denise?" David Payne recognized the CEO.

"First, let me repeat to the board that I am truly sorry for how this turned out. The lesson we should all learn is to check out our prospective donors and grantees thoroughly. And I will do whatever it takes to make things right again. If the board wants me to resign, I will. But I know I can lead this organization back to where it needs and deserves to be, and I hope to regain your trust by working as hard as I can to get us out of this mess."

"Thank you, Denise. Is there a motion on the floor?"

Discussion Questions

1. How legitimate is Mr. Wishnick's viewpoint that the board should have authority to review all grant proposals beforehand to assure they are consistent with the organization's mission and values? What are the pros and cons of this policy?

2. Why is it important that nonprofit boards have a diverse membership? What are some of the advantages and disadvantages of having such a board?

3. How much of the blame for this situation is attributable to Denise? What could she have done to avoid the situation in which she now finds herself?

4. Should the board fire Denise? If not, what other discipline, if any, would be appropriate? What should the board do to resolve the problems caused by this funder?

5. How much should the fact that Denise is a woman and minority factor into the board's decision concerning this case?

6. Why do public policy makers and the public, as well, accept the status quo with respect to the legal minimum of how much charity foundations are required to do to maintain their tax-exemptions?

Note: This case originally appeared in *The Nonprofit Management Casebook: Scenes From the Frontlines.*

Case 4
Gambling on an Outside Fundraising Consultant for the "For the Kids" Shelter

Brittany Lohman, the twenty-something CEO of the "For the Kids" shelter for runaway teenagers, was getting angry at the intransigence of her board in refusing to approve her new fundraising proposal. She tried not to display her irritation. They kept raising questions, some of which made her uncomfortable. Some of these questions were good ones that she couldn't answer. At best, she thought that the board would delay making a final decision on the proposal, which might make it too late to take advantage of what she saw as a great opportunity.

To Brittany, this should have been a "no brainer" for her board. After all, she felt certain there was absolutely nothing for the organization to lose from signing a contract with Bennett Fundraising Associates (BFA), a for-profit professional fundraising consulting and management company. At worst, the shelter would get a promised upfront payment of $400 from the arrangement, even if Vinny Bennett's plans for generating thousands of dollars in new donations for the shelter ended up a total disaster, and the likelihood of that outcome was negligible. No shelter funds would be required either as startup capital or if the arrangement resulted in any financial loss—the contract language Mr. Bennett provided to Brittany clearly stipulated that Bennett Fundraising Associates would do all of the advance work, assume all the risk, and finance all upfront costs. What downside could possibly convince her board to disapprove of this?!

Well, now after more than an hour of contentious debate, she had a better idea of some of the downsides that she admitted she had failed to consider. Still, it made sense to just do it. The proposed contract ran for only a year, and if it didn't work out, the shelter had the option simply to not renew it.

She vividly remembered the part of the pitch Bennett had made that had sold her on the concept.

"There is only one task we won't do for you," Bennett had shared with a conspiratorial smile. "You have to deposit the check we send you into your bank account. Anything else that is needed, we will do." That had been an effective close. Now, she wished he was in the room to deal with her recalcitrant board members. He would not only have glib responses, but get a sense of what she was dealing with in order to get approval for the contract.

Brittany wasn't prepared for the firestorm of opposition from board members who usually had been counted on to approve her proposals perfunctorily. This should not have even been controversial, she thought. Are they being oppositional for reasons having nothing to do with this proposal? There had to be something her board members found objectionable other than the contract. Every disadvantage of doing this was clearly counterbalanced by better reasons to forge ahead, she thought.

As Mr. Bennett himself had told her with confidence, it was not likely that this venture would lose money, and if it did, "For the Kids" would still receive $400. BFA would incur all of the losses, if any. Many other local organizations had received substantial checks from participating in this program, he intimated without naming any, because the names of his other clients, other than a handful who provided testimonials, were "proprietary."

The shelter would receive $400 immediately from BFA as soon as the contract was signed. The check the shelter would receive within two weeks of the completion of the fundraising special event conducted on its behalf required virtually no work by the charity benefitting from the program, and it could potentially amount to thousands of dollars. All the organization had to do was sign the contract, give BFA access to its mailing list of current board members and contributors and those who received its newsletter, sit back, and then cash the checks it would receive. BFA would do all of the work in generating charitable contributions through its latest collaborative program for charities.

It was all perfectly legal, and Mr. Bennett had brandished an advisory opinion from an attorney's office located in the state's largest city, or so Brittany gathered from the stationery, certifying that a charitable organization would not be violating any state or federal gambling laws by participating in this program. Also in the information packet he provided to her were testimonials from staff members of several other local charities that had participated in Mr. Bennett's program. She hadn't recognized the names of any of the organizations, none of which were particularly well-known, but she had looked online at their Web sites, and they had appeared to be legitimate.

Basically, what BFA offered to do was hold a "Texas Hold 'em Tournament for Charity" night at a local volunteer fire hall in Harristown. BFA would send mailings and emails to stakeholders of the shelter inviting them to the fundraiser, supplementing that list with its own list of hundreds of "regulars" who would attend these BFA-managed fundraisers, regardless of the beneficiary.

State law expressly prohibited gambling other than the state lottery, administered by the state to benefit education, and pari-mutuel betting on horseracing, heavily regulated with no opportunity for new entrants. But there was a loophole permitting charities with 501(c)(3) tax-exempt status to hold an annual, one-day-only, fundraising event that included gambling if all net proceeds were allocated to the charity. When the Legislature had passed this law, several safeguards were put in place. One such statutory requirement was that the event needed to be staffed and conducted entirely by employees of the charity. Few, if any, charities had the capacity or experience to stage events like this. The "one-time only annually" restriction made it not cost-effective for charities to purchase the equipment needed for these events, and few took advantage of this provision in the law, according to Mr. Bennett.

And that was where BFA came in, he explained.

What BFA offered was a service that involved doing all of the paperwork involved in hiring its own trained staff as employees of its charity clients for a single day, and having those employees reimbursed for the reasonable and actual expenses incurred in putting on the event. BFA would be in the background, orchestrating all of the management tasks, for which it would be paid a reasonable fee out of the proceeds from the fundraiser. The terms of the contract for BFA stipulated that if the event did not raise at least $400 for its charity client above any expenses paid out, that fee would be waived, and the expenses would be reimbursed by a donation made to the charity by BFA. And in the almost certain event that the fundraiser returned net "donations" in excess of this $400, BFA and the charity would split that amount 50-50 after expenses were deducted.

This arrangement was not dissimilar to a method of fundraising that had become very popular in recent years, involving arrangements between charities and local restaurants, Bennett said. Charities and cooperating restaurants would establish an evening during which the restaurant would donate a percentage of its receipts that night to a particular charity. That charity would cooperate in encouraging its supporters to patronize the restaurant on the designated evening. One difference in BFA's model was that the restaurant might at most raise a couple of hundred dollars for the charity. A BFA-managed event could possibly attract a thousand people, many of whom hadn't even heard of the charity. The funds raised typically could range from a thousand dollars to as much as twenty-thousand dollars.

"Imagine what the shelter could do with an extra $20,000," he suggested. "There is, of course, no guarantee that this will be the amount you get out of this, but it wouldn't be unusual, considering that some of our regular players attend with a roll of hundreds the size of your fist."

Mr. Bennett had explained that playing poker was quickly becoming one of America's most popular pastimes, with as many as 100 million adults playing regularly, more than double the number who had participated just a couple of decades earlier. It was quite expensive to travel to places such as Las Vegas or Atlantic City to play in states that had legalized casino gambling. Access to live, legal games had expanded as casinos on Indian reservations in additional states had expanded gambling opportunities.

Although the Internet provided virtual venues that were both legal and illegal, many players simply did not trust these sites, and there was only a minimal fraction of the excitement players felt by gambling in a lively social atmosphere.

Why should all of this money go to the government or for-profit entrepreneurs? Shouldn't charities participate in getting a piece of this action? The State Legislature certainly agreed, as they had provided for this particular law to help charities finance their good works. The only barrier to diverting some of this money to charities was a simple action of asking for some of it. This is what BFA was all about, he had told her. Everyone wins. Even those who lost money gambling had an evening out with some of their money going to a good cause.

These BFA-managed events not only would mean donations to the shelter. Attendees would have the opportunity to learn about the shelter's good work. Mr. Bennett had told Brittany that it was not unusual for the victor of the evening's Texas hold'em jackpot prize to donate his or her entire winnings back to the charity sponsoring the event. And when they did that, the charity received 50% of that donation, a windfall it would never have received otherwise.

There was a group of dedicated recreational poker players who attended the circuit of events managed by BFA, and many of them had lots of disposable income, Bennett had pointed out. Their exposure to charities that were BFA clients came only from their participation in the poker games. When they sent a check directly to the charity, which happened often, ALL of those funds went to the charity.

As an added bonus, BFA would manage and run the concession stands at the event, and "For the Kids" would receive 10% of the net proceeds from that operation, he said.

This was a limited opportunity, as there were only so many open dates to have an event managed by BFA. Once these slots were filled with other charities, there would be no opportunity to add "For the Kids." Unless the organization gave the go-ahead and signed a contract within 30 days, this opportunity would likely be lost.

But as Brittany sat in her board meeting trying to explain the details, she judged quickly that her board was less than impressed by the proposal. This was not the first time she could recall a lucrative opportunity being lost because a for-profit collaborator had been unable or unwilling to commit to a timeframe required for a nonprofit organization to process a binding decision. Many for-profit entrepreneurs became frustrated waiting for a board to approve a decision agreed to tentatively by an executive director, only to have the board delay a final decision until a board committee could make a full report at a subsequent board meeting. And board members, unlike those of a for-profit board, often did not share the same agenda.

Whereas everyone on a for-profit board shared the general goal of making as much profit as possible, there were typically many competing interests within a nonprofit board. The diversity of such a board, often viewed as an asset, also has a cost in that members often do not share the same values. As Brittany made the case for board approval of this contract, she had to concede that there were conflicting values among her board members that threatened what she thought should be routine approval.

She listened as the debate droned on and on.

"What message does this send to the community and to our young clients? Is gambling something we want to send a message to encourage?" asked Pete Hemphill, a real estate agent whom she knew was quite a gambler himself, albeit allegedly addicted to betting on sports events.

Anticipating some of these questions, Brittany had provided the board with a short position paper to justify participation, prepared using a template provided by BFA. In the paper, she noted some of the pros and cons of gambling. For example, for all but a small percentage of individuals, gambling was harmless entertainment. The event would keep dollars locally that might otherwise be diverted to other communities that permitted legalized gambling. It created jobs. It siphoned dollars away from illegal gambling, which would be available if the legal market did not satisfy its customers. And, in this particular case, it could provide an incentive for individuals to donate money that would support a worthy charity such as For the Kids.

On the flip side, there were studies that measured that 1-5% of those who gambled did so compulsively and destructively, and there were economic, psychological, and other costs involved, such as the social ills that accompanied the expansion of access to gambling.

Among these were the costs of policing and dealing with the infusion of organized crime figures who found gambling as an attractive method of generating relatively untraceable cash out of the reach of taxing bodies.

"Lots of charities have a casino night or Monte Carlo night, and I've been to a few of them myself," added Harold Fallwell, III, a used car dealer who owned several lots in the poorer areas of town. "But I've never been to one that had cash prizes, and where those who attend aren't somehow affiliated with the charity. My problem with this is that it appears to me that most of the money generated by this would go to BFA."

"I agree that this is problematic. As I read this contract, For the Kids receives 50% of the 'net revenue' and BFA receives the other half," commented Dorothy Willingham, a board member who also served as a volunteer in the shelter, playing the piano two nights each week to entertain the residents. "As I understand it, the way the contract defines 'net revenue' is revenue after expenses, and the term 'expenses' is defined in the contract in such a way that it covers the costs of personnel running the events, in addition to all of the other costs such as advertising, security, mailing, and hall rental. The way I interpret this contract is that it is possible that the 'fundraiser' for For the Kids, even if it generated let's say $10,000 in 'donations' for the event, we might only get the base four hundred dollars once all of these expenses are taken into account. BFA could pocket thousands from the management fee and using the expenses to cover its overhead."

"Okay, I would concede that, but that's $400 more than we are receiving now, and if we did this every year, we could generate some real dollars without having to do any work or incur any costs or risks," countered Steve Bartholomew, a new board member who worked as a state caseworker in the Department of Families and Youth. "I passed the fire house once when they were having one of these tournaments. I could tell the place was packed, and there were a bunch of police cars outside with their red lights flashing—I guess there was some altercation going on, which made me notice what was going on at the hall."

"Well, that brings up another question then," responded Ellen Simpson, a nurse from Harristown Hospital. "Would the shelter have any liability if something bad happened at this event? After all, the contract provides that everyone running the fundraiser is a shelter employee. I know volunteers have some protection, and nonprofit organizations have limited liability, but we have no idea who these employees would be. Would they have the same State Police background checks required of our own employees?"

"And another issue concerns me," chimed in Marilyn Able, a major contributor to the shelter who had been a charter member of the board when it was first formed almost 20 years earlier. "Doesn't anyone have any qualms about us sharing our mailing list with a for-profit provider who is using our organization's good name to earn its living?"

"Good point, Marilyn. I share that concern," responded Tim Hope, the owner of a local beer distributorship. "But even more of a concern to me, do we really want to raise money through gambling? What message does this send to the kids in the shelter, and to those in the community who we want to support us?"

There was general assent that this was an important issue. But Brittany refused to give up.

"This wouldn't be my first choice of fundraising efforts," Brittany responded. "If the board had approved the proposal I made at the last meeting, we would have invested $20,000 in hiring a part-time, in-house fundraiser who would find a way to generate enough funds to pay their salary while raising more. Fundraising takes a lot of work and effort. And money. Money we simply don't have. And I don't have the time to plan and execute the activities necessary to raise money while doing all the other things necessary to run the shelter and keep it afloat. I would prefer it if we had enough stable income from grants and donations to keep things going, but as you can figure out from hearing the Treasurer's Report, we are building ourselves a deficit that will be difficult, if not impossible, to overcome unless we do something new.

"Now, here's one way we can get a new source of revenue without any upfront costs—as we would have had if we had hired a staff person to do the fundraising in-house—or any risk. What is the problem with this! We have nothing to lose; the contract makes it clear that we will get a minimum of $400 simply by agreeing to partner with BFA, and the potential is there to get something substantial out of this!"

Rather than soothing the board, members appeared to become even more agitated, and peppered Brittany with even more questions and concerns, coming rapid fire.

I don't see anything in this contract that says the mailing list we provide cannot be used for other purposes than what we authorize, and even if it did have such a clause, how do we know we can trust this company?

Is there a list of clients? How do we know we don't have the stories of those who did not feel that this was such a good deal for them?

Have you talked with any staff of other organizations who have used the services of this company?

What is the background of Mr. Bennett? Has he operated this business in our state or other states without any problems? Who owns the company?

Is he or his company even registered as a professional fundraiser with the Bureau of Charitable Organizations? What more can we find out about him?

Brittany suddenly realized that the board would not likely give the approval she had needed, which she had all but promised Mr. Bennett would be routine. Well, maybe some of the concerns of the board were legitimate.

"Okay, I get the message," Brittany conceded. "Let me get some more information about how this would work and about who we are dealing with. But I ask that the board authorize the executive committee to act on this matter in advance of the next board meeting, as this will no longer be an option by the time the board meets again in three months. I have less than 30 days to get this approved, or the offer will be withdrawn."

"Sounds fair and reasonable, and I so move," responded the chair. "All those in favor of the motion to do this indicate by saying 'Aye,' all opposed 'Nay.' The motion has carried unanimously.

"Now," continued the chair, "let's move on to the next agenda item about what we need to do to raise the $20,000 we need to balance the current year's budget...."

Discussion Questions

1. What are some of the "red flags" in this story that might indicate that there is something not quite legitimate with BFA and its fundraising model?

2. What is the role of board and staff in deciding whether to participate in this proposed cooperative venture?

3. What are some of the ethical dilemmas involved in having a cooperative agreement with a for-profit company that seeks to exploit charities?

4. How inappropriate is it for this fundraiser to be a gambling event, compared to, for example, a meal at a local restaurant?

5. What might be some of the legal problems involved in this proposal?

6. What might Brittany have done to better research BFA and its President?

7. Discuss the problems that occur when decisions of a nonprofit organization must be made by a committee that may meet only every three months? What decisions should be the purview of the board, and when should staff have the authority to make decisions?

Note: This case originally appeared in *The Nonprofit Management Casebook: Scenes From the Frontlines.*

Case 5
Reporting Financial Misconduct at Uncommon Agenda

Jack looked at his computer screen and read the email again. And again. He felt a mix of emotions, among them apprehension, anger, disgust, fear, rage, and astonishment knowing that his life was about to change as a result of reading the content of this electronic message that was intended for his best friend rather than himself. He knew immediately that nothing good would come of this, but that it would be difficult to predict what would happen other than that it would definitely be bad.

Jack was the IT Director for Uncommon Agenda, a nonprofit, 501(c)(4) tax-exempt advocacy organization based in Washington, D.C. with field operations in six states. Nonprofit organizations granted tax exempt status under this provision of the Internal Revenue Code are designated as "social welfare" organizations rather than charities. Although 501(c)(3) organizations are permitted by law to lobby, they are prohibited by law from doing so in a "substantial" amount. In contrast, social welfare organizations are permitted to lobby to the extent they desire, and most of these organizations are formed for the primary purpose of lobbying and advocacy.

One major disadvantage of exemption under 501(c)(4), however, is that those who contribute to these organizations are not eligible to deduct contributions to them on their federal income tax returns. However, many such organizations have affiliated 501(c)(3)s that accept tax deductible contributions and then transfer those donations to fund the operations of the (c)(4). Unlike their charitable counterparts, social welfare organizations may engage in partisan political activities and support candidates for office, although there is a substantial excise tax associated with such expenditures. Many 501(c)(4) organizations, such as Uncommon Agenda, do not engage in overt partisan activity, and boast that their good government activities are nonpartisan.

The mission of Uncommon Agenda was to build support for public funding of Congressional campaigns. It worked in coalition with like-minded organizations to advocate for such funding. Although the organization solicited memberships from the public at $25 annually, most of its funding came from several large foundations that shared the vision of the organization to end the rampant abuses of campaign financing by lobbyists and others with a direct interest in legislative decision-making. Critics charged that special interests skewed public policy toward the privileged, and that the current system of campaign finance ultimately cost the public billions of dollars in wasteful spending of tax dollars and tax expenditures.

Uncommon Agenda was located in a slightly run-down office building on Connecticut Avenue in Northwest Washington, near the zoo. On most business days, the office was a beehive of activity, the phones ringing, meetings being held to plot strategy, fundraising plans being developed, and 20-something staff members who had only recently served as college interns on the Hill contacting Congressional staff to seek support for the latest version of a bipartisan public campaign financing bill.

Oblivious to most of the activity were a couple of support staff who were not directly engaged in the quest to achieve reform of campaign finance laws. One of these was Jack, the IT Director, who had a nondescript office far away from the main entrance. There was no window; his office was in an inside corridor, deep in the bowels of the 7th floor. Jack's office was lined mostly with software rather than books. Stacked high in a corner was a pile of boxes that held an assortment of equipment one might expect to find in the office of the IT head—assorted mice, cables, wireless modems, old keyboards, laptops that were in various stages of disrepair, and tools.

On most days, Jack was not particularly busy. He may have had some staff training to demonstrate to a group of employees how to use the organization's upgraded software, or to orient a new hire about how to use the existing packages that were on the network. He was also responsible for keeping the Web site in working order and sending out bulk electronic newsletters and fundraising email. On occasion, things got really busy. When that happened, such as when the system server went down or if there was a Denial of Service attack on the Web site, he was expected to work through the night when necessary to get things back in order.

But nothing in his five years in this position prepared him for the situation he found himself in today.

It was mid-March, and Washington was experiencing unseasonably hot weather, coaxing the cherry blossoms to bloom a few days earlier than the official start of the Cherry Blossom Festival still two weekends away. In mid-February, a man's heart might turn to thoughts of love. But in mid-March, it turns to college basketball. Even the President interrupted dealing with an economy that was tanking and crises around the planet to fill out his NCAA brackets along with millions of others.

On Friday afternoon, Jack had received a call on the office intercom system from Steve Pearson, the Vice President for Operations, about a problem he was having accessing his email. Steve was a congenial colleague, as well as a personal friend from Jack's grad school days. It was not unusual for Steve to join him and one other colleague, Bill Higgins, who was V.P. for Human Resources at Uncommon Agenda, to hang out together on Friday nights. They usually frequented a couple of clubs in Georgetown and got drunk together. Lately, Steve had been paying the entire tab for the three of them, explaining that he had just come into a windfall when a childless, distant aunt had died and left her nephews some money.

All of them had come to the organization at about the same time, when it was first formed with a seven-figure combined grant from three national private foundations. Steve had joined the staff first and had suggested that Jack consider leaving his job in New York to fill an opening for IT Director.

Jack was not particularly interested in the nonprofit sector in general, or the organization in particular, when he applied for that position. He would have been just as happy working for IBM or Microsoft. What attracted him were the downtown Washington, D.C. location and the likelihood that he would have a comfortable salary and not have the pressure of working in a typical corporate environment. He had interviewed elsewhere, but was attracted to the casual working atmosphere and the likely prospect that he would be in charge of the department. Actually, he would be the only member of the department, without the annoyance of having to supervise others and with no one looking over his shoulder all of the time. The people he saw in the office seemed quite happy with their jobs and were devoted to the organization's mission. This was certainly in contrast to where he had been working at the time, which he referred to as a software sweatshop where he was required to meet a quota of several thousand lines of code each week.

When Steve, one of his roommates while he was a graduate student getting his MBA from Columbia, told him about the position opening up at Uncommon Agenda, Jack had been flattered and had been delighted to consider leaving the Big Apple. He and Steve were buddies, and Steve had covered for him many times with a girlfriend who was insanely jealous of Jack seeing other women during his relationship with her. Steve had been counted on by Jack to tell more than a lie or two to preserve the relationship, and Steve never let him down. Without Steve around at Uncommon Agenda, Jack might well have left for something else.

It had only been minutes earlier that Jack felt that his life was being turned upside down. It had all started when he had heard a buzzer in the office indicating that he was being called on the intercom system. It was Steve. He expected Steve to review the plans they had for cruising Georgetown the following evening in Steve's new BMW, but instead, it was to relay a problem Steve was having with accessing his email.

"I haven't received any email for four hours now, and I know something is wrong," Steve told him. Almost all of the communications between them during office hours were by email, but without access to that mode of communication, Steve resorted to the more primitive intercom system.

"Let me check it out," Jack had said, planning to see if anyone else in the office was also having this problem. Jack himself hadn't noticed any problem accessing his work email, although such emails were infrequent except when there was an IT problem. He, like most staff of Uncommon Agenda, kept a separate email account for his personal mail. There was a written policy that every staff member was entitled to an organization email account, and the organization would respect the privacy of email sent and received on work computers. The few restrictions on this use were that the organization's computers could not be used for illegal purposes, to access pornography, or to violate copyright laws. Jack had thought this policy was flawed, since how would he or anyone in the organization determine if anyone was using the office computers inappropriately without first violating the privacy explicitly provided by the policy? In five years as IT Director, this issue had never surfaced.

Jack always encouraged new staff members to avoid using Uncommon Agenda email accounts for their personal email, and only a handful of staff members did not have separate accounts for their personal email. This was not only recommended to maintain privacy, but to save on bandwidth. With the capacity to download not only music clips but even full-length movies, Jack felt the obligation to conserve organizational resources and not overload the capacity of the server.

Jack was not working on anything in particular when Steve called, but he was still annoyed that he would be diverted from watching some of the action in the first round of the NCAA basketball tournament that was being streamed in real time to his cell phone.

A number 15 seed was hanging tough against a number two. Ah, the benefits of technology, Jack thought.

From his office, Jack had begun troubleshooting this new glitch, and came across nearly a score of emails that were caught in the network's spam filter that appeared to be potentially legitimate emails. Clicking on one of several addressed to Steve, it was clear that this particular email to Steve wasn't spam, with a .ch country code top level domain name that he didn't immediately recognize.

Reading the email, he quickly confirmed his suspicions that it was not spam. What it appeared to be was a confirmation of a bank transfer involving a transaction from the Washington Capital Bank and Trust Company to a bank in Switzerland. Reading it more closely, the transfer appeared to Jack to involve a transfer of $8,000 from an account belonging to Uncommon Agenda to a numbered account. Jack was quite certain that Uncommon Agenda didn't use banks in Switzerland, and that the organization certainly wouldn't use a numbered account. Uncommon Agenda publicly and stridently railed against the lack of transparency of the way cash for political campaigns was funneled into the system. In any case, even if the organization had a legitimate reason for getting involved in having a numbered Swiss account, it would be unlikely that Steve would have had the authority to move funds from the organization to such an account. Clearly, the Chief Financial Officer, Carol Henfield, would be the individual from the organization with authority to move funds in this way. Knowing Carol, it was quite unlikely that she would have anything to do with numbered Swiss accounts, even if the money was her own personal funds. This was not consistent with her personality, which was doing absolutely everything by the book. While liberal in ideology, she was so conservative that he surmised that she never failed to look both ways even when crossing a one-way street.

Jack's policy was to routinely delete the master file of copies of emails every month. Curious about this discovery, however, he searched in the database of archived organization emails and looked at more emails to Steve. For each of the previous four weeks, the number of weeks that old emails were still available in the system (other than on the computers of those who received them, unless they were deleted by those individuals), there was a receipt from this bank for $8,000 of funds transferred out of an account in the name of Uncommon Agenda under the total control of Steve, to the numbered account.

Jack was in shock that his long-time friend and colleague appeared to be an embezzler. Could there be some other, innocent, explanation for these transfers? Not likely, but it was possible. Embezzling would explain a few things, such as the new BMW.

But the more pressing concern was what he should do with this information. Steve was his best friend in Washington.

What if there were others in the organization involved in this other than Steve? Would his job be at risk if he reported this to the CEO? He remembered something from a recent staff meeting about Uncommon Agenda being in the process of creating a whistleblower policy. Doing so had been motivated by something that had appeared on the revised 990 annual tax return for tax-exempt nonprofit organizations. This meant that Uncommon Agenda did not currently have such a policy in force. Someone had mentioned at the meeting that there was a federal law on whistleblowing that applied to nonprofits, but that it was quite inadequate to protect anyone except under the most limited of circumstances.

Curious, he Googled "whistleblower" "nonprofit" "federal" and came up with something called the *Sarbanes-Oxley Act* enacted in 2002. Yes, that was the name he had heard at the meeting! Finding the full text of the law, he searched on some terms and found the following:

Sec. 1107. RETALIATION AGAINST INFORMANTS.

(a) IN GENERAL- Section 1513 of title 18, United States Code, is amended by adding at the end the following:
(e) Whoever knowingly, with the intent to retaliate, takes any action harmful to any person, including interference with the lawful employment or livelihood of any person, for providing to a law enforcement officer any truthful information relating to the commission or possible commission of any Federal offense, shall be fined under this title or imprisoned not more than 10 years, or both.

He interpreted that to mean that if he reported Steve's email to law enforcement authorities, he would have protection to keep his job. But if he reported this to anyone inside the organization, he would be at risk. *You would think that the organization would rather have misconduct reported internally so they can deal with it, or cover it up better*, he thought.

Jack, still shocked that his buddy appeared to be siphoning off funds from their employer at potentially the rate of $400,000 annually, took out a pad of paper and started writing out some of his options.

Among the options he considered:

1. Confront Steve. Offer to keep quiet in exchange for a share of the funds.
2. Confront Steve, and simply demand that he stop embezzling, quietly make restitution, or risk being turned in to the authorities.
3. Confront Steve, and convince him to come forward to the organization voluntarily and admit what he was doing, leaving Jack out of this.
4. Take the matter to the organization's CEO and CFO without informing Steve.
5. Take the matter to the law enforcement authorities without informing Steve.
6. Let someone know about this within the organization anonymously.
7. Do nothing.
8. Seek advice from a third party, such as a friend or attorney, before taking any action.

Jack's consideration of how to deal with this quandary was interrupted as he saw Steve stick his head into his office.

"Any progress on getting my email?" Steve asked.

"Not yet," Jack lied. "Anything interesting going on?"

"Well, I might not make it for drinks tonight, or at least until much later. There was a front page *New York Times* article this morning about campaign financing, and I've been getting lots of calls from the press as well as my field office folks."

"I didn't see the *Times* today. What was in it?" Jack asked politely, not sharing that he hadn't read the front page of the *Washington Post* that day, instead focusing on the NCAA pairings on the sports page.

"The article estimated that Obama raised an estimated $300 million for the general election, outspending McCain by about 3-1. This was after he had first pledged to accept public financing, and he eventually reneged on that commitment, becoming the first major party candidate to finance his general election campaign with private contributions. McCain only got $84 million for the general. Anyway, the *Times* story estimated that Obama raised an estimated $750 million during the entire campaign from close to four million contributors. Had he not done so, he might have gotten his butt kicked."

Jack listened, feigning interest, but he couldn't care less about campaign finance, somewhat ironic since that was the *raison d'être* of the organization that employed him. He admitted to himself that he considered the entire issue to be really boring.

But the good news was that he wouldn't have to decide what to do about Steve's "problem" today, and he could simply hang out in his office and watch some of the late first-round tournament games, or just go back to his apartment. And decide what to do.

Discussion Questions

1. How "private" should personal email be if it is sent and received from a nonprofit organization's account?

2. What are the pluses and minuses of each of the eight options on Jack's list?

3. What are the limitations of federal whistleblower protection for nonprofit organizations? What might be appropriate in an organization's whistleblower policy?

4. What are some of the objectives of having an organization whistleblower policy?

5. If you are the CEO of this organization and Jack comes to you and spills the beans, what would your response be?

6. What is Jack's legal responsibility, if any, to let someone know about this? What is Jack's ethical responsibility?

7. How important is it to nonprofit organizations that their staff be committed to the organization's mission and comfortable with the culture of the nonprofit sector, in light of the fact that nonprofit organizations more than ever employ staff who could work in business just as easily, such as Webmasters, accountants, IT professionals, and marketers?

Note: This case originally appeared in *The Nonprofit Management Casebook: Scenes From the Frontlines.*

Case 6
Public Relations Dilemma at the Harristown Hospital and Health System

"This is Roemer," answered Steve Roemer, the Vice President for Public Affairs for the Harristown Hospital and Health System (HHHS), in response to his ringing Blackberry. He didn't recognize the number that flashed on his small screen. However, the area code of 404 indicated the call was from the Atlanta area.

It was 8:30 on a Monday evening, and he was in the middle of watching an episode of *House, MD.* The mythical Princeton Plainsboro Teaching Hospital didn't have much in common with HHHS, and he was aware that most medical staff at HHHS found the show ridiculous, particularly the main character's ethics, or lack thereof. Dr. House would have lasted no longer than a day on the staff of any real hospital, they asserted, regardless of whether he could save lives no one else could, all within a 43-minute timeframe plus commercials.

Reflexively, Roemer hit the pause button on the remote and took the call. Probably nothing that was needed of him that would be on the eleven o'clock news, he judged. Most of those calls involving a request for him to do a taped interview occurred during the early afternoon, for transmission back to the studio for editing in time for the six o'clock broadcast.

Roemer was proud of the fact that he made himself available 24/7 and was accessible to reporters working on deadline. While his smartphone might ring occasionally during the middle of the night, those times were rare. A former beat reporter for a South Carolina daily, he enjoyed the excitement of working with the media, particularly when he was sought out by television stations to appear live to comment on a breaking story. Health care was a broad, high-profile topic that would find itself often as a lead story in some context in the *Harristown Morning News,* and the television news, as well.

During the five years Roemer had served as the chief public relations professional of HHHS, he had developed substantial expertise on topics ranging from medical conditions and their treatment to the complexities of hospital finance and accounting. He had visions of returning to reporting, but he was also getting spoiled by the high salary and substantial fringe benefits and privileges of working in a corporate environment with staff and other resources to help him do his job. Whoever said working in the nonprofit sector guaranteed a low salary didn't know what they were talking about.

Occasionally, at the urging of his wife, he would turn off his Blackberry during "family time" and return any calls he received later. The advanced technology of the smartphone kept him connected, but he recognized that there was also a cost to being available day or night to not only reporters, but to his small staff and his superiors at HHHS. Unlike many other nonprofit organizations, this organization did not go to "sleep" after traditional business hours, although the pace may have appreciably diminished. There was a baseline of 8 a.m. to 4:30 p.m. office hours in the administrative floor of HHHS, with meetings, press conferences, production of the weekly newsletters, and preparing flashy briefing books for upcoming board meetings, filled with eye-catching graphics. But after business hours, the hospital remained a beehive of activity, with newsworthy developments periodically occurring in the evening, throughout the night, and on weekends, as well.

Other than perhaps the CEO, Roemer was the public face of the Health System, and that telegenic face had to remain clean-shaven because of the possibility that it would be on the other side of a camera with minimal notice.

It was Roemer's responsibility to keep the public educated and happy, and to have a positive association with the name of HHHS. Although generally no news was good news, Roemer proactively engaged the local media in covering aspects of hospital activities that would put it in a positive light. HHHS was an important pillar in the community—a respected player in the city's economic and social future, and second only to the state university as the largest employer in the city. It had a brand name to protect, and Roemer was its key frontline defender.

Despite its first-rate reputation, HHHS was in a constant competition for patients, who had a choice when deciding which among the three major acute care facilities in Harristown to patronize. (There had once been six hospitals in the community, but a series of mergers had resulted in HHHS absorbing three others in the 1990s.) Increasing market share was a key component of HHHS's strategic plan, and additional funds had been allocated to Roemer's department based on the premise that good public relations could improve that statistic, as well as improve its overall net revenue.

Despite its nonprofit status, improving net revenue was the principal focus of every management decision. The hospital typically charged its patients exorbitant fees for every procedure, as did the other two hospitals in the community. However, few patients paid the regular fee schedule; most charges were reimbursed by negotiated payments from private and government insurance. Even these rates were substantially higher than costs, so that treatment of nonpaying patients could be cross-subsidized. By state law, nonprofit hospitals were permitted to make a profit, but any net revenue over expenses was required to be funneled back for the hospital's charitable purposes. Those charitable purposes, of course, included investing in the most advanced technology, increasing staff salaries, and providing substantial perquisites to those who worked there, including the use of a Skybox at the NFL Stadium at the Sportsplex across town.

Roemer had attended several games seated in this box, enjoying a lavishly catered lunch and actively participating in the advocacy and fundraising carried on there directed at invited guests, such as the State's congressional delegation and potential donors. As a reporter, he had been able to purchase tickets to only a single Atlanta Falcons pre-season game during his five years at the paper, and he had paid for those seats himself.

In addition to his other responsibilities, Roemer was also part of the team of staff who decided which programs and activities would receive financial sponsorship of HHHS, with several million dollars available annually to support concerts, youth sports, museums, the Harristown Marathon, and other events that would help the community and provide more visibility and name recognition for HHHS. He really enjoyed this aspect of the job, using the Health System's money to benefit community groups.

Roemer's face had become familiar to TV viewers as a result of on-camera duties such as explaining the changing medical status of a celebrity admitted to the facility, updating the public about a train derailment that sent scores of injured to the hospital, or decrying a recent government report documenting an increase in the uninsured.

During one week two summers earlier, he had been a constant guest on all three local newscasts in the Harristown media market following a car accident involving the Mayor of Harristown. Mayor Hawkins had suffered a heart attack while at the wheel of his city-provided Honda Accord, careening into a telephone pole. Shortly after the accident, Roemer had appeared live from the scene of the accident, with five microphones thrust into his face, and reported that Mayor Hawkins was in stable condition, but that his Honda Accord was better described now as a Honda Accordion. People still stopped him to this day to express their appreciation for that quip.

In his position, there were a number of other opportunities he had to educate the public. It was not unusual for him to be stopped on the street and recognized as a celebrity himself. He was trusted by reporters, although he certainly provided a spin on his comments that was flattering to his employer. No one would have expected anything else.

Now that he had built up a good reputation as a straight shooter, reporters came to him for both on the record and off the record comments. He liked his job. He liked being a part of the decision-making as part of the management team that ran the hospital, even though that was not a formal part of his job description. Most of the Vice Presidents, along with the President and CEO, had been there only a few years, and he felt that they valued the institutional memory he brought along with his common sense about how the public and other stakeholders might respond to consequences of a decision.

More than a few times, his advice prevented the management team from taking action that might have been a disaster. Today, however, he had been frustrated that the CEO and Vice Presidents failed to recognize the seriousness of their decision with respect to one particular sensitive matter involving a young surgeon, who was fired for attempting to perform an operation while heavily intoxicated. In this case, the doctor had been partying late into the night, but had been on call. When he responded to a page to come in to perform an emergency appendectomy, operating room nurses had complained that he was not in any condition to operate. Fortunately, another surgeon was available to fill in, and the patient had a normal procedure, unaware of the situation that might have put her at serious risk.

This was the second time the doctor had had a problem with alcohol interfering with his duties. The Medical Director had no second thoughts about firing him, and did so. However, the doctor knew that being fired for alcohol abuse would make it virtually impossible for him to be hired at another hospital. So, this doctor threatened to go public with allegations of gross negligence on the part of hospital staff, resulting in the deaths of two patients the previous year, unless the HHHS complied with a series of demands.

Apparently, hospital staff had participated in a cover-up involving a medical error. In that case, two children had been provided with lethal doses of heparin, a commonly used blood thinner, by hospital personnel. A similar medical error had made the national news in 2007 when a child of actor Dennis Quaid had barely survived such an overdose. The error was compounded by a defect in the package labeling, which failed to distinguish adequately between the weak dose administered to children and the standard dose administered to adults, which was 1,000 times more potent. After considering whether or not to disclose the medical error to the children's parents, the hospital staff had decided to simply explain to the families of the victims that the two patients had died from causes unrelated to injecting these kids with a lethal overdose. And it had issued strict verbal instructions to all staff involved in the incident to keep their mouths shut about what happened.

What the surgeon now demanded was that the hospital would have to provide him with a letter of recommendation and agree not to disclose to anyone outside of the hospital management that he had been fired or the reasons why. Second, the hospital would have to provide him with a severance payment of $500,000, which would automatically become $5,000,000, payable at the rate of $500,000 each year, if anyone in the hospital violated the first provision.

The management team had met that afternoon to decide whether or not to approve the agreement.

Roemer was hearing this story for the first time today, and he was uncomfortable. Had he been in charge, he would not have covered anything up. He would have explained the error and let the chips fall where they may. His experience was that many people understood that errors are made by professionals in all fields, although the consequences of errors in the medical field are certainly more serious than, let's say, allowing a ground ball to go through one's legs during a baseball game. But unlike a baseball game where the mistake is seen and understood by everyone in the stands, medical errors often occur without anyone knowing about them other than the staff. And the consequences can be fatal for the patient. There is a huge incentive for the staff to keep mistakes they make from the patients and their families, avoiding a lot of unpleasantness in addition to civil liability that can amount to millions of dollars in any single case.

At an afternoon meeting, where this situation was discussed among a small group of management with the chief counsel present, the team had decided to minimize the hospital's potential exposure and accept the surgeon's offer. Roemer had been the sole dissenter, arguing that the hospital should acknowledge its mistakes, suffer the consequences of being accountable for its mistakes, and not give in to what he perceived was blackmail. The chief counsel had been neutral on the decision, although she did point out that in the event this doctor was hired by another hospital and was involved in a similar incident, the fact that HHHS failed to take appropriate action rather than covering it up could make HHHS potentially liable.

Roemer was moving up the ladder in leadership of the Council of Hospital Public Relations Professionals, in line to become its next chair. The Council had an ethics code, which Roemer took seriously. Among the provisions of this code was an obligation to be accurate and truthful in representing the interests of one's employer to the public, as well as an obligation to serve the public interest. In Roemer's twelve years as information officer, he had never knowingly lied to the media or the public about a professional issue.

He knew that this would be severely tested if anyone ever raised the issue of either the medical error cover-up or the agreement HHHS management had just agreed to make with the terminated surgeon.

Although the decision made at the meeting made Roemer uncomfortable, it certainly wasn't the first time that decisions made at the highest levels of HHHS were inconsistent with his personal and professional values. However, he recognized that he was not the boss, and that overall, HHHS, despite some flaws, was operated in a manner to serve the public. And he never lied about anything, although he occasionally would tell a reporter that he was not free to comment on a particular situation.

With the TV paused, Roemer listened to the voice at the other end of the line.

"Hi, this is Steve Barton. I'm with the Associated Press in Atlanta, and I am working on a story for AP about HHHS. I'm calling with a couple questions. We are working on a story involving problems with the blood thinner heparin, which had some problems relating to contamination, as well as overdosing. One of our sources referred us to your hospital, which apparently ran into a problem with heparin overdoses last year. While researching this, we came across a story of a surgeon from HHHS who was terminated today for attempting to operate on a patient while impaired with alcohol, and found out that there was some relationship between these two incidents, which we are not clear about. Can you clarify some of this for me? I understand that you were at the meeting today at HHHS where this was discussed...."

Discussion Questions

1. How should a public relations professional deal with any conflict between the principles of one's professional ethics code and the exigencies required to represent the interests of one's organization?

2. Is Roemer obligated to talk to the reporter about the meeting? How should he respond?

3. What boundaries should individuals have between their personal lives and professional lives?

4. Is there anything unethical or otherwise inappropriate about HHHS having a Skybox for entertaining VIPs?

5. Was the decision to agree to the terms of the surgeon appropriate? What other options did the management of HHHS have?

6. If a staff member of a nonprofit is fired for misconduct, is it ethical not to take steps to inform any potential future employer of that staff member that the person has engaged in misconduct?

7. Could the hospital management have had any other options other than firing the surgeon?

8. Compare and contrast two very different types of charities that may be headquartered in the same neighborhood, such as a hospital and a food bank.

Note: This case originally appeared in *The Nonprofit Management Casebook: Scenes From the Frontlines.*

Case 7
The State Volunteer Firefighters Association's Dilemma

"Okay, I think everyone is on the call," intoned Chief Jake Weber, the crusty board chair of the State Volunteer Firefighters Association, who had served as the chair for almost 30 years. Weber had called the emergency meeting of the Association's executive board to discuss how to respond to ethics charges made against the association's executive director, Abraham Firth, by the board's current Vice President, Harold Sanders. Weber had scheduled the call with reluctance, concerned about the allegations made against the executive director, but willing to give him the benefit of the doubt. After all, for the past 20 years, Firth had been the face of volunteer firefighting in the state, and his service to the association had been exemplary.

In two decades, Firth had transformed the association from a near-bankrupt, moribund and disorganized collective into a powerful force within the first responder community in the state. He was a visible presence not only statewide, but on the national scene, as well. Whenever there was a national issue of prominence that might benefit from the expertise of someone in the volunteer firefighting community, Firth was the "go to" guy. He had made several appearances on CNN, made a short appearance in one *60 Minutes* segment, and could be counted on to deliver the association's message with the most appropriate and credible spin to state and Congressional lawmakers. Perhaps a dozen times each year, he would walk up the steps of the State Capitol and deliver testimony to various House and Senate committees, embedded with a catchy sound bite that never failed to capture the media's attention and make the evening newscasts.

Unlike many executive directors who turned over day-to-day operations to their staff, Firth was a hands-on executive director who sweated all of the details. He was worshiped by his staff, and he treated them with respect from the CFO to the receptionist. When they grew professionally, he encouraged them to find more challenging employment and continued to mentor them. More than a handful of volunteer fire companies in the state were administered by those who had first learned the business at Firth's knee.

Firth gave no indication that he was unhappy with his job or the firefighting profession in general. He was usually the first person in the office and the last to leave, and he never complained about being on call 24/7 to respond to organizational exigencies. And as a volunteer firefighter himself for more than 30 years, he knew all of the issues affecting his constituency from firsthand experience. He and Chief Weber had served as a team for two decades. Weber was the chief of a VFC in a rural area upstate and had his hands full. He knew the association's management was in capable hands, and he let Firth run the association without any micromanaging from him. Although they occasionally disagreed on policy, they worked things out quickly without any rancor. They considered each other friends.

So it was with extreme consternation and surprise when the word filtered throughout the volunteer firefighting community that someone had written a "tell all" book about his experiences within the volunteer firefighting community. The author was someone named "David Getty," and it was determined that no one by that name was known to anyone and it was likely to be a pseudonym. To old timers in the state, some of the stories sounded familiar. Only a few people in the entire country would have known about them. Extrapolating, it became clear to those who read the pirated galley of the soon-to-be-published book that had appeared mysteriously on an obscure Web site that only Firth could have written it. It had appeared on the site frequented by firefighters for only a day, in PDF format, and had disappeared just as mysteriously as it had appeared. But by then, it had been downloaded by several site visitors and was virally being circulated by the hundreds among the community of first responders.

When confronted, Firth refused to either confirm or deny the allegation, saying that it was not anyone's business.

Several board members were livid when they heard this, and Chief Weber had been deluged with calls and emails from not only irate members of his board but from staff of the volunteer fire companies that were members of the association. Weber was convinced himself that Firth was the author. And he was equally convinced that although the book would do damage to the profession if and when it was published and made available to the public, it also cast a positive light on the importance of volunteer fire companies in society, the bravery of individuals serving their communities, and the intensity of the training most members of VFCs receive. He was disappointed in several rants that appeared in the book about petty politics. And there was certainly nothing positive about the many cases described in detail in the manuscript of scandalous, and at times illegal, behavior that had been covered up.

But it was a damn good read! At times, Weber felt, he could almost smell the black, acrid smoke, and experience the adrenalin rush of racing off to a call, not knowing if it was a false alarm—as many calls were—or a serious emergency that conjured up the images of that 1991 movie *Backdraft*, which gave the public a glimpse of the heart-pounding tension involved in operations of the Chicago FD.

The outrage of those who communicated to Weber was accompanied by suggestions on how to discipline Mr. Firth for the breach of confidentiality and protocol. Other than simple outright calls for his immediate firing unless he agreed to take whatever steps deemed necessary to stop publication of the book, the board chair was called upon to require that Firth's advance and royalties related to the book become the property of the association. The justification was that all of the stories and information shared by Mr. Firth came from sources that were related to his highly paid, professional position at the association or his previous position as the administrator of a VFC.

Another board member suggested that these were ill-gotten gains, and that Firth had a conflict of interest. Knowing that he was planning to write a book, his interest in serving the association's membership was in conflict with his interest in generating titillating material that he could exploit to spike book sales, which may have colored his judgments about decision-making.

Another board member suggested that even if the book had been complimentary to the association and the profession, Firth had no right to take advantage of his position to generate his own personal wealth while he was employed professionally by the association. At a minimum, in order to access confidential records and sensitive matters, he was ethically required to obtain permission from the board, as those who shared information with him were doing so with the expectation that his access to information was predicated on the assumption that he was serving the interests of the association and its members rather than himself. In addition, the property of the association was not intended to be exploited for the personal gain of anyone, but rather intended for the exclusive use of serving the interests of the association.

Of particular concern to several board members was the fact that their executive director had publicly shared stories that embarrassed the association and the volunteer firefighting profession as a whole.

The downloaded galley Weber had reviewed revealed bombshells dropping with each page turn. There were stories of hazing of new members. There were accounts of VFCs discovering that some within their ranks had purposely set fires, and that they had participated in cover-ups of these crimes. There were stories of sexual harassment, and even sexual assault, of female volunteers. Volunteers were recruited who were under the state-mandated legal minimum age of 18. Prostitutes were hired to attend a members-only beer bash sponsored by one local VFC.

Also documented were tales of financial mismanagement and outright fraud, theft, and embezzlement. Racism, sexism, and anti-Semitism were highlighted, certainly scourges perhaps disproportionately affecting those who lived in many small towns that relied on the services of volunteer firefighters. These discrimination incidents were often magnified in rural areas that did not have the opportunity for diversity training, which might have been available in urban communities that might be more welcoming to those who were not of the "right" race or religion. Or, perhaps in just the past 20 years, the "right" gender. Women only recently had been forcibly integrated into the ranks of firefighting, and many firefighting organizations resisted this change in the culture that was forced upon them by federal laws. Women either gave up or suffered in silence. The book provided details of some of the most egregious cases of hazing of women volunteers.

But the most compelling and horrifying stories involving discrimination against volunteer firefighters revolved around what some firefighters did to those who they either knew or suspected were gay. One story centered upon one volunteer who had communicated no evidence relating to his sexual orientation, but who disliked football and liked Broadway show music, leading to stereotyped speculations about his sexuality. What his colleagues did to him to show their distaste would turn the movie about this book from a PG-13 to an R rating, if it ever did become a movie, which appeared to be a distinct possibility. The salaciousness of some of the stories made it quite possible that someone would find bidding on the book's movie rights to be attractive.

For his part, the author had made it clear that most volunteer firefighters were patriotic, hard-working, and put service to their communities paramount. There was nothing in the book that condoned the inappropriate behavior. There was little in the book that the board members who were either volunteer firefighters or who worked with them professionally found surprising, likely to have been embellished, or fabricated.

The fact that this book was likely to have been written by Firth gave credibility to stories they read that they were hearing about for the first time. Yet there was something unsettling for those in the firefighting community to find out that it was one of their own who was responsible for what was likely to be a public relations nightmare. If published, the book would likely cast a cloud over the profession that would impugn the integrity of the majority for the actions of a small minority.

After Weber determined who was present, he launched a discussion of the matter at hand and what should be done.

"This is Felicia. I actually enjoyed reading the book. But I see two distinct issues that are problematic with this situation," commented Dr. Felicia Howser, an associate professor for the State University who was a specialist in nonprofit law and ethics and the only female on the board. "The first issue, which is of paramount concern, is the potential, if not actual, conflict of interest, involved in Abe being involved at all in writing this book.

"We are paying him to be a staff member, and we should expect that this creates a requirement of loyalty to the organization. He has an obligation to represent our interests publicly and be discreet with how he shares information that he receives in the course of his job that we have a right to expect should be kept confidential. When he writes this book, it creates a dual relationship on his part.

"He has to choose between whether to represent the interests of the publisher and make the book interesting enough to generate substantial sales, or whether he represents the interests of the organization that pays his salary. There may be a value to the readers to consider his thoughts on these issues that are internal to the Association. But it certainly doesn't have much value to us to have our dirty laundry aired in public.

"The second issue is, even if we were to require that we approve the book in advance, there is a question in my mind as to whether the income derived from this activity belongs to Abe."

"Hightower here. I think any money generated by this book belongs to the Association," chimed in Gregg Hightower, a VFC administrator from Oshman, on the east coast of the state. "If he made money playing in a rock band, the money would clearly be his. But in this case, he is taking obviously confidential and sensitive information that he would otherwise not have any access to and making money from telling the world about it. But even if he gives us the money, I think he should be fired regardless. He's made some of us look like immature fraternity boys, and it is not fair for us to be paying him a cent more. I want to be on record that if he isn't fired soon, Oshman VFC will put its Association dues payment in escrow until he is fired."

"This is Vinnie Altman from Troy VFC. Gregg has a good point, although I don't see what we would accomplish by firing Abe, who by consensus is a terrific executive director. I don't see the possibility of finding anyone better to replace him. But I do see the need to discipline him for the breach of confidentiality. I suggest we let him know that we think this book violated the confidentiality of our association, and that we move to suspend him for two weeks without pay."

"At this point, we don't know definitively that he wrote the book, although his fingerprints are certainly on the passages I read," interrupted Harry Sanger, in a booming bass voice that was so distinct and unusually loud that no one required him to first identify himself before his comment. "Jake is a good friend of his; maybe the two of them can sit down, have Jake explain why we are so pissed at this, and see if Abe himself is willing to admit that perhaps writing this book while still employed by us was not such a good idea. Maybe he is willing to voluntarily donate all or part of the proceeds to some charity as a sign of good faith, or better still, simply inform the publisher that he has had a change of heart and is withdrawing the book from consideration."

"This is Williams," intoned Tom Williams, a driver of a hook-and-ladder for Griffin VFC. "I think we should fire the S.O.B. He violated our trust. I don't know how I can have a private conversation with him in the future about a sensitive matter without thinking that he is taking notes and I'll read about it in his next book."

"I'll talk to Abe, as Harry suggested, but I think it is wishful thinking to expect that this book will never be published in substantially the form that we have seen. But maybe we can use our influence to have it toned down a bit. Anyway, I think we do not have any consensus within the executive committee," summarized Chief Weber. "So I will put this on the agenda at the next board meeting in two months. By then, maybe I'll have more information about what actually happened and some more options on what we can do about it. In the meantime, thank you all for participating, and I'll see you at the board meeting."

Everyone took this as the cue to hang up, other than Williams.

"Jake, you've got to deal with this; that's why we pay you the big bucks to be the chair. Make it right."

"I hear you, buddy. I'm not happy about this book, either, but as you can tell from this call, there is no clear consensus on what to do, and the options we have are limited. Even if we fire him, as you suggest, we could be hit with a lawsuit for wrongful discharge, and it could cost us plenty in legal fees even if we won. Let me talk with Abe, and see if I can resolve this to your satisfaction. Firing him doesn't help anyone, and I think the best interests of the association would suffer, although I see your point about needing to talk to Abe without the conversation appearing in print."

"Okay, Jake. Regards to Wilma."

"Regards to Althea, and let's get together after the board meeting and check out that new restaurant on Almand Street."

"Bye, my friend."

"Bye."

Discussion Questions

1. What constraints can/should a nonprofit organization put on the behavior of its executive director related to how that individual spends his or her free time?

2. Is there an implied requirement that a nonprofit employee act with loyalty to an organization that employs him/her?

3. Who has the authority to fire an executive director: the board, the executive committee, the board chair?

4. What could the board have done to avoid this situation?

5. Did the executive director in this case act unethically?

6. Does the organization have any claim to the money the executive director received for writing this book?

7. Is it a problem for any organization to have the same board chair for decades? What are the pros and cons of permitting this?

Note: This case originally appeared in *The Nonprofit Management Casebook: Scenes From the Frontlines.*

Case 8
The One (Wo)Man Band Running the Kenmore Midget Baseball League

Looking at a street light outside the second story window of the Clubhouse, Sarah determined that it was still snowing lightly. The Borough's maintenance crew had plowed out the parking lot in Kenmore Borough Park in response to her telephone request earlier that day, as she had expected. No one else would have thought to make that call, she mused, and there might have been no place for cars to park otherwise because of the foot of snow that had fallen earlier in the week. *Without me, this organization would be only a skeleton of what it is now,* she thought.

A couple of cars were still pulling into the parking lot of the Clubhouse, but Sarah prided herself on starting board meetings exactly on time.

With two minutes to go before the digital clock in the Clubhouse hit 7 p.m., Sarah imagined how the scene outside of this window would be different six months hence, the sun still relatively high in the sky and the temperature hovering in the low '90s, perhaps 70 degrees warmer than it was now. She could almost smell the pungent odor of the mustard that would be spread liberally atop the soft pretzels sold from the concession stand housed in the Clubhouse's first floor, the pretzels often stale, soggy, and delicious!

She delighted in the smell of the freshly mowed grass, the baseball diamond manicured with care by her two sons.

Among the sounds were a cacophony of dogs barking, babies crying in their mothers' arms, the chatter of players shouting encouragement to their teammates, and parents and coaches shouting out instructions. And, of course, the occasional "pong" of aluminum striking a ball. "Swing, batter!"

In the scene she conjured up, there were also younger siblings of the players ignoring the action on the field, instead playing tag with each other or catching lightning bugs and grasshoppers, the latter to use as bait to catch sunfish in Kenmore Creek. Midget League, for kids 10-12, was truly an intergenerational activity. Grandparents, and even great-grandparents, would attend games, some making the trip from the parking lot to the temporary stands using walkers.

Her reverie was interrupted by her Blackberry chiming the tune "Take Me Out to the Ball Game," indicating that it was 7 p.m. and time to start the meeting.

"The board meeting will come to order," announced Sarah Goodling, banging the ceremonial gavel that was presented to her at a board meeting of the Kenmore Midget Baseball League, Inc. two years ago. Two more parents entered the room as she spoke. They quietly took seats around the large folding table and reached in the center of the table for a printed agenda. The gavel had a small plaque on its handle, lauding her for ten seasons of distinguished service as chair of the League. Her re-election this year was again by acclamation; for the past eight years, she had run for the office unopposed. Most board members were parents of players and rotated off the board when their kids aged out of the program and moved up to juniors.

Kenmore Midget Baseball League had operated in Kenmore since shortly after World War II. In the 1960s, the organization had incorporated as a 501(c)(3) tax-exempt nonprofit organization. It formally incorporated for several reasons, but the principal motivation was to respond to the liability exposure members of the organization thought they might have from injuries players and spectators might suffer as a result of being hit by stray balls. An added benefit of this status was that individuals who made donations to the organization could deduct their value on their federal income tax forms.

League expenses consisted chiefly of equipment, field rentals, insurance, paying umpires, maintaining the fields, and painting the Clubhouse. In addition to an annual dinner dance fundraiser, income came from a modest $50/season fee assessed to players in the league (waived if a family could not afford it) and from tax-deductible contributions by team sponsors whose logos adorned the uniforms, ads sold for the program book, and signs put up on the electric scoreboard. Sarah had been particularly proud of the scoreboard, for which she had found funding by requesting an earmark from a friendly state legislator who himself had played Midgets in Kenmore back in the 1970s.

Substantial additional income came from the brisk business generated by the field's concession stand, which had been operated by a local restaurant that was served by Sarah's food distribution business. That relationship was good for the equivalent of two team sponsorships each season. The agreement between the League and the restaurant was that 15% of proceeds would go directly to the League, and as an added bonus, the players playing in the game would receive a free hot dog and lemonade after the final out.

Volunteer parents staffed the concession stand each game, and this was the major activity in which parents engaged that contributed to the League's operations. The concession stand typically had a steady stream of customers whenever there were games. Many of the customers visited the stand without having any connection to the games, attracted to the reasonable prices for slushies, soft pretzels, roasted peanuts, grilled hot dogs, hamburgers, ice cream novelties, and popcorn. It was not unusual for the cash receipts at the end of an evening doubleheader to exceed $700. After each evening, when the concession doors were shuttered, Sarah would personally collect the cash from the register, count it, place it in a cash bag, and make a night deposit at the Kenmore Community Bank, another team sponsor.

Sarah was generally acknowledged as the glue that held all of the pieces together. Those close to the program's operations knew that she was not only the glue, but for the most part, was the pieces, as well. It was common knowledge that Sarah was indispensable to having a successful season. Almost single-handedly, she recruited coaches, arranged the schedule, hired the field maintenance crew (for the past two years now, comprised exclusively of her twin sons, who had once been stars for Kenmore's Allstars), ordered bats and balls, recruited sponsors, and made sure the uniforms were ordered.

She attended to every detail, including proofreading the designs of the uniforms to make sure the names of the sponsors were spelled correctly. The first year she had chaired the League, she had delegated that task, and was embarrassed to find that the Kenmore Indians sported jerseys that season sponsored by "Katy's Jewlers." Katie, the store owner, had expressed her disapproval, but had been mollified by being offered a free ad in the next year's program booklet. Sarah never delegated that task again, nor most others.

During the summer, Sarah was a professional volunteer, devoting much of her day to the League while her husband ran the family business. Each season, those who served on the board could count on Sarah to be a busy worker bee, making sure every task was completed. On the wall of the Clubhouse, in addition to team pictures of players and coaches, was tangible evidence of recognition of her efforts, of which she was justly proud. Among them was a copy of a proclamation of Kenmore Borough Council commending Sarah for her achievements, alongside a resolution passed by the State House recognizing her ten years of leadership as chair of the board.

Sitting in the stands watching the games on a warm summer evening was heaven to Sarah, basking in not only the sun, but the glow of knowing that this was a masterpiece she had created. Each year, she had added to this masterpiece until the facility and program were the envy of not only nearby communities, but of those around the state who visited, seeking advice on how to emulate the success of the Kenmore program. This year, she had arranged for the construction of pro-style dugouts, complete with a water fountain, courtesy of a cousin who ran a construction company. He had given her a good price and had completed the work well before the deadline. Among the accoutrements added in recent years were an electric scoreboard, a clubhouse (where this board meeting was being held) that housed the concession stand, and net-enclosed batting cages.

Although she solicited ideas for these improvements at board meetings, she generally decided on her own which new feature she would add. This was a closely guarded secret. Universally, there was admiration among the board for how she found ways to make the program better each year. A few board members might grumble about what they perceived as heavy-handed tactics, but no one disputed that the results she achieved were well worth the occasional ruffled feathers. Most respected the fact that Sarah did her homework before engaging in a project on behalf of the League, and she was not perceived at all to be a loose cannon risk taker. Admittedly, she was aggressive in building the League, and she acknowledged that there was some validity to the saying "you can't steal second base with one foot on first."

It was a relief for virtually every board member when they got a notice in their email in January that a board meeting was to be scheduled at the Clubhouse located on the grounds of the Kenmore Midget Field. This served as verification that Sarah was again willing to not only serve as board chair, but likely would make all of the arrangements for the coming season. There was anticipation about what new, creative physical improvements would be made to the fields (or, as sometimes occurred, had already been made in the fall before the construction season came to a halt and before the field was ready for seeding and painting).

Sarah, on the other hand, lived for Midget Baseball, even now that her kids were grown. She was in charge and the League was hers to run without much interference from anyone. In previous years, when she first began taking a leadership role, she had delegated many of the tasks to other parents. But she found that it was rare that anyone else could produce the results required to assure that the product each summer was up to the high quality standards that she demanded and that the kids deserved.

Eventually, parents learned to let Sarah do everything herself and stay out of her way. They knew that Sarah's commitment would solve any problem that might come up, and it certainly saved them a lot of aggravation to let her do all of this work behind the scenes, which she apparently reveled in doing. On one level, they felt that they were exploiting her, but if she was willing to do all of this work, what was the harm? It wasn't like they were capitalizing on this by sitting at home eating bon bons. Most parents of players were busy with work, and in the evenings, they did chores, shopping, and helped their kids with their homework. If they were able to squeeze out an hour or two to relax with a shared TV program with their spouse or perhaps one night each week for a movie, they considered themselves lucky.

Being the parents of eleven-year-olds was so much different than it had been for their own parents. Midget League was not the only activity that required their attention. There were music lessons, religious school classes, and any other number of organized activities that required chauffeuring their kids and often waiting until the activity was completed to drive them home.

Almost to a parent, watching their son or daughter play in the Kenmore Midget League was something they looked forward to well before their child reached the eligible age to compete. Because everything about the program was first class, parents from outside Kenmore clamored for the opportunity for their kids to play their Midget baseball in that community. At first, the board had resisted opening up the program to outsiders in nearby communities, but eventually, it embraced doing so. More playing fields were added in Kenmore Park to accommodate the additional demand for teams.

At its peak the previous season, 10 teams of 14 players each were competing in the Kenmore Midget League. It was not unusual for the stands to have crowds exceeding 100 watching the games. Many graduates of the program went on to play high school and college baseball. Although no one had as yet reached the Big Leagues, two former players were playing AA minor league ball and were in a position to be called up to the Bigs in September.

After so many years of doing this work, Sarah could produce results effortlessly compared to having parents do their share and make a mess that she would have the task of cleaning up. Sarah knew which businesses in the community to squeeze for sponsorships, how to avoid scheduling games on religious holidays, which kids needed to be on separate teams, and how to placate the demands of "Little League Dads" who demanded that their teams consist of the best players. Dealing with some of these parents was the toughest part of Sarah's job, and she often had to serve as the sole arbiter when her coaches were unable to deal with the abuse they had to take for not starting a particular player. Or for taking that player out of a game "prematurely" to let a less talented player meet the League's requirement that each player on the team plays at least two innings in the field.

Sarah had even dealt with one mom who had heaped a constant tirade of abuse on the home plate umpire. Sarah had calmly informed that mom out of earshot of curious onlookers that her behavior was unacceptable and a violation of League rules—and that if she continued her behavior, she and her son would not only be banned from participating in any further competition, but that her husband would somehow find out who she was spending time with every Wednesday morning. The mom had backed down without indicating which threat had intimidated her the most.

Sarah had boundless energy when it came to League business, although during the season, everything else was relegated to secondary importance. One of her brood, in high school, had grown up in Kenmore Midgets, and was a promising pitcher, scouted by several major league teams. Another was an All-American college wrestler who also played for State on its baseball team. Sarah knew that without the experience of playing Midget baseball, many of the kids in Kenmore would have turned to drugs or a life of crime, and they might very well have become permanently entangled within the criminal justice system.

She was proud of her accomplishments. Several years earlier, she had even been nominated to receive one of the daily "Point of Light" awards, created in response to a call by President George Herbert Walker Bush in his 1989 inaugural address and spearheaded by the Points of Light Institute.

Although she was not independently wealthy, Sarah and her husband ran a successful local food distribution business, and they were more prosperous than most parents with kids on the teams. When she found out that a kid with some talent lacked a glove or proper cleats, she often reached into her own pocket to provide them. She was delighted when one of these kids started calling her "Mom," and other players started doing this, as well, making her feel proud. In some sense, they were all like her children to her.

In December, Lenny's Family Restaurant, the restaurant that operated the concession stand, had been forced to close because of lease problems. The owner had decided to move the restaurant to Centertown, more than fifty miles away from Kenmore. This development meant that the League would not only have to find two new team sponsors, but also find another operator for the concession stand.

This new problem didn't faze Sarah at all, as she was a problem solver. Sarah judged that she could kill two birds with one stone and turn lemons into lemonade, perhaps literally in this case. If her board had no objection, she would propose to take over the concession stand management, and continue the terms of the previous agreement, running everything through her husband's food distribution business. The revenues she would receive would pay for sponsoring the two teams that the restaurant had sponsored, and more so. She also calculated that doing this would compensate her for some of the countless hours she put in during all of these years of service. And it would solve a big problem, as it could take a lot of effort to find someone else to provide for concessions on short notice.

It would also help stop the constant nagging of her husband, who continually was complaining that Sarah's devotion to the Midget League, including long hours, was having a harmful effect on the family business and their own relationship, as well. Her husband suggested that it was not fair that Sarah did all of this work without any compensation, while others benefited and did virtually nothing. With no kids in the program any more, her dedication and generosity were being taken advantage of, he persistently pointed out.

Considering how much work went into each successful season, most of it done by Sarah single-handedly, it should be a paid position, he contended.

After consulting with her husband, she wrote down more details of her concession business plan that would bring some income into the household to compensate her for all of the work she was doing, without having to propose to the League that it hire her to do this work in the future. Obviously, if she decided for any reason not to continue doing this work as a volunteer, it would be difficult, if not impossible, for the program to continue. She made a note in her Blackberry to add this item to the board agenda, thinking that it was appropriate for the board to consider what she planned to do to solve this last-minute problem.

"The next agenda item is replacing the partnership agreement we had with Lenny's Family Restaurant to manage the concession stand. I've talked this over with my husband, and we are willing to take it on with the same terms of 15% of the revenue going to the League. My business will sponsor the two teams, and we will use parent volunteers as before. Things can go on and we won't miss a beat.

"Does anyone object?"

Discussion Questions

1. Was it a problem that the concession stand was operated by a restaurant that had its food distributed to it by the board chair of the League?

2. What is the board's responsibility to question this proposal, and what is an appropriate response?

3. What problems might arise when an organization has one major committed volunteer who does all of the work? What might happen to the organization if that person burns out or otherwise becomes unable or unwilling to perform those duties? What leverage does that person have to make sure the board acts as he/she desires?

4. How should anyone in a nonprofit organization with authority to hire workers do so? What are some of the problems with how Sarah handles this process?

5. Would the governance structure of this organization benefit by having committees?

6. Beginning around the early 1990s, the term "midget" became known as a derogatory and offensive term. Discuss how you would handle a situation as the chair of the Kenmore Midget League if a board member offered a motion to change the name of the organization to the "Kenmore Youth Baseball League" and to forbid the use of team names that may have been used in this League for years that are considered offensive to some people, such as "Indians," "Redskins," and "Braves." Is it ethical to continue to use the term "midget" and other offensive terms in the name of an organization?

Note: This case originally appeared in *The Nonprofit Management Casebook: Scenes From the Frontlines.*

Case 9
The Professor's Farewell

Dr. Stephen Richards locked the door behind him, tested it carefully, and made the short trek from his office in the Social Sciences Administration Building to a classroom in Harrison Hall, behind the Woodson Library. It was a trip he had made hundreds of times. More than likely, this would be the last such trip in his academic career.

It was Friday, the last day of summer term, and few students were on campus. He remembered back when he had first arrived here, the ink on his Ph.D. diploma hardly dry, never suspecting that he would possibly be teaching the same courses for the same department at the same institution for four decades.

In those four decades, he had physically changed along with the campus. His beard was now grey, and his bones creaked when he walked down the polished granite stairs to the department's bank of elevators. Perhaps he had put on "only" two extra pounds each year, but they added up. Now 73, his obesity was only one of his chronic health problems, exacerbated by age and lack of exercise.

In contrast, the University had aged more gracefully, expanding away from the town's main street in three directions, sprouting up buildings of modern glass and concrete that changed the character away from the ivy-covered brick walls that he had known when first arriving. The University had a voracious appetite, particularly in the 1970s and 1980s, consuming nearby parking lots, small businesses, student and other low-income ramshackle housing, a couple of factories, and even a hospital. The acquisition of land for expansion was accomplished with some of the same ruthlessness, although not on quite the scale, as the early settlers of America had shown expanding westward at the expense of the indigenous population.

When he first taught here, locking doors of his office behind him had been unnecessary. But times had changed, not only on urban university campuses, but on relatively isolated bucolic campuses such as Tidwell University, as well. Several weeks earlier, someone had broken into the department's offices and made off with seven computers. Just this summer term, there had been two sexual assaults reported on campus, an armed robbery, a carjacking, and several dorm room break-ins.

On this Friday morning, the air was pungent with the odor of burning leaves. Although fall term was still three weeks away, leaves were dropping on campus, creating piles for a multitude of grey squirrels to scamper through, chasing each other playfully. Students were playing touch football on the quad, adjacent to the classroom building. *Oh, to be 19 again*, he mused.

I'll miss football, he thought to himself, reveling again in the memory of Tidwell just missing out on being in the NCAA Division 1 title game the previous season. When it came to football, the Tidwell administration gave that program a virtual blank check, even when there was a hiring freeze and a temporary ban on using department money to pay academic conference attendance expenses.

Tidwell had done everything legally possible, and sometimes not so legally, to improve its chances for national prominence that accompanied success on the gridiron. "Student" athletes were recruited to play for the institution, some of whom were functionally illiterate. For the glory of Tidwell, some students were provided with not only room, board, and books, but also full-time tutors and special classes. That was the best that could be offered, once the NCAA put a stop to the gifts of cash, cars, and clothes to star recruits from sports-obsessed alumni.

Some professors at Tidwell had resigned several years earlier rather than yield to the substantial pressure from the administration to give certain football players a break on their grades so they could remain eligible to play. Eventually, the administration had wised up and sequestered most of the football squad in their own classes, with their own professors, away from the "real" students. Doing so was expensive, but it had been a great investment. Donations from proud alumni soared with the nearly undefeated season last year, enough to fund not only the costs of the football program but of Tidwell's entire lineup of NCAA Division 1 sports for both men and women.

Although perhaps only a third of the football team's entering freshmen ever graduated, none of them ever questioned whether they were being exploited. On the contrary, most would have said their five years at Tidwell were the best of their lives, even if most were relegated to working in dead-end jobs rather than becoming millionaires as high draft choices on an NFL team, as many had expected to be when they accepted a scholarship offer to play for the legendary coach of Tidwell, Buckets Henry. It had been rumored for years that Coach Henry's salary was more than ten times that of the President of Tidwell, confirmed when the federal government required the top salaries of tax-exempt nonprofit organizations to be disclosed on the organization's 990 federal tax return. The line-item on the return, of course, did not include the income Henry received from his radio show, endorsements, and royalties on products.

The consensus was that since the Tidwell president had never personally led a Tidwell team to an undefeated national championship 13-0 season and a major bowl bid worth almost $15 million, the salary shelled out to Henry was worth every penny. Although this money had to be shared with other schools in the conference, the spike in sales of official clothing and souvenirs with the school's logo as a consequence of success on the gridiron more than compensated for this.

Twice in its history, the Tidwell board of directors had been forced to make a choice between keeping either the school's president or the football coach. It had not been one of the tougher decisions it had had to make.

Other than a year off almost 20 years ago for a well-deserved sabbatical leave, Dr. Richards had not missed teaching fall term in his 40 years with the University. This would be something he would miss the most. There was something magical about fall term. He would sometimes sit outside on a bench in the quad in early September, adjacent to one of the residence halls, and watch parents drop off their sons and daughters. Many of these children, now young adults, would be having their initial experience of being on their own, away from home for any extended period of time.

If it had been his choice, Dr. Richards would have continued to teach until he died or was unable to stand up in front of a classroom. And with the amazing state-of-the-art technology to which he had access, even the inability to stand up in a classroom would not have deterred him from physically being able to teach classes. The University had an active online master of public administration (MPA) program, and several years earlier, Dr. Richards had experimented by teaching one of the classes. It simply wasn't his cup of tea, he remembered. He could not look into the eyes of his students and see whether what he was saying was sinking in. Overall, he found that teaching online required much more work on his part. He did appreciate that the online environment encouraged his students to think about a response to a question. In a classroom, his students appeared to be in a competition to raise their hands first and be recognized (at least those who deigned to participate, which seemed to be declining with every passing year). Online, the playing field was leveled.

On the other hand, he could barely keep up with the rigors of online teaching. He did not have a good experience; the department had been forced to bring in a Ph.D. student to take over his class after the fourth week after students complained that he was two weeks behind in responding to classroom posts.

A realist, he recognized that the University would likely try to exploit the advantages of online education, as it could charge students full price for courses without all of the high overhead of having support facilities. It was indeed a lucrative enterprise. But he remained skeptical that students really learned anything of value. His department had lately been advertising for online adjuncts, recognizing that it could pay salaries that might be a third of what it would have to pay for recruited assistant professors, and it would avoid having to pay any benefits, as well. The jury was still out, in his mind, over whether students were learning anything by typing into a keyboard, perhaps in the middle of the night with loud rock music in the background and the air filled with marijuana fumes.

But who's to say they are learning anything of value in conventional classes, he mused. *Things have changed so much in 40 years.*

It was not really his choice to retire. He really wasn't sure why the department's leadership found him to be expendable after 40 years. Being a tenured faculty member, he technically couldn't be fired. In his younger days, he had considered the tenure process simply another strategy colleges and universities had adopted to institutionalize mediocrity.

No one in the administration had ever directly asked for his resignation; rather, it was a series of explicit and implicit messages, some subtle, some not so. Perhaps the first sign of his falling out of favor was his appointment to the Parking Appeals Committee. His applications to attend various academic conferences, once approved routinely, were now denied. He became more suspicious after he judged that his student advisor caseload had inexplicably doubled. He noticed that not only the administrators, but even faculty members whom he had mentored, were beginning to avoid him. Last year, he had received an email notice that his office in the department's headquarters would need to be vacated to make room for a new research and teaching institute. He was able to harness what little political power he still had to reverse that decision of the academic dean, with whom his relationship had frayed since his failed attempt to thwart the University from accepting a sizeable donation from a convicted felon.

One obvious message came from his deteriorating course assignments. Lately, he was assigned to teach courses that were typically assigned to junior faculty, and at times of the day that were not particularly pleasant, such as this current class assignment at 8 a.m. on a Friday. Eventually, he was not assigned to teach much at all. Although this freed him to pursue more opportunities for his research, he knew that his *raison d'être* was teaching. Most of his research, he knew, would never be communicated to those who could use it to make the world better in any way. Rather, it would be published in academic journals that hardly anyone, even his colleagues, would even open, if only to see whose articles got published. When he had an article published in one of these journals, he could count on kudos being offered by his friends in the department and in his field. But he was well aware that hardly anyone actually read the articles, not that it would have changed any behavior in the world if anyone had read them.

At first, he fought against the pressure to retire. Last year, with resignation, he recognized that it was an uphill battle to continue to resist, and that the joy of teaching was dampened by the frustrations of dealing with an administration that he felt was openly hostile to serving the educational needs of students, making their own needs paramount. And the students seemed more interested in partying than learning.

Students today expected getting an "A" simply for showing up, he lamented. The grade inflation in recent years induced this attitude to some extent. And no wonder; professors were often judged by their student evaluations, and students who expected to get good grades gave their professors good evaluations. Students had the process of taking the easy way out down to a science; they shared intelligence on Web site databases to find out which professors were "easy." When he was a student himself, Richards had been more interested in determining which professors were good teachers. The good grades came through hard work. Getting an "A" was an achievement back then. Even then, flunking out was a real fear, even for students who had done well in high school.

Maybe it really is time for me to retire, he thought, entering the classroom. *I remember when the business of the University was run by educators whose sole concern was educating its students. Today, if there is an interest in preserving educational standards, it seems more that this is to preserve the value of the University's "brand name" rather than prepare our students to respond to global challenges. No wonder football has become such a high priority.*

Harrison Hall was a completely renovated and retrofitted building of classrooms, wired for the 21st century. Most of the funds for the renovation had been donated by William Jayson Harrison, whose net worth had been estimated at $400 million at the time of his conviction for insider trading violations. He had served his sentence in the federal penitentiary at Allenwood, often considered one of the "country clubs" for federal white collar criminals. There had been serious opposition from some board members and faculty about accepting the $30 million gift from Harrison to fund the classrooms, particularly since it was predicated on the requirement that the Hall bear the donor's name.

Richards himself, as a member of the Faculty Senate at the time, had argued against accepting the donation. He had pointed out that just as for-profit companies pay for the naming rights of stadiums, there is a tangible value to the donor for doing so. So, at a minimum, if the University wanted to prostitute itself (the very phrase he used) by selling its good name to benefit a convicted felon, the University should consider naming the building after Harrison as a fee for service, and should not issue Harrison a substantiation letter acknowledging that the $30 million was a gratuitous donation and thus eligible for a tax exemption.

As expected, the motion was made to endorse acceptance of the gift and it carried by a large majority. The school needed the money. Although tainted, a dollar was a dollar. From that day on, he had noticed his relationship with his department leadership, most of them 20 years his junior, had begun to fray.

He entered the classroom at exactly 8 a.m. He saw again that most of his class of 16, mostly upperclassmen in his Nonprofit Management Seminar class, had not yet arrived. Most needed three elective credits that could be squeezed into their schedules on Fridays to avoid delaying their graduations, and they were understandably not particularly interested in the topic of the class.

Some, he suspected, had simply blown off the final class. Several years earlier, he had announced that being late to his classes was rude and disruptive, and that the door of his classroom would be locked from the inside when the clock's second hand hit twelve, the time the class was to start. That policy lasted exactly one week; four students who had been late the following week had jointly complained to the academic dean, and Richards was curtly informed that he should be a bit more accommodating to "customers."

The school had been on a Total Quality Management kick at that time. In successive years, it had gone through other business fads, including Management by Objectives, Future Search, and Business Process Reengineering. In virtually every case, the "reform" was accompanied by evaluations, surveys, tons of forms to fill out, and, as he had predicted, had resulted in little if any improvement in the efficiency or effectiveness of the University's programs and activities.

What he thought was the last straw, convincing him to consider his retirement, was a budget department policy that courses would be cancelled if they were not self-supporting. This meant that Richards' favorite Ph.D. seminar electives would not be held as scheduled, as it was unlikely that the population of Ph.D. students in the small program would support enrollment at the required minimum.

 He had tried to organize a protest. If the institution would only offer courses that broke even or made a profit, how could they justify seeking donations? The response from his colleagues was lukewarm at best. No one wanted to rock the boat anymore, certainly not like almost everyone had seemed willing to do in the turbulent sixties when he had arrived on campus. He remembered an anti-war rally in progress on the quad when he had arrived for his interview. Students had briefly occupied the president's office, demanding an end to the ROTC program on the campus.

In the last ten years, the largest campus protest he remembered was one organized by the student newspaper when the board had approved a tuition hike of 10%.

He took his usual place behind a small lectern and looked over his class, its ranks depleted even more than its typical 75% attendance rate. When he had been an undergraduate, he had attended classes wearing a tie and jacket. Today, anything more than shorts and a T-shirt would be considered formalwear. The young women pretended to be oblivious to the effect their low-cut halter tops were having on their male colleagues, but likely were well aware. He, himself, pretended not to notice.

Students from all social classes sported spiked haircuts. Pink dyed hair. Nose rings. Fingernails looking more like talons with designs on them. And tattoos!

Students came to class with laptops, iPods, Blackberries, and other electronic gadgets that had been out of a science fiction comic book at the time he had been an undergraduate and now were *de rigueur* for almost everyone. All he had taken to class as a student was a book, a notebook to take notes, a pencil, and an empty, open mind, which he expected the professor to fill with wisdom. Today's student demanded two hours of entertainment and an opportunity to chat.

Professor Richards looked up, smiled as warmly as he could muster, and began the class.

"Good morning, everyone. This is the last class of summer term, and I hope you've enjoyed it as much as I have. I'd like to begin by going back to basics and discussing what makes an organization a nonprofit, what makes it a charity, and what is the difference between these two, and how nonprofit organizations differ from other organizations in government and the business sector."

His eyes met Roger, his best student, perhaps the only one who took the class seriously, who studied, and who he thought might have actually paid attention to his lectures. "Roger, let's begin with you. Why is Tidwell University considered a nonprofit, charitable institution?"

"Well, none of the excess revenue over expenses inures to the benefit of the trustees, and Tidwell offers scholarships to the needy."

"That's a good start. Now, let's assume that you are paying the full cost of your education, and something happens, so your parents no longer can pay your tuition. Should we assume that Tidwell will give you a discount of some kind, or treat you like any other for-profit business? What I mean is, will you be given a break based on your ability to pay, or will you be thrown out on your posterior, and escorted from the classroom if you expect Tidwell to act like a charity?"

"Thrown out on your ass, obviously," came a response from a possibly anorexic young woman with a nose ring and black lipstick, sitting in the back row.

"Now, look around this campus. It is about five times as large as it was when I first started working here 40 years ago. The annual budget of Tidwell University is perhaps $1 billion annually, in round numbers. The income Tidwell receives from its $12 billion endowment is more than that, because it has hired staff who invest its money in all sorts of business enterprises and securities. One could argue that the main business of the Tidwell Corporation is to generate wealth from its investments, and that education is simply a side business. So, if you accept that, why does Tidwell deserve to be tax-exempt?"

"Don't foundations have to distribute 5% of their assets annually?"

"No, this federal requirement doesn't apply to educational institutions, and even if it did, the 5% rule includes reasonable administrative expenses.

"Now, how many of you think Tidwell pays any property taxes? If Tidwell pays some of its endowment fund managers seven-figure incomes—certainly more than our university president earns—you might argue that it values this side of the 'business' more than education. So, how can it justify receiving a property tax exemption that by any estimate has a value more than the amount of scholarships Tidwell provides to needy students? Remember, we have already agreed that if you can't pay your tuition, you are barred from attending classes and are forcibly ejected from the campus, using our taxpayer-subsidized campus security force if necessary."

He didn't wait for any answers.

"And it is not like students know what they are getting into when they start here freshman year. Tuition was just $5,000 when I started teaching here; each year it increased by about twice the CPI. What other business can get away with offering a product to its customers without knowing in advance what the price is going to be, and having that product virtually worthless unless you pay up in full and graduate?

"What is the value of a four-year university education at Tidwell University if you take being awarded a diploma out of the calculation? Put another way, how much would you be willing to pay for it? And let's assume you could agree to have a four-year degree from Tidwell with the proviso that at the end of the four years, you would have your diploma, but everything you learned would be wiped clean from your memory? That is, you have the legitimate credential but not the learning, skills, or knowledge?"

Unlike in other class sessions, he saw evidence that his students were beginning to respond to his questions. At least they appeared to be shifting uncomfortably in their seats.

"Without having to go to school, take tests?"
"Without the partying and Bowl Games?"
"I would probably pay more for that than what the current tuition is!"

"Now, what if I told you a little secret about how Tidwell is run. This year, Tidwell's budget office sent a memo to all of the academic deans informing them of a new policy stating that each class we offer, with limited exceptions, needs to generate at least as much in revenue as its expenses. In other words, if a class has enrollment that is too low to generate a break-even point for the course, it will be cancelled. This, of course, is why this course was scheduled originally for spring term and is being offered in the summer—in addition to the fact that Tidwell pays professors less for teaching summer courses than for fall or spring courses. What are some of the unintended consequences of this?"

"Well, for one thing, students who need courses to graduate might not find the course offerings they need."

"How about, how do you justify asking alumni to donate—with the implication that their donations are subsidizing the education of students, when by definition, there is no longer a need for subsidization?"

"Is this why my class in strategic planning last term was taught by an adjunct faculty member?"

"Actually like, you know, one of my classes was taught by a master's graduate student. I bet he was barely paid at all. There were 30 students in the class, and we each were paying $600 per credit hour, or $1,800 for the class. I would expect that would generate some net income. Let's see, $1,800 times 30...."

"But you are forgetting that for every class like those, there are full professors earning six figures who might only be teaching a class or two each term, and who are instead getting paid out of your tuition money to do research. Research is an important part of teaching institutions such as Tidwell University. And there are costs, such as when the University pays the equivalent of hundreds of thousands of dollars to me to do research rather than teach, I send this research to an academic journal, which then publishes it—and charges the University to buy a subscription to that publication, and charges again for the right to make copies.

"Believe it or not, I get a notice from the journal telling me when my article appears that I have the right to purchase copies of my article. Once in a while, the journal offers me a small discount!"

"Are you making this up?"

Something about the story he was telling about research triggered a deluge of more stories, which he began nonstop. He could hardly focus on the class in front of him. Forty years of frustrations came out like a flood, induced by the ambivalence of emotions he felt upon reflecting that this was likely to be his final class. He couldn't help himself. For the next 90 minutes, Dr. Richards launched a monologue and shared with his class why he thought the education system was a failure, and why Tidwell University was in need of reform if it wanted to break the culture.

Why are professors usually such bad teachers? Because getting one's Ph.D. doesn't require any training on how to teach. I am certified to teach Ph.D. students, but I can't teach seventh grade in the Tidwell school district, because I don't have the certification required to do so...

When I first started here, there was virtually no crime. Ten years ago, the University saw the need to construct a building to house the expanded security department, which monitored the campus inside and out using a sophisticated video camera system. The institution now had an entire police force that was as large, and as well-trained, as that of the town of Tidwell itself. Four patrol cars are in the fleet. Each year, the security department puts in a request to purchase several AR-15 automatic assault rifles—the civilian version of the M-16—although the administration routinely denies funding for these—but it is only a matter of time before this request gets approved, now that college campuses have been victimized by mass shootings.

Did you know that you have the right to see reports of crimes on the Tidwell campus? The Congress enacted the Student Right-To-Know and Campus Security Act of 1990. *The law was further amended in 1998 to require most institutions of higher learning, including Tidwell, to keep a public crime log, and to impose sanctions against institutions that fail to accurately disclose crime on campus. This is one more example of how government regulates nonprofit organizations differently from business organizations. Before the federal mandate, Tidwell was quite protective about keeping its crime incidents to itself, so as not to blemish the institution's reputation. I remember how many eyes were opened when the first report of crime on campus was made public, and the internal debate that had preceded publication of the report on how to sanitize it as much as possible.*

He railed against the tenure system, which he suggested protects the mediocre. He criticized the disconnect between research and practice. He pointed out his view that tuition was higher because senior faculty members were being paid six-figure salaries for having a minimal teaching load, and the school was top-heavy with assistant deans each receiving high salaries and lucrative benefits who did the work previously performed by deans.

No subject about his experience at Tidwell was taboo.

...which raises another, related issue. Probably scores of faculty members have been involved in dealing with cover-ups involving alleged cases of sexual harassment at Tidwell, which in decades past had typically resulted in the victim quietly being forced to leave the University and little or no sanctions imposed on the perpetrator. Federal laws have been enacted to apply protections against sexual harassment on all workplaces, such as Title VII of the Civil Rights Act of 1964, *and on educational institutions receiving federal subsidies, such as Title IX of the* Education Act Amendments of 1972. *These laws give students legal ammunition to fight professors who thought of their students as potential members of their own private harem. This is another example of government regulation directed at nonprofits...*

He noticed several students peering down at their watches. It was 9:50, time for the class to be dismissed. Dr. Richards had just been getting warmed up. There was so much more to tell these poor souls who were trapped by the system.

"As some of you know, this is my last class before I retire. I have enjoyed teaching, and I hope that I have made a positive impact on the lives of my students. I didn't become a millionaire teaching. I did accomplish some things, and I have enjoyed it. So, I can only say 'farewell' and hope you learned something useful here, and will put to good use what you learned in this nonprofit management seminar. If you haven't provided it yet, please don't forget to turn in your final paper to me now or email it to me by close of business today. Class dismissed."

The students gave him a standing ovation, as was customary at the conclusion of the last class of a course. He waited in the room until every student had left. Then he laid his head down on the desk, tears streaming down his face.

Two students left the classroom together, their arms draped around each other's backs. One male with spiked bleached hair and one female. Both were wearing earrings. His hand was buried in the back pocket of her jeans.

"Bit of a pompous, self centered jerk, don't you think?"

"I've had worse. At least he didn't give us a final exam. Gotta say, his two-hour rant for the entire last class was a bit over the top. How did you stand it?"

"I spent most of it playing Free Cell on my iPhone, and then I got bored, so I spent the rest of the time writing rude messages on my friends' Facebook walls. I know it's only 10, but let's go back to my dorm room and get wasted."

Roger, the professor's best student, went to the library to return some books. After he had done so, he sat in a corral and checked to see if anyone had posted any responses to his blog, which he had written and posted during Richards' class. Roger had dutifully chronicled the professor's entire rant in detail. *Should definitely get some comments on this one,* he anticipated. He was disappointed to find no responses yet, but the day was young. And, he was delighted by an @reply on Twitter, responding to his tweet about his new blog post. It read: *im a reporter for the Wash Post. Luvd yr blog today. Doing an article on ed reform. Pls call me. 202-334-7300 steve reedman*

Discussion Questions

1. Review the public crime reports submitted by your campus's security department. Is anything surprising to you? What might be some of the reasons colleges and universities resisted the regulation to make these reports public? What might have been some of the reasons why the Congress enacted it over their objections?

2. Should donors to charities that condition their donation on naming a building after them be entitled to a tax-deduction?

3. What are the pros and cons of a charity accepting a donation from a convicted felon?

4. Why should Tidwell University be exempt from local property taxes? How much community benefit should institutions be providing before they are deemed to be eligible for such an exemption?

5. What are some of the unique aspects of nonprofit universities that make them different from other charities?

6. What are some of the unique aspects of nonprofit universities that make them different from for-profit or government institutions of higher learning?

7. Professor Richards remembers the days when students expressed their advocacy by holding rallies on campus. Discuss how social media such as Facebook, Linkedin, and Twitter have given students new tools to coordinate their efforts when they seek change. How has social media changed the educational culture? How might it change in the future as a result of these new tools?

Note: This case originally appeared in *The Nonprofit Management Casebook: Scenes From the Frontlines.*

Case 10
Doctoring the Résumé—Giving the Third Degree to the Director of Research at SCRC

Dr. Mary Parker, executive director of the State Children's Research Consortium (SCRC), was sitting in front of her computer screen when she made a shocking discovery. She was aimlessly surfing the Internet in her office between meetings, at this particular moment, seeing what new posts of interest were made on Facebook. She had another meeting in ten minutes, for which she had procrastinated preparing. No matter; she had confidence she could wing it adroitly.

This new development was certainly more important. If what she read on this one particular posting about her most valuable staff member was true, she would rather pack up her briefcase, go home, and hide under the covers for at least a week.

Normally, she would have felt a bit guilty about indulging herself in such an activity on work time. But yesterday, while she was spending a few minutes decompressing after a tense meeting on her organization's potential budget shortfall by clicking on some links her cousin Lisa had shared via email, she had come across news of a study conducted by researchers from the University of Melbourne on Internet surfing in the workplace.

According to the study, a large majority, 70% of the workers who were the study's sample population of 300, engaged in Workplace Leisure Internet Browsing (WLIB). WLIB was defined by the author of the study as browsing the Web for information and reviews of products, reading online news sites, playing online games, keeping current with friends' activities on social networking sites, watching videos on YouTube, and similar non-work related activities. What was surprising about this study was that the researchers determined that workers who engaged in WLIB were, overall, more productive than those workers who didn't spend work time on the Internet, at least when WLIB was limited to not more than 20% of work time. The researchers theorized that Internet surfing and other personal use of the Internet during work time afforded an unobtrusive break that helped workers' brains regain their concentration for work tasks.

With a chuckle to herself, she remembered one staff member she had had to let go for spending almost all of his time doing personal business while at work. She imagined that had he read the article, perhaps he might have decided to spend a few hours each day actually doing the work he was being paid to perform, as doing this might have made him think he would be able to focus better doing his personal business—at least so long as his time doing actual work for SCRC didn't exceed 20 percent of the time in the office.

Dr. Parker often accessed the Internet for personal purposes during work hours, but usually for only a brief time. Certainly nowhere near the 20-percent threshold. She was a busy member of the staff, dealing with five full-time researchers and a cadre of ten administrative and other support staff, not including herself. She used to feel guilty stealing a few minutes of down time, reading the latest posts on the *American Idol* blog or looking for a bargain on a new smart phone at Amazon.com. Her guilt during these forays away from her official duties in her office was somewhat assuaged after having read about the study. Now, if she could only find something about a study with a similarly counterintuitive conclusion that those who eat at least one bar of chocolate each day were more successful in losing weight than those who didn't!

The Consortium's primary mission was to conduct research to improve the health outcomes of children. Although some of the studies the Consortium conducted required its researchers to collect their own data, the organization mostly analyzed existing data, such as that collected by the State's Health Care Cost Containment Council (HCCCC), a quasi-governmental organization that was a collaboration of the State Department of Health and the State Hospital Association, authorized by a statute enacted a decade earlier by the State Legislature. Many of the research studies conducted by SCRC were commissioned by the HCCCC. Funding for these studies came mostly from the HCCCC and from grants from some of the largest and most prestigious national foundations concerned about the health of children.

SCRC was incorporated as a federal, tax-exempt 501(c)(3) organization, with a board consisting of a balanced mix of health researchers, hospital administrators, elected officials, community advocates, academics, and representatives of think tanks in the state. Doing so provided many advantages compared to creating the organization simply as a research arm of the Department of Health. Generally, the board stayed out of Mary's way, and she had developed a close relationship with her funders.

Although Dr. Parker suspected others on her staff wasted working time playing computer games, arranging personal trips, or reading movie reviews, she wouldn't have considered cracking down on this practice. She never monitored how her staff used their time, provided they accomplished what needed to be done. She trusted their judgment in using their time. If they required an afternoon off to attend to some personal business, she routinely granted it, provided they did not have important deadlines that would be missed. She did not feel it was necessary to hold her staff hostage until 4:30 p.m. each work day.

Mary often enjoyed using the Google search engine to take a break from the pressures of running the largest research organization in the state devoted to children's health. Periodically, she would Google the names of her employees and their families and visit the social networking profiles of those who had one. She took pleasure in learning about her coworkers' personal lives. Many of the professional staff had joined the organization when she had four years ago, and everyone was collegial and friendly. It was not unusual for staff members to invite the entire SCRC staff to their life-cycle events. There were staff outings to sports events, picnics, and occasional dinners. It would have been natural for the staff to be segregated culturally along the lines of educational achievement. It was important to her to make sure that those who had their Ph.D.s treated those who didn't as equal, valued members of the team.

Dr. Parker would have been the first to admit that her role was mostly administrative and political. She had been a researcher once herself, but her current role was to assure that the SCRC had the resources it needed to fulfill its mission and keep all of its stakeholders happy. Perhaps her most important task for the organization was recruiting some of the best talent around to design and carry out the research that she knew would be used by state and local government, foundations, and practitioners in the field to improve the health outcomes of children, many of them disadvantaged. And, of course, doing what was necessary to retain these staff and keep them happy and motivated.

One of the best decisions she had made, she had thought, was hiring Harry Hauser as the Director of Research. Dr. Hauser was amazing, and his commitment to the mission of the Consortium was unquestionable. He was responsible for the five-member research department, all of whom had Ph.D.s. No study had ever been conducted by the organization since his arrival that did not have his creative signature visible somewhere on it, increasing its chances to avoid any threats to internal and external validity. In some cases, his research designs were a work of art, and several state laws were directly attributable to the data he collected and analyzed.

She was in the habit of cleansing her browser's history after each WLIB session, so as not to be embarrassed if anyone was snooping on her computer. This time, she bookmarked the Facebook page she had just accessed. She also printed out the page, as well, and placed it in a secured personnel file cabinet. More than likely, this particular post would be deleted as soon as Harry saw it.

Now, as she stared at the Facebook page on her computer screen for perhaps the tenth time, she could hardly believe what she was seeing, and wondered whether it might simply be a mistake. After all, there was no system in place that verified the accuracy or reliability of what one read on the Internet. Most of it was unfiltered, giving any single individual with a modem, some free open source software, and a Web hosting account the power to publish anything at any time. Social networking sites such as Facebook eliminated the need for even some of these minimal requirements.

What had shocked her was a comment on Harry Hauser's Facebook wall. Harry was one of Dr. Parker's 89 Facebook "friends." All of what she read on Harry's Facebook wall today was benign, other than one glaringly disturbing post. It was by all appearances from an Arkansas woman, a former colleague of Dr. Hauser's from a previous research job. She had been simply catching up with him, one of several new friends he had added this week. The post was written in a friendly manner and didn't appear to be malevolent in any way. But what Dr. Parker distilled from the posting was that Dr. Hauser had been dismissed from a similar research position in Arkansas four years earlier for exaggerating his academic credentials.

Dr. Hauser was, according to the post, Mr. Hauser. It raised the strong possibility that he had never received a Ph.D., although at the time of his dismissal from the Arkansas position, he was apparently quite proficient, if not gifted, in conducting research.

Dr. Parker had remembered building her staff and making a phone call to the executive director of that Arkansas organization that was Hauser's previous employer. Dr. Hauser's, or rather Mr. Hauser's, boss had praised his work, but had mentioned, somewhat cryptically, that he had left for personal reasons, and he had parted company on good terms. If the post was true, it wouldn't have been improbable that the terms of separation with that employer had been that his supervisor would have agreed not to disclose anything substantive about the reasons why Hauser had left the organization.

Dr. Parker considered how to deal with this upsetting situation. If the Facebook post was accurate, Dr. Hauser had won the keen competition for his well-paid position based on false pretenses. He certainly demonstrated that he had the expertise and qualifications to continue in the position if she decided to simply ignore what she had found. On the other hand, ignoring this information, she judged, made her complicit to his alleged fraud, and it wasn't fair to keep someone on her staff who was dishonest, even if this meant losing a valued employee.

She considered seeking advice from a friend (a real friend, not a Facebook friend), or sharing what she learned with the current board chair, an older philanthropist who usually told her to do whatever she needed to do, provided it was ethical and consistent with the organization's mission. However, she decided that once she shared this information with anyone, it would be only a matter of time before others learned of this. And even if she decided to keep it to herself, others could learn about Hauser's fraudulent credentials in the same manner as she had.

On one hand, she knew that silence was complicity, and it just wasn't right to ignore this information. And on the other hand, she knew that Hauser's research, using the substantial resources provided by the Consortium with funding from both public funds and prestigious foundations, was so valuable that thousands of lives of children at risk could very well be improved if she simply kept mum about what she had discovered.

This was shaping up to be a classic ethical dilemma.

Dr. Parker's ethics training in graduate school had prepared her to deal with ethical dilemmas, or so she thought. She recalled the two primary approaches to ethics—*teleological,* based primarily on the outcomes of a decision, and *deontological,* based primarily on principles. In this case, a teleological approach militated for keeping her mouth shut as long as possible, knowing that the greater good would be served. And a deontological approach suggested her taking action on the principle that Hauser should be held accountable for his dishonesty—assuming the Internet post was accurate. And she truly hoped it wasn't.

She considered estimating the costs and benefits to each of the stakeholders of the organization, including herself, of various responses. She made an attempt to be a rational decision-maker, using her graduate degree nonprofit management training. The basic model she remembered was a seven-step process called RESPECT. In short, it called for:

- Recognizing the moral aspects of the dilemma,
- Enumerating the guiding principles,
- Specifying the stakeholders and their principles,
- Plotting the various options to resolve the problem, and evaluating these alternatives,
- Consulting with others, including the stakeholders, where appropriate, and
- Telling the stakeholders what your decision will be.

This model sounded reasonable in the crucible of a class, but in a real situation, she found it to be hopeless. There were too many variables, the issues were too complex, and the reaction of any single stakeholder to the news of Harry's deception, or rather alleged deception, in the calculation was unpredictable.

It was time for her next meeting, and she was so preoccupied with this new problem that she was unable to focus on the topic, which was whether to change the Consortium's health benefit plan and other fringe benefits to accommodate same-sex partners. Her distraction was noticed by other staff members around the table, but they plodded on until there was agreement to end the Consortium's current discrimination against gays and lesbians in committed relationships and propose this policy change for board approval.

When she returned to her office, she decided that her course of action would be to go with what her gut told her was the right thing to do, rather than weighing the costs and benefits through some calculation. Maybe the Facebook posting was a practical joke, she thought, thinking that this was unlikely. Almost every Ph.D. she knew who received a degree in the social sciences was more than willing to volunteer, unasked, the horror stories of his or her matriculation experience, the hazing, the senseless rewrites of dissertation chapters, and the months of delay until a dissertation chair set aside the time to read anything. Harry had never mentioned much about his doctoral experience at Princeton, which she found to be unusual. He had been reticent in response to her sharing her own story as an ABD student ("all but dissertation"), which had been the two worst years of her life.

Anxiety was mounting for her about how to deal with this, or whether to deal with it at all. The safest course was to simply sleep on it for at least a day. But she suspected that she would be unable to sleep soundly, knowing that this 800-pound gorilla in the room would make it difficult for her to have the interaction with Harry during working hours that she needed to do her job.

If only he wasn't such an important part of the success of this organization, she thought. The decision would be easy. But, she lamented, by all measures, Harry Hauser was a crackerjack researcher, regardless of whether he was Dr. Hauser or Mr. Hauser. His research designs were elegant. Although others performing research in the social sciences were content to distribute a survey to a sample population with a perfunctory Likert scale and simply publish the results, Harry found ingenious experimental designs that provided much more confidence that the answers to the research question posed were reliable and valid.

Harry had contempt for surveys, which he was unable to disguise even when doing so would have been appropriate. Surveys provided an opportunity for people to either lie, exaggerate, or self-delude themselves in order to please the researcher or be deceptive about personal issues. He was fond of illustrating this assertion by relaying the story of the Milgram experiments conducted in the 1960s. She remembered this as if it were yesterday, although it had in fact been several years ago.

Using newspaper ads and direct mail, Milgram recruited male individuals to participate in an experiment lasting an hour, for which they would be paid $4.50, paid whether or not the subjects completed the task. Subjects were told that they would be involved in an experiment that would test the effect of punishment inflicted by a teacher *on learning, and would play the role of the teacher or learner. Unknown to the subjects, they always were picked to play the role of teacher, and a paid actor in cahoots with the experimenter was trained to play the role of learner. The learner, who made sure he informed the "teacher" that he had a heart condition, would pretend to receive a shock administered by teachers, and occasionally scream in mock pain and beg for mercy. The subjects were subjected to a 45-volt electric shock, as an example of the punishment the learner would receive with a wrong answer. They were then told to administer a shock to the learner when the learner gave a wrong answer to a question. Not knowing that the learner was not really a participant like themselves, they "administered" severe electric shocks when asked to by the experimenters. Most of the teachers were willing to administer electric shocks to the learners, who pretended to writhe in extreme pain and discomfort, and more than half (26 of the 40 subjects) administered "shocks" of 450 volts with either little or no encouragement from the experimenter before the experiment was halted.*

Today, the methodology of this experiment is considered unethical. And it is. But if the methodology were carried out by traditional surveys, the result would be closer to the results obtained by Milgram when he asked his Yale senior psychology class what percentage of teachers they would predict would be willing to administer the severe shocks—which was less than 2%.

What point had Harry been making with this? He had continued with the punch line of the story.

> *Imagine the Milgram data had been collected relying on surveys administered to participants, as is the typical data collection tool for most social science research—*

> *Question #1: If you were asked by an authority figure to administer a 450-volt, potentially fatal shock to a heart patient, would you do so?*

> *Question 2: If "no," what would be the highest voltage you would administer?*

Using this philosophy, Harry's research often made the local news and occasionally made the national news, and certainly his research designs were legendary. The organization had exploited Harry's reputation for finding ingenious ways to answer sensitive questions by applying for a series of grants from the Hughsport Foundation. These grants not only funded all of Harry's salary, but also covered a good share of the general overhead of the organization. These grants not only had financial benefit, but there was a certain level of prestige that accrued whenever the Hughsport Foundation approved another grant.

Harry's contributions to the organization went beyond his research talents and his ability to attract outside funding from grantors. He was a model employee. Mary considered him to be a personal friend.

After the meeting on same-sex benefits, Mary returned to her office and tried to work. Instead, she began looking at movie reviews on the Web. Her thoughts returned to her dilemma, and she couldn't focus on the reviews.

She decided to confront Harry directly, to simply press his intercom button and ask that he come to her office. If anything, she might find some swift resolution. He could vehemently deny the truthfulness of the Facebook post, which would require her to investigate further. Or he might admit his subterfuge and beg to remain on staff. Or he might simply resign. Each of the three posed serious risks for the organization. This would likely be a distasteful confrontation, regardless of how sensitively she handled it, but she admitted to herself that as executive director, this was part of her job to do. Her instincts were to pose a simple question and to listen as much as possible.

She paged him to her office, and his head popped in.

"Sit down, Harry."

"Everything okay?"

"No. I just learned that you may not really have a Ph.D. from Princeton. If this is true, I haven't given much thought to what should be done about this, but I wanted to hear directly from you whether this was true or not."

She saw his face redden.

"It's true," he admitted. "I don't have a Ph.D. from Princeton. I was ABD at Princeton, but never got the chance to defend my dissertation. I kept running into roadblocks. The closer I thought I got, the farther away I seemed to be. And then my wife got pregnant, we had our first child, and you already know this, our kid had health problems. Eventually, he was diagnosed with autism. That has been one of my motivations for working with the Consortium, helping to identify treatment protocols to deal with problems such as what my son is experiencing. As a result of all of the stress of the Ph.D. program, needing to earn a living, and being a caregiver for my kid, I had to abandon Princeton when I was this close to finishing," he said, his fingers in the air indicating that he was really close.

"The truth is, I was as close to getting my Ph.D. from Princeton as one can get, and it certainly wasn't my fault that I didn't get through the last hoop they put in front of me. Obviously, my work here is good and respected nationwide, and the fact that I didn't get my Ph.D. diploma from Princeton didn't affect the quality of my research. My Ph.D. is really from Coolidger University. I could tell you more about this, but it is not something I am proud of. The short answer is that Coolidger is a diploma mill. It was the only way I was going to be Dr. Hauser.

"I lied on my application to work here. I admit that. I am sorry. If you want to fire me, I will understand. However, you might consider the option of disciplining me for lying on my job application in some way we can mutually agree, and keeping me on staff here. I need the job. I like working here. My research is first rate. No one has ever complained. Obviously, the mission of the Consortium is important to me, and I think everyone is served by letting me continue to do the job you hired me for, for which I am qualified."

"I appreciate your honesty," Mary shared. "I don't know how to respond, but there are issues here that I have to think through, such as who should be aware of this, and what authority I have to make the decision. So, give me the rest of the week to sort through this, and I'll meet with you to decide how we will address this."

"Again, I'm sorry. I always expected someone would find out eventually. Believe it or not, I am actually relieved that you now know about this." He got up and left her office.

Dr. Parker considered the option of simply keeping the information to herself and telling Harry to terminate his Facebook account, or at least remove the offending post and remove that former colleague as a Facebook friend. After all, it wasn't the same as if Dr. Hauser was claiming to be a medical doctor and performing surgery. Unlike in medicine, those without being formally trained in research can be quite capable of doing research. There is no requirement that researchers be licensed or even have any particular educational training. The proof was in the pudding that Dr. Hauser, or rather Mr. Hauser, knew what he was doing when it came to performing social science research, and his work was respected.

Clearly, he would not have been considered for the position with only a Master's degree, regardless of his abilities. The recruiting notice explicitly required an earned doctorate for applicants to be considered.

Epilogue: Five years later, Dr. Parker, still the executive director of the SCRC, comes across a news item about a research study, in which Dr. Harry Hauser is the senior project manager. It mentions that Dr. Hauser received his Ph.D. from Princeton University.

Discussion Questions

1. What are some of the advantages the SCRC enjoyed by having incorporated as an independent nonprofit organization compared to being an office within the State's Department of Health?

2. What boundaries should there be between the personal and professional lives of staff members of a nonprofit organization? Should an executive director encourage or discourage staff to share time away from the office?

3. Should Hauser be fired simply because he misrepresented his credentials when he was hired, or are there other ways to discipline him while keeping him in the organization?

4. How might this development affect the credibility of the research he has already completed for the foundations and government agencies that commissioned his research?

5. Should Dr. Parker inform the funders of Dr. Hauser's past research that he lied about his credentials?

6. If Dr. Parker does fire him, does she have an obligation to tell funders who are expecting Hauser to be the senior project director for several major current grants?

7. If she does choose to fire him, what obligation does she have to disclose to future employees that he had misrepresented his credentials?

8. How much time is "permissible" for workers to do personal things such as surfing the Internet during work hours without being disciplined?

9. Was Dr. Parker's strategy for dealing with her initial confrontation with Hauser a good one? How else could she have approached this?

Note: This case originally appeared in *The Nonprofit Management Casebook: Scenes From the Frontlines.*

Nonprofit Ethics Scenarios

1. Patty is working late at the State Association of Veterans Organizations. She hears some light tapping on the windowpane, and looks out the window to determine how hard it might be raining. Her office overlooks the office building parking lot. She notices that one of her colleagues, Tom, the organization's government affairs officer, is loading boxes of bubble envelopes into his SUV. Immediately, she suspects that Tom, who recently started a home eBay business selling sports cards, has likely taken these from the supply closet for his personal use. Feeling a bit guilty that she may have jumped to a false conclusion, she leaves her office, walks down the long hallway to the supply closet, and confirms that the four boxes of these bubble mailers that were recently placed there by the office manager are no longer there. Patty and Tom have worked together for several years, and they have a good relationship. She decides to simply ignore this, as it is not her job to police the organization and she doesn't want to get anyone in trouble, particularly Tom.

a. Is Patty acting unethically by not reporting Tom's behavior?

⤷⤷⤷   ⤷⤷⤷⤷⤷   ⤷⤷⤷

2. Jackie is a home health aide for Harristown Hospice Services. Her job is to make home visits and help a hospice nurse provide health services to patients who are receiving hospice care in their own homes. The organization provides a car to Jackie, but forbids her to use that vehicle for personal use. Jackie has bristled at this restrictive policy. Initially, she used her vehicle to pick up personal prescriptions from a local pharmacy on the way to visiting her patients, and dropping off laundry, and didn't give it a second thought. Lately, she has begun using the vehicle as a replacement for her personal vehicle, rationalizing that her salary is quite low compared to those of her colleagues who work for for-profit counterpart organizations. She thinks that the possibility of anyone finding out about her use of the car is remote, and that the organization would look the other way if it did find out and take action against her, as she felt she was a valued employee who would be difficult to replace. And she knows firsthand that other employees of the organization have occasionally violated this policy, although perhaps not to the extent that she has currently been doing.

a. Is Jackie acting unethically by using the vehicle for personal use?

b. What alternatives might Jackie pursue if she strongly believes that this policy is too restrictive?

⤷⤷⤷   ⤷⤷⤷⤷⤷   ⤷⤷⤷

3. Katrina is the executive director of the Midtown Bar Association Library. Her national conference was being held at a luxury hotel in Orlando, Florida, 500 miles away from where she lives. She decides that because of the location, it makes sense to turn this conference into a family vacation. Rather than spend almost a thousand dollars on a flight for herself, she arranges for herself and her husband, with her two children, to travel by private vehicle, with her husband and her sharing the driving.

At the conference, she uses the organization's credit card to charge the entire cost of her suite at the conference hotel, and some of her family's travel expenses including gasoline, justifying this as offsetting some of the savings her organization realized because of her driving to the conference rather than flying—savings that would not have accrued if she had not had her husband with her to share some of the driving.

a. Is Katrina acting unethically by having the organization paying for any expenses that related to her family's trip?

b. Is she acting unethically if she decides instead to reimburse the organization for any incremental expenses that are attributable for her family's presence on the trip?

c. How might she handle this issue in advance if she decides she does not want to violate any ethical principles, but would like to consider having her family with her to this conference?

ৎ ৎ ৎ ৎ ৎ ৎ ৎ ৎ ৎ ৎ ৎ

4. Bill is the executive director of the State Track and Field Festival, a statewide association that administers an annual Olympic-style track meet. He has served in this position for almost three decades, and is considering retirement in the near future. His youngest son, Bill Jr., was recently laid off from his job at the local meat packing plant. Bill has always dreamed that one of his sons would follow in his footsteps, and he sees an opportunity to turn this vision into a reality. He offers his son a newly created position of assistant executive director, with the intent of teaching him everything he knows so that when he retires, Junior will carry on the organization's mission. Although some members of Bill's board of directors voice some opposition, over the years, Bill has selected many of the board members who serve on the board, and he is able to convince a majority of the board to fund this new position, and authorize him to recruit and hire whomever he wants. Junior is delighted to work for his Dad, although he knows virtually nothing about the duties he will be required to do in the new position, and certainly has no experience in managing a nonprofit organization should his father retire.

a. Is Bill acting ethically in hiring his son for this position?

b. Was Bill acting ethically when he selected board members to serve on his board?

ৎ ৎ ৎ ৎ ৎ ৎ ৎ ৎ ৎ ৎ ৎ

5. Allyson serves on the board of the State Association to Abate Women's Domestic Violence. In her professional life, she is the publisher of a series of magazines geared to women's issues. The board has agreed to publish a monthly magazine for its stakeholders, and Allyson has taken an active role in convincing the board that this would be a valuable addition to the communications strategy of the organization. Because of her experience, members of the board suggest that Allyson's organization produce the magazine. Allyson agrees to do this, and offers to provide a reasonable discount for providing these services.

a. Is Allyson acting ethically by offering to provide these services?

b. Was Allyson acting ethically by participating in the debate on whether to have a magazine?

c. Would Allyson's offer be more appropriate and ethical if she offers to provide these services at cost?

d. How might the board have structured decision-making on this issue to make sure the process of deciding whether to have such a magazine, and deciding who does this work, to make it ethical?

જ જ જ   જ જ જ જ જ   જ જ જ

6. Mary is the conference planner for the State Association of Volunteer Firefighters. Her brother was recently hired as the head of sales for the Conference Retreat Center 12 miles from the state capital. Mary suggests that the organization's state conference next year be held at the Conference Retreat Center.

a. Is Mary acting ethically by making this suggestion?

b. Can she avoid the appearance of any impropriety by making the suggestion, but agreeing not to participate in the decision to have the conference at the Retreat Center?

c. Can she avoid the appearance of any impropriety by making the suggestion, by advocating for having the conference at the Retreat Center, but by disclosing that her brother is the new head of sales at the Retreat Center?

જ જ જ   જ જ જ જ જ   જ જ જ

7. Priscilla is the receptionist for the Harristown Area YMCA. She has a lunch meeting scheduled today with a committee consisting of parents from her son's school to plan a fundraising event. She does not have a photocopy machine at home, and decides to make five copies on the YMCA's photocopy machine of a newspaper article from today's paper on how groups might raise funds for various causes to hand out at the meeting.

a. Is Priscilla acting unethically by making these copies?

b. Is your answer different if Priscilla is making one copy? Fifty copies? A thousand copies?

c. What should an organization's policy be with respect to making photocopies on the organization's copier for personal use? What sanctions should there be for violating this policy?

જ જ જ   જ જ જ જ જ   જ જ જ

8. Geraldine is the Webmaster for the Harristown Family and Children's Service. Geraldine's Web site is designed to provide the organization's stakeholders and the public with information that will be useful to improve the quality of their lives, regardless of whether they are paying clients or not. Geraldine routinely surfs the Internet for interesting published articles about the issues of concern to the Service, and copies them to the Web site so that everyone can view them. There is no charge to anyone for viewing these articles, and Geraldine considers this to be a valuable public service.

a. Is Geraldine acting unethically by posting these articles?

b. Is Geraldine violating the law by posting these articles?

c. What should the policy of the organization be with respect to posting published articles such as these?

ஃஃஃ ஃஃஃஃஃ ஃஃஃ

9. Pam is the executive director of the Wildtown Nature Center. The Nature Center started ten years ago with only one paid staff member, but as a result of grants and bequests, the Center has expanded its staff by leaps and bounds, and now has more than 30 paid staff and scores of volunteers. Her board has asked to draft a comprehensive personnel policy. Not thinking it is necessary to reinvent the wheel, she surfs the Internet and finds a document that serves as the personnel policy of a similar organization thousands of miles away. By simply changing the name of the organization and a few other cosmetic tweaks, she submits that personnel policy document as her own to the board.

a. Is Pam acting ethically by adopting this document as her own?

b. Is she acting ethically if she adopts this document as her own, but discloses to the board that the language came principally from a document she found on the Web?

c. Is she acting ethically if she first asks permission from the organization that originally formulated the personnel policy to use it for her own organization?

ஃஃஃ ஃஃஃஃஃ ஃஃஃ

10. Jasper is the executive director of Down by the Old Main Stream, a nonprofit organization that serves severely disabled children. A generous donor has provided a $1,000,000 grant to the society to provide for a camp serving such children, but only for that purpose. Jasper was in the middle of a painful, but necessary process of shutting down a respite care program serving the parents of severely disabled children because of a lack of funds. Knowing that it would take several years before any new camp could be established, and scores of parents would be severely affected by the loss of services provided by the respite care program, Jasper decides to temporarily divert some of the funds from the camp grant to keep the respite care program from shutting down, justifying this in his mind by the fact that this diversion is temporary until replacement funds could be found, no one would find out about this, that much more good would be provided by the organization by doing this, and that the use of this money is certainly consistent with the mission of the organization to serve those who are severely disabled.

a. Is Jasper acting ethically by temporarily diverting funds from the grant for this purpose?

b. Are there any other alternatives he might consider if he feels uncomfortable with diverting these funds?

c. If he chooses to divert these funds, even temporarily, should he be disclosing this to anyone?

ஃஃஃ ஃஃஃஃஃ ஃஃஃ

11. Mia is the executive director of the Harristown Rape Crisis Center. One of her friends from college, Penelope, was recently fired from her job as the government relations officer for a local college, and asks Mia if she knows of any similar positions that might be available. Mia's organization has a government relations officer, Sandy, who has done a relatively good job for the organization, but Mia does not feel that she has become friends with this staff member, and it would be great to have someone work for her whom she can be friends with, as well, in the same way she and Penelope were in college. Mia decides to ask Penelope to work for her and fire Sandy, an "at will" employee.

a. Is Mia acting ethically if she hires her friend and fires Sandy?

b. Is Mia acting legally if she does this?

12. Alisha is the CEO of Shaping Young Minds Day Care Center. One of her employees, Malory, is having personal problems at home, taking care of a chronically sick parent who is keeping her up at night. She suspects that Malory is using amphetamines to stay awake during working hours. Malory has been a valued employee for almost ten years, and has never had any discipline problems. Before now, there has only been circumstantial evidence that Malory has a drug problem. The day care center has a strict policy that staff members may not use illegal drugs, and those that do are subject to being summarily fired. Today, Alisha accidentally notices that Malory fails to return the meds intended for one of the children with ADHD, and slips it into her pocket, and heads for the bathroom. Alisha follows her into the bathroom, and confronts Malory, asking her to empty her pocket. Malory at first refuses, then starts crying, and admits she has taken the Ritalin tablets intended for one of the clients. She begs for her job, explaining that she has been doing this only since her mother has kept her awake at all hours, and she needs the job to pay for her mother's care during the day. She threatens suicide if she is fired. Alisha agrees to look the other way, provided Malory stops stealing the Ritalin.

a. Is Alisha acting unethically by not firing Malory?

b. What other options might be available to Alisha rather than either firing Malory or looking the other way?

13. Steve is the CFO for the Outlidge Nursing Home, a nonprofit long term care facility. Recently, the executive director, Harold, has discovered by accident that Steve never received his MBA from Cornell, as he had claimed on the résumé he had submitted when he first applied for the position five years ago. In fact, he didn't have an MBA at all. The job opening notice for the position clearly stated that an MBA was a prerequisite for qualifying for an interview. Harold has to admit that Steve has done an exemplary job guiding the financial management of the home, and certainly demonstrated sophistication in dealing with the financial affairs of the organization, and was well-liked and respected by his colleagues. Harold discusses this issue with his board chair, and the board chair tells Harold that he should do what he thinks is appropriate. Harold decides to fire Steve effective immediately, who with three kids and a large mortgage, would clearly be devastated by this decision.

a. Is Harold acting ethically by summarily firing Steve for exaggerating on his résumé?

b. Is there any discipline short of firing that might be appropriate for Steve's transgression?

ৰ্঵ ৰ্঵ ৰ্঵   ৰ্঵ ৰ্঵ ৰ্঵ ৰ্঵ ৰ্঵   ৰ্঵ ৰ্঵ ৰ্঵

14. Trent is a senior development officer for the Greenspace Wildlife Preserve. One of the administrative assistants for the organization, Teresa, has made a formal complaint against Trent for sexually harassing her. The executive director, Pamela, has suspected that this complaint has some truth to it because of some previous behavior that she has observed firsthand. Informally speaking with other female staff members, she is amazed to find that virtually every female staff member in the organization has had a bad experience with Trent at one time or another. Some of these staff members have reported being stalked by Trent, directly propositioned, and touched inappropriately. Pamela decides to fire Trent. She calls him into his office, and explains the evidence against him. Trent denies all of the allegations, but admits that the organization for which he worked for previously let him go for similar allegations, which he attributes to his good looks and animal magnetism, and women who just don't understand his friendliness and mistake it for something more sinister. He agrees to leave the organization quietly, in exchange for four weeks of severance pay and an agreement that Pamela will provide a reasonably good letter of recommendation for him, and not disclose the reason he is leaving. Pamela accepts these conditions for the good of the organization, and breathes a sigh of relief that she may have avoided a messy and long legal battle.

a. Has Pamela acted ethically by accepting the conditions Trent proposed?

b. How should have Pamela handled this matter to have acted ethically?

c. What might be the consequences of another organization hiring Trent without knowing about his past employment history?

ৰ্঵ ৰ্঵ ৰ্঵   ৰ্঵ ৰ্঵ ৰ্঵ ৰ্঵ ৰ্঵   ৰ্঵ ৰ্঵ ৰ্঵

15. Kelly is a committed fundraiser for Friar College, a 4-year liberal arts college in California and she is evaluated partially on the number of face-to-face visits she makes with alumni. She is also a committed marathon runner, and was quite proud to qualify for her first Boston Marathon, held on the third Monday of each April, Patriots Day. She decides that if she schedules meetings in Boston to meet with alumni and other potential donors, she can pad her statistics for face-to-face meetings, avoid having to take a couple of vacation days to compete in the marathon, and have the college absorb most of her travel costs for the trip, including airfare, hotel, and food expenses. She pays for the marathon entry fee out of her own pocket, and vows not to put the cab fare to Boston Commons, where the buses take runners to Hopkinton for the start of the race, on her expense account.

a. Is Kelly acting ethically by scheduling donor meetings in Boston during the week of her race?

b. What expenses she incurs should she absorb out of her own pocket for this race and what might she be ethically able to charge to the college?

∽∽∽   ∽∽∽∽∽   ∽∽∽

16. Harley is the CEO of Harristown Housing Project, a nonprofit housing organization. He is also the owner of a for-profit business that sells condominiums. Prior to 2008, he made hundreds of thousands of dollars flipping condominiums. But in 2008, he overextended, and was poised to lose millions, and defaulting on some of his personal debt. He explained the situation to his board, and requested that the board approve a loan of $900 thousand to help keep his personal business afloat. Harley offers to pay a market rate of interest in return for the loan. The board treasurer, noting that it had the money in its accounts and was receiving only 3% interest, agreed that the organization would benefit by doing this loan. Harley suspected that the loan may or may not be enough to forestall personal economic disaster, but grasping at straws, he was willing to do whatever was necessary to save his personal business. He hinted that he would be forced to leave the organization if it failed to approve this loan, as he would have to generate more income to meet his needs than would be available from his nonprofit job. The board approved the loan.

a. Was the board acting ethically in approving the loan?

b. Was the board acting legally in approving the loan?

∽∽∽   ∽∽∽∽∽   ∽∽∽

17. Harry is the new chair of Returning Warriors Helping Hands, an organization to provide veterans with services such as counseling, housing, and mental health services. He has discovered that the organization is spending much more on fundraising services than it is providing in actual program services to its constituency. He believes that there isn't an arms-length relationship among the organization's staff, board, and for-profit fundraiser. He makes a motion at the next board meeting to declare the five-year contract with the fundraising organization null and void, and that the Treasurer should be prohibited from making any more payments to that fundraising organization until it raises at least as much money as it bills the organization for its fundraising services.

a. Is the Chair acting ethically with this motion?

b. Is the chair acting legally with this motion?

c. What alternative actions can the Chair pursue if he believes that there is an unethical relationship between the organization and its fundraiser?

∽∽∽   ∽∽∽∽∽   ∽∽∽

18. Steve is the new founder of the Harristown Prostate Education Foundation. He recruits nine members from the community to serve on his foundation's board of directors. As a condition for serving on the board, he requires each board member to lend the organization $5,000 and donate at least $2,500 each year so the organization has startup funds to hire staff, rent an office, and pay expenses relating to programming. The requirement is included explicitly in the organization's bylaws.

a. Is the founder acting ethically?

b. Is the founder acting legally?

ও ও ও   ও ও ও ও ও   ও ও ও

19. Rebecca is the executive director of the Drink Responsibly Education Council, a 501(c)(3) tax-exempt nonprofit organization whose mission is to educate students about the dangers of binge drinking. One of her staff members, Linda, asks to meet with her, and tells her that she was recently arrested and charged with DUI. However, she says that it was her boyfriend who was actually driving the car erratically, and during the police chase, she agreed to change seats with him and take the fall because her boyfriend already had two DUI charges pending against him. Rebecca is astonished by this information, but agrees not to fire Linda. However, as a friend, she encourages Linda to tell the police the truth.

a. Is Rebecca acting ethically?

b. Is Linda acting ethically?

c. Does Rebecca have any obligation, legal or ethically, to let the police know the story Linda told her about the arrest?

ও ও ও   ও ও ও ও ও   ও ও ও

20. Peter, who runs a nonprofit "meals on wheels" organization, is seeking creative ways to generate revenue to stave off what appears to be certain bankruptcy for his organization. He decides to drive through the office parking lot late at night when no one is likely to be watching, and slowly crash the back of his car into the side of one of the organization's vehicles, causing modest damage to the back door of the vehicle with virtually no recognizable damage to his own vehicle. He will wait until one of his drivers reports that there was damage done to the organization's vehicle. He expects that his insurance company will routinely write out a check to the organization for the damage, which he will deposit into the organization's checking account rather than using the check to repair the damage. He justifies this by recognizing that the agency has received little return from its vehicle insurance policies, and that the money would be used for a good cause rather than making an almost unrecognizable increase in the profits of the national insurance company.

a. Is Peter acting ethically?

b. Is Peter violating any laws?

ও ও ও   ও ও ও ও ও   ও ও ও

21. Briana is a 20-something single woman who works in the strategic communications department of the Association for Computer Technology in Higher Education, a national association headquartered in Washington, D.C. Particularly on hot summer days, Briana dresses in skimpy clothing, showing lots of skin and causing a distraction to her coworkers. Her immediate supervisor, Harriet, is hearing complaints from the other

females in the office, and she senses that the males in her department are indeed spending a lot of time around her, ogling, and whispering about her around the water cooler. Harriet calls Briana into her office, explains her distaste for Briana's choice of wardrobe, and demands that she dress more modestly or face repercussions. Briana responds that her clothing is her own business, and in the absence of any formal organizational dress policy, she has the right to wear whatever she wants. She claims that she is being discriminated against because of her attractiveness, and implies that any action taken against her will result in a discrimination suit. She leaves in a huff.

a. Is Harriet acting ethically by providing an ultimatum to Briana?

b. What other options may be available to Harriet to respond to the perceived problem?

ợ ợ ợ   ợ ợ ợ ợ ợ   ợ ợ ợ

22. Harry has just been asked to volunteer for a nonprofit organization, Boyleton Arts Association, to set up its computer system. Conscious of the limited financial resources of the organization, Harry purchases a low-end laptop with lots of hard drive space available. He then loads the laptop with the latest versions of word processing, spreadsheet, desktop publishing, presentation, and Web Page software, which he has personally purchased for his own personal and business computers. He doesn't charge the organization anything for providing this software—only for his out-of-pocket costs for the computer, printer, and accessories.

a. Is Harry acting ethically?

b. Is Harry acting legally?

c. What other options might Harry pursue if he wants to provide standard software to the organization in an ethical manner?

ợ ợ ợ   ợ ợ ợ ợ ợ   ợ ợ ợ

23. Tidwell University's chief development officer, Ted, receives a call from "Wild Bill" Hanford, one of its best known alumni, requesting a meeting to discuss a possible major gift. Hanford was recently released from a federal prison in Allenwood, PA, having served a 3-5 year sentence for insider trading. At the meeting, Mr. Tidwell asks if the university would consider a $30 million donation for the purpose of building a new facility to house Tidwell's business school, with state-of-the-art technology embedded in the building. The only requirement would be the building would have to be named "The William Hanford School of Business." Ted thanks Mr. Hanford for his offer, and replies that it would need to be a decision of the entire board to decide whether to accept such a donation for this purpose. Two months later, the President of Tidwell puts the issue before the board of the institution. The board approves it.

a. Can the board ethically approve this donation?

b. If the donation is approved and provided, should Mr. Hanford be provided with a substantiation letter permitting him to take a full tax deduction for his donation because of the tangible value in having the building named after him?

c. If the donation is not accepted with the strings attached, is there some middle ground the board might pursue to not offend this major donor and generate needed funds to finance its programs and do so ethically?

⋇ ⋇ ⋇   ⋇ ⋇ ⋇ ⋇ ⋇   ⋇ ⋇ ⋇

24. A major donor, Jasmine, approaches Tina, a major gifts officer for the Harristown Art Museum, a 501(c)(3) tax-exempt, nonprofit organization, with a proposal. Jasmine has inherited an art collection of five Picasso paintings valued at $25 million. She discovers that she is liable for inheritance taxes on the value of the collection in excess of $5 million. What she would like to do is "donate" the collection to the museum to avoid inheritance taxes, with the proviso that she can keep the art collection displayed in her home and the museum is prohibited from selling, lending, or other transferring the collection until after her death. The museum would be required to keep the arrangement a secret, other than providing the typical substantiation letter to Jasmine, and agreeing to pay for a routine appraisal of the collection. Tina doesn't think this would be a problem, and tells Jasmine that the museum would be delighted to accept her donation.

a. Is this proposed arrangement between Jasmine and the museum ethical?

b. Is this proposed arrangement legal?

⋇ ⋇ ⋇   ⋇ ⋇ ⋇ ⋇ ⋇   ⋇ ⋇ ⋇

25. Carl, the sole proprietor of a professional fundraising company, approaches the "Save the Kids Foundation" with a proposal to rescue the organization from its near fatal experience whereby it lost its entire endowment of $10 million in the Madoff pyramid scandal. Carl proposes to raise at least $5 million for the Foundation within the next two years, and agrees to not require any fee other than a flat 10% of the amount he raises beyond out-of-pocket expenses that are agreed to by his client in advance.

a. Is this proposal by Mr. Plansky ethical?

b. Is this proposal legal?

⋇ ⋇ ⋇   ⋇ ⋇ ⋇ ⋇ ⋇   ⋇ ⋇ ⋇

26. Robert, a member of the Jewish Community Center, receives an invoice for $3,218 for the catering and room rental for his son's Bar Mitzvah celebration. He calls the executive director of the center, and suggests that the center provide him with a substantiation letter documenting that he received no goods or services of value, and in exchange, he will write a check to the Center for $4,000. The Center will receive this additional $782 sum to use as it wants, and Robert will benefit from the tax deduction that he would otherwise not receive, so it would be a win-win situation.

a. Is the proposal by Robert ethical?

b. Is the proposal by Robert legal?

c. Who wins or loses if the JCC executive director agrees to Robert's proposal?

⋇ ⋇ ⋇   ⋇ ⋇ ⋇ ⋇ ⋇   ⋇ ⋇ ⋇

27. The Harristown Musical Association generates income by a partnership it has with a for-profit company that sells donated vehicles. The partnership works by having the nonprofit organization solicit the donation of surplus vehicles. The for-profit partner picks up the vehicles, processes all of the paperwork for the donor to receive a tax deduction, and then sells them at a hefty profit. The charity typically receives 10% of the sale price of the vehicle, but has almost no direct costs itself, so it risks nothing by accepting the vehicles for donation. The Harristown Musical Association purposely avoids finding out how much these vehicles sell for and how little it receives from this partnership so that the arrangement is not threatened, and it can plausibly respond that it doesn't know how much profit the for-profit partner made on the sale. However, the donors do receive a substantiation letter from the charity, and the charity, according to IRS regulations, informs the donor when the sale price of the vehicle is less than $500. Rarely does that value exceed $500 in the case of that particular vendor because he often buys the vehicles himself for use in his auto parts business.

a. Is the charity acting unethically if it solicits donations from individuals, knowing that most of the revenue accruing from the donation of the donated vehicles accrue to the for-profit partner?

b. Is the charity acting unethically if it purposely keeps the donor unaware of amount of the donation actually received by the charity in exchange for the donation?

c. What can the IRS do to assure that donations intended for charitable purposes are not siphoned off by private companies exploiting the brand name of a charity?

ళ ళ ళ   ళ ళ ళ ళ ళ   ళ ళ ళ

28. The Harristown Wildlife Preservation Foundation is a 501(c)(3) nonprofit, tax-exempt charity committed to preserving the environment in the Harristown region, and establishing a wildlife preserve to preserve the natural habitat of flora and fauna in the region and provide for education about the environment. The Genoa Oil and Gas Company is beginning to survey nearby acreage for its potential to generate natural gas from Marcellus Shale deposits. To improve its public image, following a series of local newspaper reports that its exploration wells have ruined the water supplies in the area, Genoa approaches the Foundation and offers to provide a $100,000 donation to support the Foundation's education programs. The board, grateful for any financial help it can get, accepts the offer.

a. Is the foundation being ethical in accepting the donation?

b. If not, under what conditions might it be ethical to accept the donation, if any?

ళ ళ ళ   ళ ళ ళ ళ ళ   ళ ళ ళ

29. Steven is a senior fundraiser for a local United Way. He has recently been elected Chairman of the Board of the Kidney Disease Research Foundation, a 501(c)(3) nonprofit tax-exempt organization. At his first board meeting, he tells the senior fundraiser for that organization, Harry, that he can be helpful finding prospects to purchase tickets to the Foundation's annual fundraising ball. The next day, Steven examines his database at the United Way and compiles a list of 250 likely major donors who should receive invitations to the Research Foundation's fundraiser. He copies the names, addresses,

phone numbers, and some personal data on his flash drive, converts it into an Excel file, and sends it to Harry by email.

a. Is Steven's action ethical?

b. Is Steven's action legal?

c. If not, to what extent may Harry use the information he has from his job at the United Way to promote fundraising for the Kidney Disease Research Foundation?

30. Melissa, a fundraising associate for Harrelson University, is an attractive, blond, 30-something, who has a vivacious personality. She has been having lunch occasionally with a Harrelson alumnus, Emerson, scion of a wealthy oil magnate, with the intent of convincing Emerson to make a major gift to the University. Melissa has noticed that Emerson has drifted off occasionally during their lunch meetings, calling her by the name of his late wife, and demonstrating lapses of memory. She thinks he may be starting to have symptoms of Alzheimer's or perhaps some other dementia, and is motivated to begin closing the deal before his family takes legal action and obtains power of attorney over Emerson's financial affairs. She does not think the university would fare well if Emerson's family gets complete control over his wealth, and she thinks all of the work she has done would be wasted. She convinces Emerson to meet with her for lunch the next day, and brings with her papers that provide for Emerson pledging half of his wealth, $40 million. She winces as Emerson appears unable to sign his name on the papers, and she leans over to help him. She rationalizes that she does not stand to benefit by this gift, that thousands of students of Harrelson will benefit, and that when Emerson was perfectly lucid and sharp, he always expressed a desire to leave a lasting legacy and assist his alma mater in its mission to become a better institution.

a. Is Melissa's behavior ethical?

b. Is Melissa's behavior legal?

c. What would you do if you were in Melissa's position?

31. Baruch is the CEO/President of the Jewish Advocacy Center. His organization has built up an endowment of more than $1 million, partly as a result of his aggressive investment strategy, with a diversified, yet socially responsible portfolio, and his board has rewarded him appropriately. At a recent board meeting, the newly elected Treasurer, Manny, made an impassioned pitch for the center to move all of its investments out of accounts managed by several well-known traditional brokers into accounts managed by a single financial manager, Bernie Madoff. Manny suggested that through both good times and bad, Madoff's brilliant management has paid off handsomely, with investment returns far exceeding the average. Baruch is intrigued by the almost "too good to be true" track record of Madoff, but argues strenuously that it is foolish for the Center to put all of its eggs in one basket, regardless of the rate of return. But the board sides with Manny, and passes a resolution for all of the current accounts, other than enough to pay bills for a year, be transferred to the management of Mr. Madoff. After giving this some

thought, Baruch decides to simply ignore the board resolution and move only 10% of the Center's endowment out of the current accounts.

a. Is Baruch acting ethically?

b. Is Baruch acting legally?

c. What alternative strategies, if any, might Baruch pursue if he strongly believes that moving the accounts is not a wise decision?

დ დ დ   დ დ დ დ დ   დ დ დ

32. Ariel is the executive director of the Coalition for Women's Survival, a ten-year-old 501(c)(3) nonprofit tax-exempt organization dedicated to educating young men about the scourge of sexual violence against women. Each year, as part of her job description, she prepares a detailed, balanced budget consisting of income expected and expenses. After much wrangling and give and take compromise, her board of directors approves the budget after making modifications. Once the budget is approved, Ariel perfunctorily files it and ignores it. She feels that the business operations of her organization are too turbulent to be tied to a spending plan that was devised as much as 18 months before spending is required, and that it makes much more sense to see the board-approved budget as a useful guide, but certainly not as a directive. So, she spends as she thinks necessary to achieve the stated mission of the organization, and usually gets close to the income and revenue projects, even though she tends to have little memory of the individual line-items that comprise her annual budgets. So far, no one on the board has caught on to this, and she certainly isn't going to volunteer anything.

a. Is Ariel acting ethically by ignoring her board's approved budget?

b. How much flexibility should an executive director have over line item spending before it is ethical to ask the board to approve changes?

დ დ დ   დ დ დ დ დ   დ დ დ

33. Peter, a nurse practitioner, works for the nonprofit Johnson City Hospital that encourages its medical staff to volunteer at a nonaffiliated nonprofit community health center. Peter enjoys this volunteer work, but feels uncomfortable that the clinic is understaffed, pays salaries at a fraction paid to those in comparable positions at his hospital, and is starved for funds to pay for basic supplies of all kinds when the same materials are overflowing in the supply closets of the hospital. Just last week, he was unable to obtain the syringes he needed to administer flu shots to those in the community who were otherwise unable to afford them. Peter decides to make a list of the supplies needed by the clinic, and systematically, without drawing any attention to himself, siphon off small quantities of these supplies from his own employer each week and transfer them anonymously to the clinic.

a. Is Peter acting ethically?

b. Is Peter acting legally?

c. What alternatives might Peter pursue to his behavior if he had any qualms about carrying out his plan?

જ્જ્જ્   જ્જ્જ્જ્જ્   જ્જ્જ્

34. Nevin, a bank vice president, is the newly elected Treasurer of the Harristown Family and Children's Service, a 501(c)(3) nonprofit tax-exempt organization. The total cash assets of the Service have never exceeded $100,000 at one time, not very much in Nevin's world of dealing with accounts, often worth millions of dollars. However, he feels embarrassed that the checking accounts of the Service are with a local competitor's bank. At the next board meeting, he offers a motion that the Service's checking and savings accounts be moved to his bank as soon as possible.

a. Is Nevin acting ethically by offering this motion?

b. Is Nevin acting legally by offering this motion and participating in the discussion?

જ્જ્જ્   જ્જ્જ્જ્જ્   જ્જ્જ્

35. Harriet has been the executive director of the Harristown Chamber of Commerce, a 501(c)(6) nonprofit tax-exempt organization, for almost 20 years. She has never married, and the Chamber has become her entire life. It is not unusual for Harriet to be working in the office 12 hours each day, being the first one to arrive in the morning and the one to turn out the lights in the late evenings, which may be filled with meetings and telephone calls. For the last several years, she has gotten in the habit of having the support staff of the Chamber run her personal errands, justifying that her herculean work hours simply leave little or no time to do this herself and that the organization is better served if she devotes the time for those mundane tasks to her professional life. Some of the staff who are asked to do these errands are sympathetic and understanding, and are quite willing to help. But lately, she has noticed that some appear to be resentful. Fortunately, no one so far has given her a flat "I won't do this for you."

a. Is Harriet acting ethical when she asks her staff to run personal errands when she is devoting the time saved by this to the work of the organization?

જ્જ્જ્   જ્જ્જ્જ્જ્   જ્જ્જ્

36. Perry is a development associate for the Tyne Foundation, a nonprofit organization that raises funds to support development in third world countries. Perry has been a development officer for more than 30 years, and many of his friends are those he has met as colleagues in the field. At gatherings such as meetings of the Association of Fundraising Professionals and other conferences, he often has gathered with his colleagues to share stories about the fundraising craft, some from personal experience, some second-hand, some perhaps apocryphal, but almost always interesting. For the past 20 years, he has been writing these stories down, and has several loose-leaf notebooks filled with handwritten notes. More than half of these stories are taken from his own personal experience as a fundraiser for Tyne, and he would be the first to admit that when they become public knowledge, Tyne would find the disclosure of some of the material embarrassing, even if the statute of limitations has run out on anything that might have been criminal. He is about ready to retire, so he doesn't worry too much about how Tyne's senior management might react. And being an author has always been a lifetime dream of his. Today, he decides to start the ball rolling by asking his secretary at Tyne to start typing up his notes after swearing her to secrecy about the content,

and announces to his wife that he plans to submit a letter to his boss announcing his retirement plans later this week.

a. Is Perry being ethical?

ཚྭ ཚྭ ཚྭ   ཚྭ ཚྭ ཚྭ ཚྭ ཚྭ   ཚྭ ཚྭ ཚྭ

37. Horace, the executive director of the Harristown Energy Assistance Fund, a 501(c)(3) nonprofit tax-exempt organization, finds it hard to concentrate at board meetings whenever Bridget, the board treasurer, is even in the room. Horace, who is divorced and thirty-something, feels an electricity that he never felt even at the beginning of the five-year relationship he had with his wife, or rather, ex-wife, who never quite satisfied him emotionally. By the time he filed for divorce, their marriage had deteriorated into one of convenience, where they avoided each other as much as possible, and each had moved on to relationships that were more satisfying. He had had a series of casual affairs even while married, but none had provided the sparks that he experienced simply being around Bridget. And after just a couple of board meetings, he began to suspect that the feelings were mutual, and not just "sport flirting," as he had been engaged in with colleagues in the past, but never considered actually doing anything about it while he was married or after. During the past few months, particularly since it was budget season, he and Bridget had opportunities to meet alone, typically at public restaurants, and crunch the numbers. At recent meetings, the discussions between them had become more personal, and she sounded interested in him. Flattered and willing, he let her lead, and it wasn't too long before she simply suggested that their next meeting be at a local hotel room. He agreed, knowing what was likely to follow.

a. Is Horace being ethical?

ཚྭ ཚྭ ཚྭ   ཚྭ ཚྭ ཚྭ ཚྭ ཚྭ   ཚྭ ཚྭ ཚྭ

38. Dave is the newly elected president of the Harristown Running Club, with 500 members. The 30-year-old organization is a tax-exempt 501(c)(3), and its mission is to represent and advance the sport of running in Harristown. While perhaps half of the members are women and there are a sprinkling of minorities among those who pay the $20 annual dues, the self-perpetuating board consists of 11 white males, only one of whom is under the age of 50. Dave has no problem with this; it tends to make reaching decisions much easier when all of the board members are older and male and have been running together for several decades, and share much of his perspective and vision. Seven years ago, the board did have a black woman on the board, but she tended to vote against the majority and ask too many questions. She quit after only attending three board meetings, and no one on the board expressed any regret about her decision to leave. And the fact that more than half of the board members attend Dave's church means that he can communicate easily in an informal way outside of board meetings. He remembers that the Club did have a Jewish member once years ago, but had become incensed and resigned in a huff when the board had voted to have a pig roast on the Rosh Hashanah holiday to avoid a conflict with major Club races.

a. Is the HRC Board being ethical by not having any women or minority members on its board?

b. Was the board being ethical by scheduling a pig roast on Rosh Hashanah?

జ్ఞ జ్ఞ జ్ఞ   జ్ఞ జ్ఞ జ్ఞ జ్ఞ జ్ఞ   జ్ఞ జ్ఞ జ్ఞ

39. Leslie is part of the political elite of the community, or at least aspires to be. He has landed a plum position on the board of the Kessler Chocolate Company, where he earns a six-figure honorarium for simply attending four corporate board meetings each year. As a former elected member of the state legislature, he is expected to offer political advice to the corporation which, since all of the board members are long-time personal friends anyway, he would feel comfortable providing for free. As part of his service, he is expected to serve on the board of the corporation's captive charity, for which he is paid an additional high five-figure stipend, and for which he is also expected to serve without making any waves or questioning the leadership. This reminds him of when he was a first-term member of the state legislature, and was expected to vote for whatever the leadership wanted without question, in exchange for financial help getting reelected, the approval of pet projects in his district, and a lifestyle augmented by taxpayer funded perks. At the board meeting of the Kessler Chocolate Foundation, the Chair of the board is suggesting that the salary of the officers of the board be increased from $100,000 to $150,000 annually. Leslie thinks that is perhaps excessive for a position that is typically volunteer, but recognizes that if he plays his cards right, he could become an officer within a few years and never have any money worries again. With the rest of his colleagues on the board, he votes to approve the chair's motion.

a. Is Leslie being ethical by voting on the chair's motion?

b. Is Leslie being ethical by serving on this board?

జ్ఞ జ్ఞ జ్ఞ   జ్ఞ జ్ఞ జ్ఞ జ్ఞ జ్ఞ   జ్ఞ జ్ఞ జ్ఞ

40. Jennifer is the executive director of the Women's Education Network of North Dakota, a 501(c)(3) nonprofit tax-exempt organization. She is attending her annual professional conference at the Hope Springs Retreat and Conference Center in Palm Springs, California. She looks forward to her conference every year, and thinks of it as a paid vacation. While there are a few actual working sessions where her colleagues discuss issues that affect their professional tasks for their respective organizations, the culture has evolved more to escaping the day-to-day rigors of being in a high-pressure environment and simply relaxing, with conference organizers taking great pains to make the conference as enjoyable as possible for attendees. Golf outings, luaus, shopping tours, whale watches, and tennis tournaments, and evening shows far outnumber these working sessions. Jennifer spends some time at the beach, escaping the often frigid temperatures of her home base in Fargo, ND. This morning, after a sumptuous breakfast that is included in the conference registration, she decides to make an appointment for a massage and pedicure, and charges it to her room rather than using the organization's credit card. One of the perks of being an executive director of a nonprofit where my salary is much lower than what I could earn in the private sector is taking advantage of this week of relaxation, she muses.

a. Is Jennifer being ethical?

b. Are those who organize this "conference" being ethical?

జ్ఞ జ్ఞ జ్ఞ   జ్ఞ జ్ఞ జ్ఞ జ్ఞ జ్ఞ   జ్ఞ జ్ఞ జ్ఞ

41. Bill is an adjunct faculty member at the local state university, where he teaches nonprofit management at the graduate level. One of his students, Lisa, the CEO of a small nonprofit that runs an animal shelter, approaches him after class and asks him if he can help her with a real-life problem. Her board has asked her to create a strategic plan, and she thinks Bill would be the best person to be hired to facilitate the process. She wants to know if Bill is willing to do this for the shelter, for which he would be paid $75/hour, probably much more than he is being paid to teach the class. Bill is quite busy with his own job, in addition to his teaching duties, but he has one kid who will be starting college in the fall, and he thinks the money would be welcome.

a. Is Bill being ethical by accepting the work offered by Lisa?

ം ം ം   ം ം ം ം ം   ം ം ം

42. Linda, the executive director of the Wildwood Day Care Center, is a very spiritual person. She believes that everyone has the right to believe whatever they want to with respect to Jesus and His role in their lives, but she strongly believes that everyone who does not accept Jesus as their Savior is going to Hell. She does make an effort to treat nonbelievers fairly, but makes it a point to not hire anyone who doesn't share her enthusiasm for a fundamentalist Christian perspective. While the Center is officially nonsectarian and serves clients from all religious faiths, Linda sincerely feels that her faith and those of similar-thinking co-workers is what creates an environment that improves the quality of the facility. She starts each staff meeting with several minutes of prayer, and no current employees have expressed any concern about this, although her exit interviews with past employees have indicated that this made some uncomfortable— evidence to her that their employment in this organization was not a good fit.

a. Is Linda being ethical by imposing her personal religious views on the workers she supervises?

ം ം ം   ം ം ം ം ം   ം ം ം

43. Harold is the executive director of the Monessen Falls Dance Studio, a nonprofit 501(c)(3) organization. While many of the dancers who participate in the programs of the Studio are women, the staff tend to be gay white males, like Harold. Harold tries to hire gay men, knowing that these individuals are often discriminated against when finding employment in traditional organizations, nonprofit or otherwise. Today, Harold is interviewing Tim, a candidate for the position of chief financial officer. Tim has an impressive résumé, and has served as the CFO for several arts-related nonprofits during a 20-year career. Harold knows that he cannot directly ask Tim if he is gay because of the limitations in the state human relations law. But he asks subtle questions that he expects will provide evidence about Tim's sexual orientation. He thinks this is fine, since the intent is not to discriminate against anyone who is gay but just the opposite. Tim mentions that he and his wife were bringing up their two kids in a neighboring state, but that his wife recently took a position with the Monessen Community College. Harold, assuming that this indicated that Tim was not gay (although not necessarily the case), thanks Harold and decides not to hire him.

a. Is Harold being ethical?

ം ം ം   ം ം ം ം ം   ം ം ം

44. Rose is a professional singer, who organized the Harristown Early Music Consort consisting of herself, a recorder player, and a lute player. For several years, they have performed in coffee houses, schools, and arts festivals, mostly for minimal pay (if any) and being fed. Lately, word of their talent has spread, and they are beginning to receive more offers for their performances, some of which pay quite well. Rose has decided to create a nonprofit organization, mostly to avoid liability exposure, and also for tax reasons. The board of the new organization consists of herself, the recorder player, and the lute player. For each performance, she asks the organization hiring the group to make a check out to the "Early Music Consort," which is deposited into the consort's checking account. Then, after paying for any out-of-pocket costs related to the performance, such as travel, food, and insurance, she divides up the remainder equally, writing a check for that amount to each of the three members.

a. Is Rose being ethical?

ও ও ও   ও ও ও ও ও   ও ও ও

45. Doug is a well-heeled philanthropist who has been making sizable donations to the Harristown Futures Fund, one particular local charity whose mission is to restore historic buildings in Doug's community of Harristown. Doug recently asked the executive director of the charity, Peter, to consider making a grant to restore one particular building, a hotel on Main Street that was owned at one time by Doug's grandfather. Peter explained to Doug that this particular building did not meet the organization's criteria, and that his board had voted 12-6 against accepting this project, although Peter agreed that it did make sense to keep the building from being turned into an indoor shopping mall, as was being proposed. Doug wasn't happy with this answer, but understood that Peter's organization had some constraints. Doug decided to do whatever was necessary to restore that old hotel, which brought back many memories to him whenever he passed it. He decided to create his own 501(c)(3) where he could make all of the decisions with how his donations would be used, rather than having to depend on decisions made by almost 20 local community members whom he did not know, and who were unlikely to share his love for that hotel. Doug hired a consultant to do all of the paperwork to create the organization, incorporate it, and apply for 501(c)(3) federal tax-exempt status. He wanted to make sure that he would retain complete control over how his donations would be used. So, in his first official act as Chair, he appointed to his board of directors himself, his wife, Ann; his son, Steve; Steve's wife, Olivia; and his brother, Tom. With that board composition, it would be unlikely that Doug would be unable to see his dream of preserving the hotel from being destroyed.

a. Is Peter being ethical?

ও ও ও   ও ও ও ও ও   ও ও ও

46. Debbie is a recent graduate of Tappler University with a B.A. in Communications, and was delighted to have found a part-time position as the director of the Wilson-Area Vintage Thrift Shop, a small store that accepts donations of vintage clothing and sells it to the public. Debbie receives very little in salary and no benefits, and is struggling to pay off her student loans. While she has been hired part-time, she finds that she is devoting much more than the 20 hours per week to her job—more like 40 hours. She

cannot afford any health insurance, and is terrified that a major illness will make it impossible for her to pay her rent and food expenses, which her meager salary barely covers. Proceeds from the store support the programs of her employer, the Bratton Mission, that helps those with alcohol and substance abuse addictions reintegrate into the community. Debbie is a one-woman band at the center, being its only paid staff member. She solicits and processes donations, sorts the clothing with a small staff of part-time volunteers, pays the bills, mans the cash register, and deals with the myriad problems that accrue in running what amounts to a small business for a nonprofit organization with only minimal supervision. Debbie loves her dog, and keeping her pet is virtually her only indulgence. She has an outstanding $110 invoice from the vet, and has no funds to pay it until she receives her paycheck in a week. She decides that given the circumstances, she needs to borrow money from the Thrift Store's cash register to pay this bill, and replace it once she receives her paycheck from the Mission. Since she handles the bookkeeping for the Thrift Shop, she knows she can do this without anyone finding out, and she knows she can pay the money back once she gets her paycheck.

a. Is Debbie's behavior ethical?

b. Is Debbie's behavior unethical even if she pays the money back the next day?

જ⁀જ⁀જ⁀   જ⁀જ⁀જ⁀જ⁀જ⁀   જ⁀જ⁀જ⁀

47. Gerald is the chair of the board of the Harristown Youth Athletic Association, and he has been in a heated discussion with the executive director of the organization, Melissa, about the terms of the contract with a for-profit fundraiser the organization wishes to hire. Melissa, who is a member of the Association of Fundraising Professionals (AFP), insists that it is unethical for fundraisers to receive compensation based on a percentage of the amount they raise. Gerald sees nothing wrong with this, and thinks the fundraiser will certainly be motivated to raise much more money if there is a direct incentive to produce results. Melissa counters that this direct incentive also motivates the fundraiser to engage in unethical and deceptive practices. Gerald, an attorney, is reviewing the contract of the professional fundraising organization that Melissa has recommended. The contract specifies that the fundraiser is paid a flat fee regardless of the amount raised for the Association. Melissa has added language to the contract that specifies that in addition to not permitting the fundraiser to receive a percentage of the amount raised, the fundraiser is not permitted to pay his staff, including the telemarketers hired to actually make the calls to potential donors, a percentage based on the amount they raise individually. Gerald deletes this line from the contract, signs it on behalf of the organization, and sends the final copy to the professional fundraising organization for signature.

a. Is Gerald's behavior ethical?

જ⁀જ⁀જ⁀   જ⁀જ⁀જ⁀જ⁀જ⁀   જ⁀જ⁀જ⁀

48. Oliver is the board chair of the Alliance for Progress in Harristown, a 501(c)(3), nonprofit tax-exempt organization. His nemesis on the board for the past several years has been Manachim, an Orthodox Jew who has been a constant irritant to Oliver, who he feels is purposely being oppositional to much of Oliver's vision for the organization. Oliver has a list of important projects he wants the board to approve, and he knows that Manachim will likely skewer Oliver's plans. Manachim often comes up with justifications

for thwarting what Oliver wants to do, and those justifications tend to sway a majority of the board. Oliver comes up with a bright idea—schedule the next board meeting for Yom Kippur, the holiest day on the Jewish calendar. That way, Manachim will not be able to attend and do his mischief.

a. Is Oliver being ethical by scheduling the board meeting on a Jewish holiday?

         ళ ళ ళ   ళ ళ ళ ళ ళ   ళ ళ ళ

49. Barbara is head of prospect research for Wellsworth College, a private, nonprofit 501(c)(3) tax-exempt institution of higher learning. She has been working with one major donor, Benson, for several years, and they have met socially on many occasions, with both spouses being included. At their last meeting, Benson, who is quite wealthy and has several vacation homes, offers Barbara the use of his Cape Cod beach house for a week at a time when Benson is not using it. And he has mentioned on more than one occasion that he might leave something in his will for Barbara, who has been a true friend and made it possible for Benson to provide for his favorite alma mater, Wellsworth, which contributed so much to his success as a businessperson. Barbara feels close to her old friend, and thanks him for the offer, planning to spend a week-long getaway at the beach house during the summer.

a. Is Barbara being ethical by accepting the use of this vacation home?

         ళ ళ ళ   ళ ళ ళ ళ ళ   ళ ళ ళ

50. John is the chair of the Philosophy Department for Orwells University, a private, nonprofit institution of higher learning. There is an opening for a new faculty member, and John is chair of the search committee. One of his former students, Oliver, has recently received his Ph.D. from a prestigious university, and John is certain that Oliver would be terrific in this job. He calls Oliver, and Oliver informs him that he would be delighted to take a job in this department under the leadership of his mentor. John's university has procedures for hiring that require a search committee to be formed, the job be advertised nationally, three finalists for the position be identified from among candidates, and the three finalists be invited to campus for interviews. The process was quite unnecessary, and even counterproductive, John thought, knowing that two candidates would be giving up two days of their lives and his department would be tied up for more than a week going through the motions of finding the successful candidate, with thousands of dollars in unnecessary expenses to comply with the college's procedures. But John sees no way around this, and guides his committee in selecting two lesser qualified finalists compared to some others who apply for the position. John knows these two competitors will not provide much competition for his protégé, in the unlikely event he gets some resistance for his choice for the position.

a. Is John acting unethically?

b. How might a process for selecting faculty be redesigned to make it fairer to both the school and to faculty candidates?

         ళ ళ ళ   ళ ళ ళ ళ ళ   ళ ళ ళ

51. Harley is a megadonor to Hanson-Smith University. He asks the development officer soliciting him, Christine, about whether Harley's nephew's application to attend the university has been accepted, rejected, or accepted for attendance at a less prestigious satellite campus. Christine knows quite well that rejecting Harley's nephew's application will result in a decreased annual gift from him. And she knows that the process of accepting and rejecting applications is ongoing, and will not become public for several weeks. She agrees to intercede on behalf of Harley and pledges to communicate to her boss that Harley's donation might be enhanced with a positive response to his nephew's application for admission.

a. Is Christine being ethical by agreeing to communicate this information to her institution?

b. Is the institution being ethical if it is influenced by such a communication?

᪥ ᪥ ᪥   ᪥ ᪥ ᪥ ᪥ ᪥   ᪥ ᪥ ᪥

52. Frank is a development officer for the Prentiss-Gabe Foundation. While reviewing a confidential background check he commissioned from a private investigator he has hired to check out prospective donors, he discovers that one of the wealthiest and prominent members of the community, Roger, has a past criminal record of fraud. If this became widely known in the community, Roger's reputation in the community would be tarnished. Frank decides he could leverage this knowledge subtly without overtly threatening Roger, but letting him know that he knows about Roger's past, and that a donation to the foundation would help provide scholarships to needy children.

a. Is Frank's plan to increase donations from Roger ethical?

᪥ ᪥ ᪥   ᪥ ᪥ ᪥ ᪥ ᪥   ᪥ ᪥ ᪥

53. Tori, who recently is in remission from leukemia, wants to start a nonprofit organization to help find a permanent cure for the disease. She is quite aware that there is a well-established organization, the National Leukemia and Lymphoma Society, which raises millions, if not hundreds of millions of dollars for this cause already. However, that organization never responded to her request for a job interview. She decides that she wants to leave her job as a cashier for the local diner and raise money for the cause full-time, and serve as the executive director, providing herself with a modest salary (although somewhat better than what she receives from her current position) and benefits. She starts compiling a list of the tasks she must complete to incorporate, file for federal tax-exempt status, and file with the state charitable solicitation regulation bureau. She thinks she has the drive and motivation to raise lots of money, having successfully raised almost $20,000 to pay her doctor and hospital bills through her personal Facebook page. At first, she thought of calling her new organization "Tori's Quest," but thought this might not communicate what the organization would be about. So, to enhance the likelihood of getting donations, she decided to closely mimic the name of the established organization, perhaps hoping that this would help the new organization with its fundraising success. She decides to incorporate her new startup as "The National Leukemia Research Society, Inc.", and hopes that if some donors contributed to her organization unintentionally, the money would still support the same cause.

a. Is Tori's plan to use a name similar to that of the existing organization ethical?

ꕥꕥꕥ ꕥꕥꕥꕥꕥ ꕥꕥꕥ

54. Jacqueline is the CEO of the Wilson City Blood Bank, a 501(c)(3) nonprofit tax-exempt organization. Two weeks ago, one of her staff members, Rick, admitted to her that he had inadvertently lost a flash drive at a sporting event that contained very sensitive data on each of the 3,243 blood donors who had contributed to the blood bank during the calendar year. Included in the lost data were birthdates, social security numbers, and addresses, including data on scores of individuals who were asked not to donate because of how they answered very sensitive questions about their sexual and medical history. So far, there have been no indications that the data has been found by anyone or accessed in any way. Jacqueline recognizes that it is quite possible that the data will never be found or accessed in any criminal way. Jacqueline is hesitant to inform all of her donors because of the embarrassment it would cause the Bank, and it might give donors pause for donating again if they find out that their data were compromised. And it would be expensive to inform everyone, and there might not be much anything donors could do about it. She decides to wait a month or two more before informing anyone, including her board of directors, and directs Rick not to tell a soul about his mistake or risk being summarily fired.

a. Is Jacqueline's behavior ethical?

b. If Rick stays silent, is his behavior ethical?

ꕥꕥꕥ ꕥꕥꕥꕥꕥ ꕥꕥꕥ

55. Ariel is the Executive Director of the Harristown Social Services Foundation, a 501(c)(3) nonprofit tax-exempt organization. She is faced with making very unpopular budget cuts, because in her view, her board is resisting raising the fees it charges to clients. Ariel knows that there are some areas of the budget that could be cut without sacrificing client services, both quality and quantity. Yet she feels that if she cuts some of the "fat," such as staff conferences, the annual staff parties, the staff retreat, training, and health care benefits, employee morale would likely suffer. So, she realigns the budget. She leaves those areas intact and instead focuses on cutting programs she knows her board strongly supports, expecting that they will come to their senses, restore these programs to reasonable budget levels, and finance this by raising client fees, only rational option.

a. Is Ariel's behavior ethical?

ꕥꕥꕥ ꕥꕥꕥꕥꕥ ꕥꕥꕥ

56. Orrin is the executive director of Outside the Box, Inc., a think tank that does research for the Department of Defense. He suspects that one of his employees, Jeanette, has doctored some of the data relating to a particular research grant, and has a too cozy relationship to a particular defense contractor that stands to benefit from the results of the research. He confronts Jeanette about her project, and she admits what she has done, confesses that she received two first-class, round-trip plane tickets to Hawaii along with a pre-paid stay for two at an all-inclusive resort in Maui, and offers to resign. Orrin accepts her offer. He then directs his administrative assistant, Steve, to figure out what paper trail there might be that might serve as evidence of wrongdoing by Jeanette,

including email, and visits to Jeanette by this defense contractor. Orrin resolves to take it upon himself without any delegating to see how the research data can be reconfigured to make it right—and leave no evidence that there was something wrong to begin with. Steve spends the entire weekend at the office, deleting emails from Jeanette's computer, shredding memos from her files, and deleting computer printing runs of her computer simulations. On Monday, after he is assured by Steve that there is no trace of the "Jeanette problem," as he refers to it, Orrin contacts the grant officer at DOD in charge of the project, and lets him know that his researcher has resigned, there will be some delay in providing the deliverable, but that he will assure that it will be of high quality. Smiling for the first time in days, he congratulates himself for yet another successful trip through a minefield, and begins focusing on the next swamp he needs to drain for his organization.

a. Is Orrin's behavior ethical?

b. Is Orrin's behavior illegal?

ళ ళ ళ ళ ళ ళ ళ ళ ళ ళ ళ

57. Nathan serves as one of 24 board members of the Harristown Symphony Orchestra Association. Nathan, now 82, used to be a member of the orchestra. Once he retired, he was asked to join the board. Nathan likes to hang out in the offices of the orchestra, sticking his nose in among the staff, sometimes helping out as a volunteer, but mostly making a nuisance of himself. He continually orders the staff around, telling them how to do their job, creeping them out by taking notes as he watches, criticizing and often countermanding the directions the staff have received from their supervisor and/or the managing director. He demands to see all of the bookkeeping and expense accounts, and berates employees, particularly the major gifts fundraising staff, for spending more than a few dollars on an out-of-town dinner.

a. Is Nathan's behavior ethical?

ళ ళ ళ ళ ళ ళ ళ ళ ళ ళ ళ

58. Rachel is the executive director of the Baytown Food Bank, established in 1972 to accept donations of food, mostly nonperishable, from the public and distributing it to the needy. A personal friend of Rachel's, Katherine, who works for a foundation, tells Rachel of a funding opportunity that may be of interest. The Foundation is looking for a reputable nonprofit organization partner to organize rides for senior citizens to take them to doctors' appointments. She suggests that Baytown Food Bank could generate net revenue from the grant, which could help Baytown expand its services beyond the Baytown city limits, an objective that has been in the Baytown Food Bank's strategic plan, but has always been delayed because of a lack of funding. Katherine tells her friend that she would do what she can to steer the grant to the Food Bank if Rachel would like her to do so. Rachel thanks Katherine and Katherine agrees to grease the skids, and sends Rachel the forms to apply for the grant. Rachel applies for the funds the days after she receives the application forms.

a. Is Katherine's behavior ethical?

b. Is Rachel's behavior ethical?

ംഃ ംഃ ംഃ   ംഃ ംഃ ംഃ ംഃ ംഃ   ംഃ ംഃ ംഃ

59. Barry is the president of Ornland University, a private, nonprofit university. The Dean of Science, Rocco, tells Barry at a staff meeting that a female teaching assistant has complained to him (Rocco) that she was sexually assaulted by a tenured male faculty member. Rocco reminds Barry that this is the third incident in which a female student has complained about the behavior of this particular faculty member, and it is likely that the charges are founded in fact. Barry and Rocco discuss the political implications of having such an incident, whether or not it had occurred, being splashed on the front pages of the local newspaper, and the effects such a report might have on applications for admission and donations. Barry and Rocco agree that the best way to handle this is to do whatever it takes to keep the incident from becoming public knowledge, and authorizes the dean to make a large financial settlement to the woman out of a slush fund established for purposes such as this, in exchange for not filing charges, and an even larger settlement offer if she agrees to sever her relationship to the university and continue her studies at another institution—provided she agrees to keep everything totally confidential.

a. Is Barry's behavior ethical?

b. Is Rocco's behavior ethical?

ംഃ ംഃ ംഃ   ംഃ ംഃ ംഃ ംഃ ംഃ   ംഃ ംഃ ംഃ

60. Mindy is the executive director of the nonprofit Medical Testing Services of Harristown. Mindy has a good relationship with her board, and prides herself in dealing with as many problems as she can without resorting to having the board deal with controversial issues. To her, the perfect board meeting involves a nice lunch at a fancy hotel, a series of dog and pony shows by herself and her key staff members, accepting the kudos from grateful board members, and a quick adjournment by the chairman. But today's telephone call from the investigative reporter from the local newspaper has caused her concern. The reporter, Carl, tells her that he understands that Dr. Richard Hastings, the organization's Chief Medical Officer and Vice President in charge of Laboratory Operations, never really graduated from medical school, and that all of the laboratory results from the organization may be called into question as a result of Hastings' lack of qualifications. Mindy, shocked and blind-sided by this news, masks her surprise and dismay, and calmly replies that she has "no comment." As luck would have it, her board meeting is the following day. She decides that as executive director, it is her duty to fix the problem with the minimum amount of damage, and she makes the decision not to mention this telephone call at the board meeting.

a. Is Mindy's behavior ethical?

ംഃ ംഃ ംഃ   ംഃ ംഃ ംഃ ംഃ ംഃ   ംഃ ംഃ ംഃ

61. Petunia is the Director of Purchasing for the Citizens for a Saner World, a 501(c)(3) nonprofit tax-exempt organization, dedicated to reducing tensions among the global nuclear powers. The organization has affiliates in 40 states and 30 foreign countries,

and all purchasing for the organization must be approved by Petunia. As the senior officer who buys supplies, travel, giveaways with the organization's logo, telephones, and computers, Petunia is courted by manufacturers and distributors, hoping to convince her to steer the multi-million dollar business of the international organization their way. To entice her, it is not unusual for her to receive thank-yous from suppliers in the form of boxes of cookies, movie tickets, and flowers. But yesterday, she received two open tickets to Hawaii from a company that has been courting her to choose them to handle the organization's travel business. She considers herself a professional, and doesn't expect that receiving these tickets will influence her decision to choose this company over several others who are equally courting her for this business. So, she decides to keep and use the tickets, and sends a thank-you note to the travel company's sales rep.

a. Is Petunia's behavior ethical?

ও ও ও   ও ও ও ও ও   ও ও ও

62. Fred is the executive director of the Harristown Holocaust Education Center. As part of his job, Fred authors a teachers' guide for use in high schools so teachers have the material they need to educate their students about the Holocaust. Fred has spent more than two years preparing these materials, and has freely used all resources at his disposal, including his staff for research, and consultants hired by the Center. He has an idea to submit the Guide, with minor modifications, to a commercial publisher, who accepts the manuscript. Fred directs that the royalties be sent to him rather than to the Center, justifying that he is the author of the work, and thus is entitled to all of the royalties.

a. Is Fred's behavior ethical?

ও ও ও   ও ও ও ও ও   ও ও ও

63. Geraldine is the President and CEO of Holsteed Community Hospital, a small nonprofit community hospital in a rural area. A major donor, Alex, has offered to provide a $35 million donation to build a research center adjacent to the main building of the hospital. His stipulations for receiving the grant are that the building is named after his wife and himself, and that the construction is awarded to his son's company. Geraldine thinks she can finesse both conditions by getting variances approved by the board, which has rules in place requiring a rigorous bidding procedure for capital projects. She thanks Alex, and tells him that his conditions will not be any problem.

a. Is Geraldine's behavior ethical?

ও ও ও   ও ও ও ও ও   ও ও ও

64. David is the Chairman of the Board of the state's Bowling Promotion Association, a 501(c)(6) tax-exempt nonprofit organization, which represents the interests of bowling alleys before the state legislature and executive branch. The current executive director, Genevieve, has just resigned, having eloped with the organization's lobbyist, who also submitted his resignation. Both have relocated to another state, leaving the management of the organization in disarray. At the emergency board meeting held to discuss this situation, David tells the board he is willing to serve as the executive director of the organization for the next two years, if the rest of the board approves, but that he still

wants to continue as the Chair of the Board. He is willing to serve at the same salary as Genevieve. He asks if there is anyone who objects to this, and no one responds.

a. Is David's behavior ethical?

b. Is the board acting ethically?

ॐ ॐ ॐ　　　ॐ ॐ ॐ ॐ ॐ　　　ॐ ॐ ॐ

65. The Board of the Harristown Community Hospital and Healthcare System, a 501(c)(3) tax-exempt charity, is considering a proposal being made by its president and CEO, Michael, to increase its net revenue in the wake of likely massive cuts to its Medicare reimbursements. He is proposing that the hospital shut down its emergency room at its location in the inner-city of Harristown, and invest the millions of dollars being saved by doing this to create satellite clinics and walk-in health centers in the surrounding suburbs. Michael and his CFO, Courtney, explain that the emergency room is draining the hospital of its reserves, and that the satellite centers in the suburbs offer a lucrative investment that can make up for the forecasted revenue shortfalls emanating from Medicare cuts. He dismisses the protests from the only African-American on the board joined by only two others who live in the city as not recognizing the realities, and suggests that the emergency health care needs in Harristown can be served by a regional hospital that is located ten miles away in the neighboring community of Indiantown.

a. Is the President and CEO's proposal ethical?

ॐ ॐ ॐ　　　ॐ ॐ ॐ ॐ ॐ　　　ॐ ॐ ॐ

66. Victor is Vice President for Development for the nonprofit Brochton Medical Center, a 501(c)(3) nonprofit tax-exempt organization. He has a team of assistant vice presidents who help him raise nearly $40 million annually for the Center, and an additional $30 million for its capital campaign. Victor drives his staff hard, but pays them well and entices them to work even harder by sponsoring competitions in which high performers are rewarded, and prizes are offered for extraordinary closes on major gifts. This year, he offers two tickets to the Superbowl and two airfares and a hotel suite for four days in New Orleans to the Vice President who closes the most total gifts in the calendar year.

a. Is Victor's compensation program ethical?

ॐ ॐ ॐ　　　ॐ ॐ ॐ ॐ ॐ　　　ॐ ॐ ॐ

67. Betty is the CEO of the Grobman Foundation, Inc., an operating foundation, and she is frustrated with the performance of her chief fundraiser, Bernie, who follows both the letter and the spirit of the ethics code of his professional association, the Association of Fundraising Professionals. He rejects her pleas that he be a bit more aggressive rather than being so "nice," a quality that she feels is resulting in lost opportunities to maximize gifts. She decides to fire him, and replace him with Franklin, who she sees will be more aggressive in utilizing the latest strategies and techniques, including social media. Franklin also has no qualms about pushing the envelope with respect to prospect research, exaggerating the foundation's needs, appealing to guilt, and bullying donors to give more. But he has a history of improving fundraising wherever he has served the chief fundraiser. He refuses to join the AFP, suggesting that they are too timid to accept fundraising practices that get results.

a. Is Betty's behavior toward Bernie ethical?

b. Is Franklin's behavior ethical?

༄ ༄ ༄   ༄ ༄ ༄ ༄ ༄   ༄ ༄ ༄

68. Brian serves as the senior policy advisor for the Gantry Institution, a Washington-based think tank. By day, he soaks up knowledge, and occasionally writes white papers for his employer. By evening, he hits the speaker's circuit, charging as much as $1,000 plus expenses for an hour speech. He used to share some of his speaking fees with the organization, but no longer does so, as he feels that his time after 5 p.m. is his own. He refuses to tell his employer about these speaking engagements and the amount of money he makes from them, saying that it is none of their business.

a. Is Brian's behavior ethical?

༄ ༄ ༄   ༄ ༄ ༄ ༄ ༄   ༄ ༄ ༄

69. The Anti-Racist Society is one of the most financially successful nonprofit organizations in history. Its fundraising machine is well-oiled. Despite having assets of a quarter of a billion dollars, seven times its annual expenses, it continues to fundraise aggressively, and typically spends millions of dollars less than it raises.

a. By continuing to raise funds aggressively when it has more than enough money to reasonably pursue its mission well into the future without doing so, is the Society's behavior ethical?

༄ ༄ ༄   ༄ ༄ ༄ ༄ ༄   ༄ ༄ ༄

70. Heartland Hospital, a 501(c)(3) nonprofit tax-exempt institution located on a beautiful lake and a sprawling, well-manicured campus, is nationally known for the quality of medical care delivered by its staff. It attracts some of the best medical professionals, partially because of its attractive location, but perhaps more from its penchant for offering lucrative salaries and perks to its staff. A few years ago, the institution purchased a marina and a private golf course, and encourages its employees to use these facilities, and charges them almost nothing. The institution has always provided millions of dollars annually in "charity" care, and the leadership has always highlighted the exact amount in its presentations to the public. The leadership recently hired a nationally recognized public relations firm after a series of newspaper articles in the regional newspaper chronicled some of the less attractive and embarrassing policies of the institution. Among those were paying its CEO a seven-figure salary, providing NFL tickets and other perks to local government officials who might be in a decision-making capacity with respect to the validity of the hospital's local tax exemptions, providing incentives to its medical staff for scheduling more bypass surgeries—which tend to pad the bottom line and are often highest on the list of the most unnecessary surgeries—and finding ways to discourage admissions and transferring patients whose government subsidies for care are not likely to result in net revenue for the institution. The series did

confirm that the millions of dollars in so called charity care provided by the institution was indeed accurate, although in almost every case, the institution used aggressive collecting agencies and a team of sophisticated lawyers to harass patients into paying all or part of their debts, and only after all of their strategies were exhausted did the hospital list what was still owed as "charity care."

a. Is Heartland Hospital's behavior ethical?

જી જી જી   જી જી જી જી જી   જી જી જી

71. Connie is a therapist at the RFM Counseling Center, a nonprofit 501(c)(3) tax-exempt organization that provides services to veterans with PTSD. Connie has dreamed about starting her own practice, but is insecure about whether such a private practice would be financially viable, with two kids to support and soon to be applying to college. Connie decides to test the waters before diving full-in, and retain her full-time position at the Center, and put out her shingle in a private office located just one block away. At first, she discreetly tells her clients at the Center that she has a private practice as well, offering convenient evening hours, and providing a discount. Later, once she realizes that she can make a go of it, she offers her resignation, and sends a welcome letter to each of her former clients, soliciting them to continue where they left off at her new place of employment.

a. Is Connie's behavior ethical?

nnn nnnnn nnn

72. The State Legislature was considering legislation that would open up a local wildlife preserve near Harristown to limited hunting. The board of the Harristown Wildlife Protection Association, a nonprofit, tax-exempt 501(c)(3) organization, was considering how to respond. There was rapid agreement that the organization should launch a public education campaign to educate the public about why enacting legislation to do this would be unwise. The Secretary of the Board, Kimberly, was the owner of a public relations organization with a decade of experience in formulating campaigns of this type, one of the reasons he was solicited to join the board several years ago. There is some discussion about whether to find an organization to do this campaign that is not directly connected to the organization, but it is clear that Kimberly has the experience to do this kind of work. The board passes a motion that Kimberly's company should be hired to do the campaign, provided that this work is provided "at cost."

a. Is Kimberly's behavior ethical?

b. Is the board's behavior ethical?

જી જી જી   જી જી જી જી જી   જી જી જી

73. Donald is the CEO of Health Research Consortium, a nonprofit 501(c)(3) tax exempt research organization with clients consisting mostly of local governments and foundations. For research involving issues relating to Obamacare and its effects on local governments, HRC is the go-to organization, chiefly because of its two leading

researchers, Ben and Earl, who have national reputations for understanding and analyzing the complexities of the Affordable Care Act. Since passage of the Act, the HRC has been flooded with research grant opportunities, some of which have even been unsolicited, as local governments and now, even for-profits, have sought to benefit from the knowledge and expertise of these two researchers, as well as their support team. But all is not well at HRC. Ben and Earl are gay, and have been living together for 20 years. Once Massachusetts approved legislation authorizing gay marriage, the couple announced that not only were they going to Massachusetts to be married, but they would be staying there permanently to live and raise a family. They gave their two weeks' notice, and everyone wished them well at the farewell party held in their honor. But Donald knew that Ben and Earl were the backbone of several pending contracts. It might not be impossible to replace them in the long term, but in the short term, their absence would be problematic. Donald was not sure how the grantors would respond if they knew that Ben and Earl were no longer involved in the projects. He decides that he will divulge this fully if the contractors raise any questions, but unless and until they do, he will keep this as quiet as possible and try to find other staff who will be tasked with completing the work.

a. Is Donald's behavior ethical?

ও ও ও   ও ও ও ও ও   ও ও ও

74. Bill, the Director of Communications and Social Networking for the Friends of the Kraft Lake Nature Center, a nonprofit 501(c)(3) tax-exempt organization, has recently hired Lorraine as his new administrative assistant. Lorraine is a young, attractive redheaded woman who has recently gone through a messy divorce. Bill is also divorced, and is looking for a relationship. For the first few weeks, their relationship has been entire professional. But since they have been working closer together, they have developed a friendship, and Bill begins to fantasize that it could become much more than that. He decides that the best course of action is to simply ask her out, and that if this doesn't work out successfully, he can simply hire another administrative assistant or just pretend nothing happened. He does ask her to dinner, and she accepts with a smile. He thinks this could be the start of something meaningful, and he envisions that his life is changing for the positive.

a. Is Bill's behavior ethical?

b. Is Lorraine's behavior ethical?

ও ও ও   ও ও ও ও ও   ও ও ও

75. Quad Fundraising Services (QFS) is a for-profit professional fundraising firm that specializes in providing services to small nonprofit charities that have no internal fundraising staff. Quad handles all fundraising duties, using a bank of trained telemarketing staff, and a sophisticated direct mail operation. QFS is expensive, but they promise that the charity will receive at least something for being added to its client list, and the costs are reasonable considering the upfront investment a charity might have to make to purchase mailing lists and train staff, something QFS has already done. Brad,

the CEO of the Harristown Environmental Improvement Fund, decides to hire QFS. QFS raises nearly $450,000 from its telephone and direct mail campaign, and, after expenses and a reasonable fee, presents a check to the Fund for $5,200, money that will go a long way considering the meagerness of the Fund's budget. Brad is grateful he had the foresight to find a professional fundraiser to do all of this dirty work so that he could focus on the actual mission of the organization.

a. Is it ethical for Brad to hire Quad Fundraising Services?

જ જ જ   જ જ જ જ જ   જ જ જ

76. Katelyn is the admissions director for Harristown University, a private, nonprofit 501(c)(3) tax-exempt, independent institution of higher learning. Katelyn's job involves constant travel, and she accumulates more frequent travel miles than she knows what to do with. She and her husband have used these miles to travel the globe, visit family, and travel to sports events and concerts. Years ago, her husband suggested that these miles really belong to the university, because it had paid for the fares that generated them, but she dismissed him as being ridiculous. But she now donates hundreds of miles each year to her favorite charity, the Make a Wish Foundation, and wonders if perhaps she really is required to declare the value of these miles as compensation on her personal income taxes.

a. Is Katelyn being ethical by not declaring the value of the frequent flier miles as income received from her employer when she takes a charitable deduction for the donation of these miles?

b. Is the institution she works for being ethical by not reporting the value of those miles to the IRS?

જ જ જ   જ જ જ જ જ   જ જ જ

77. Josephine is the Communications Director for the Montrose Association of Nonprofit Organizations (MANO), a nonprofit 501(c)(3) tax-exempt organization formed to bring together nonprofits in Montrose to collaborate on advocacy for the sector, and provide joint purchasing and insurance opportunities. Josephine's husband is running for State House, and she is doing everything she can to support his candidacy. She knows that if he is elected, the nonprofit sector will have a strong, active voice in the state legislature. Today, because her husband is conducting fundraising coffees in their home, Josephine is working in her office, using her computer to create flyers, and printing out hundreds of copies to place under the doors of her neighbors seeking support. At eight o'clock, a group of her friends are meeting with her there to pick up these flyers, and stuff thousands of envelopes in the MANO conference room. She remembers to order four pizzas for delivery.

a. Is Josephine's behavior ethical?

b. What alternatives might be available to her if she wishes to completely separate her political life from her professional life in the nonprofit sector?

જ જ જ   જ જ જ જ જ   જ જ જ

78. Bella is the chief financial officer (CFO) for the Summer Dreams Foundation, a 501(c)(3) whose mission is to send inner-city kids to summer camp in a bucolic, rural setting, who might otherwise not be able to afford this experience. The camp receives substantial revenue from a tree harvester who cuts down trees on the camp property and processes them into furniture products. Bella is wrestling with whether she should file a 990-T with the IRS, disclosing unrelated business income and paying a tax on it. Bella knows that the enforcement of Unrelated Business Income Tax (UBIT) laws is quite spotty, and the money that the organization would pay in taxes would be better spent on providing more kids with camp. Bella decides not to file the 990-T.

a. Is Bella's behavior ethical?

ဆို ဆို ဆို   ဆို ဆို ဆို ဆို ဆို   ဆို ဆို ဆို

79. Louisa is the project director for a grant from the Johnson Foundation provided to her employer, the Citizens Vote Project. She is delighted that her work on the grant is just about finished, and everything relating to this grant has appeared to go well. The final deliverable has been delivered. The only task remaining for her to receive the final grant payment installment is for the program evaluation to be completed. The Johnson Foundation has provided a list of peer reviewers who may be selected by the grantee to perform the evaluation. Louisa looks down the list and sees that one of these evaluators happens to be one of her best friends, Jane. She decides to choose Jane as the evaluator of the grant.

a. Is Louisa's behavior ethical?

ဆို ဆို ဆို   ဆို ဆို ဆို ဆို ဆို   ဆို ဆို ဆို

80. Hallie is the newly elected Chair of the Women's Advocacy Center of Harristown, a 501(c)(4) nonprofit organization established in 1973 that advocates on behalf of the healthcare needs of pregnant teenagers. Hallie is relatively new to the organization and to Harristown, having served on the board for just two years. But the membership has been impressed by her dedication to the mission and her indefatigable efforts to raise funds for the cause. Prior to coming to Harristown, she had served on many other boards in a leadership capacity, and the board had no qualms about electing her chair of this all-volunteer-run organization. Hallie dives into the work of the organization, but learns of a serious problem with the organization's legal status. Apparently, the organization has never filed 990 tax returns for years, and she finds out the IRS had dropped the organization from its Master list of tax-exempt organizations in the 1980s when its communications to the founder of the organization did not receive a response— not surprising since the founder had died only a few years after the organization filed its incorporation papers. Hallie knows that the organization has operated quite well for years without knowing of this problem, and would likely continue to fly "under the radar" for many more years, benefitting by the fact that as a c(4), those who make contributions to the organization may not take a deduction for their contributions on their personal income taxes, making it less likely that the IRS will audit them. So, why open a can of worms?

a. Is Hallie's behavior ethical?

ç ç ç   ç ç ç ç ç   ç ç ç

81. Viola, Betty, and Fran are volunteers at the Amazing Grace Thrift Shop in Haroldson. They enjoy their work there, because they support the mission of the organization, and spend time gossiping and trading shopping coupons. Everyone who works there is real nice. One of the best things about the Shop is they are the first staff people to assess the suitability of the material donations, in the form of clothing and household goods, and their job is to eye-ball the donations, throwing in the trash bin what is too worn or nonrepairable, and sorting the rest. Fran keeps a box by her side as she sorts the donations, deciding if there is anything new coming in that she wants for herself. When she finishes, she takes her box to the cash register, pays the usual cost for each item, and takes the box out to her car. Then she returns to the Shop to continue with her other volunteer duties.

a. Is Fran's behavior ethical?

ç ç ç   ç ç ç ç ç   ç ç ç

82. The American Disaster Relief Fund (ADRF), a 501(c)(3) charity, raises money to support relief efforts in American cities suffering from natural disasters. After Hurricane Sandy, the ADRF launched a massive ad campaign in local newspapers and on the Web soliciting donations from those touched by the disaster, showing horrific pictures of the destruction. On its donation page, in almost unreadable fine print, there is a disclaimer that says that "your donations may be used to fund general administrative expenses of the ADRF and for future natural disasters like Sandy."

a. Is the Fund acting ethically in its fundraising pitches?

ç ç ç   ç ç ç ç ç   ç ç ç

83. George, the father of three children who were killed in a school house fire tragedy in which seven students perished, establishes a charitable nonprofit to accept donations for financing the educational expenses of siblings of those who were victims of the tragedy. George has three other children, and hopes the money raised will be enough to put his eldest daughter through college.

a. Is George acting ethically by establishing a charity to support the expenses of his own family?

b. Is George acting legally by doing this?

ç ç ç   ç ç ç ç ç   ç ç ç

84. Bridget is the President and CEO of the Pennsylvania Heart Disease Education Fund, a nonprofit 501(c)(3) tax-exempt organization. She receives a letter in the mail proposing a partnership between her organization and the manufacturer of a new cereal. The literature provided in the letter describes the cereal as a healthy alternative

to a typical eggs, bacon, and whole milk breakfast. Putting that aside, the cereal is high in sugar, salt, and cholesterol, but certainly much lower in calories than the other breakfast pictured on the box. In exchange for the Fund providing its seal to the manufacturer to use as an endorsement on its packaging, the manufacturer will pay the Fund $10,000 annually. Bridget knows that the $10,000 will go a long way in advancing the mission of the organization, and could save hundreds of lives, even if the cereal might not be the most ideal formulation for someone seeking to improve their heart health. But it is clearly a better alternative than the full breakfast of eggs, bacon, and whole milk it is intended to replace. She agrees to the proposal.

a. Is Bridget acting ethically by providing this approval?

ও ও ও   ও ও ও ও ও   ও ও ও

85. Neva is the executive director of the Historic Preservation Society of Harristown County, a nonprofit 501(c)(3) tax-exempt organization. One of the area's real estate developers, with whom Neva has had run-ins in the past as a result of his, in her opinion, unprincipled irresponsible conversions of historic landmarks in the county into modern condominiums, has sent the organization a contribution of $40,000 without any strings attached. This contribution was never solicited, and she is suspicious about his motives. However, she recognizes that $40,000 will pay for a full-time fundraising staff person that is called for in the Society's strategic plan but never funded, and that the salary check for that staff person will still be able to be cashed regardless of the source of the money. She immediately writes a grateful substantiation letter to the developer, with an abject apology for her behavior towards him during their last confrontation.

a. Is Neva acting ethically by accepting this donation?

ও ও ও   ও ও ও ও ও   ও ও ও

86. Santos is an assistant development officer for the Wild City Foundation, a nonprofit 501(c)(3) tax-exempt organization. He is recruited by a foundation in a neighboring community that solicits many of his current organization's donors, and agrees to leave Wild City for a higher paycheck and more job responsibility. As he cleans out his desk, he remembers to download the Excel file that has the data about his accounts, recognizing that it might take many months to reconstruct this data from memory, and it would save him hours of needless work. He also has access to the accounts of his colleagues in his office, but he believes taking those might be unethical, even though it certainly would be useful to have this material.

a. Is Santos acting ethically?

ও ও ও   ও ও ও ও ও   ও ও ও

87. Mark Is the Executive Director of the Save the Wildlife Fund of Harristown, a 501(c)(3) dedicated to preserving natural habitat in Harristown. The annual performance reviews of his staff of 20 are coming up within a couple of weeks, a task Mark admits he doesn't enjoy, but which is required by the job description approved by his board. His own performance

review is also due, and one of the criteria on which he is judged is his effectiveness in raising funds for the organization. This week, Mark has on his calendar meeting informally with each staff member for about ten minutes, soliciting their annual gift to the Save the Wildlife Fund annual campaign. He knows that the timing of his solicitation makes sense, as it likely results in higher gifts than if it occurred during the winter during less than peak periods of organizational activity, which used to be when he carried out this task.

a. Is Mark's behavior ethical?

ৎৎৎ   ৎৎৎৎৎ   ৎৎৎ

88. Brad and James, two colleagues, are having lunch together. They are discussing their respective charitable gift annuity programs and efforts each is making to convince well-heeled donors in their respective communities to sign up for these. Brad is a bit loose with the tongue as a result of being on his third vodka and tonic, and mentions one particular client. James knows this client, and thinks he can offer him a much better deal than Brad's organization. When James returns from the office, he makes a call to that donor, doesn't mention anything about his conversation with Brad, and simply tells him about the additional tax benefits of donating to James's organization using this vehicle compared to traditional charitable gift annuities that he might be considering elsewhere.

a. Is Brad's behavior ethical?

b. Is James's behavior ethical?

ৎৎৎ   ৎৎৎৎৎ   ৎৎৎ

89. Vinnie is the communications director for the Save Our Guns Foundation, a 501(c)(3) tax exempt organization that provides education, limited advocacy, and firearms training. Vinnie designs a "Voter Education" flyer that details the voting records of each member of the state house and senate, and members of Congress, with respect to Second Amendment issues. The flyer rates each lawmaker using a scale of zero to four guns, with four being awarded to those who support the positions of the National Rifle Association, to which virtually all of the board and members of the Foundation belong. A team of volunteers organized by Vinnie hand out these flyers at area malls and gun shows, and certain legislative districts will be targeted to receive mailings of this flyer a week prior to the election.

a. Is Vinnie's behavior ethical?

ৎৎৎ   ৎৎৎৎৎ   ৎৎৎ

90. Tara is the Assistant Vice President for Development at the Harristown Area Community College. Tara serves on the board of the Freedman Arts Festival, and this year has agreed to manage the festival's fundraising efforts. She boots up her WealthEngine computer program at the office and uses the search tools to identify prospects she might approach to donate to the cause.

a. Is Tara's behavior ethical?

ᢦ ᢦ ᢦ   ᢦ ᢦ ᢦ ᢦ ᢦ   ᢦ ᢦ ᢦ

91. Allyson is a curator of the Harristown City Museum, a 501(c)(3) tax-exempt organization. She is an art lover, and is frustrated that the museum lacks the capacity to exhibit hundreds of interesting pieces of art that languish in the basement storage room. She has just moved into a new apartment, and decides to borrow some of these pieces to furnish the walls of her apartment. She types a memo outlining which pieces she is borrowing, signs it, and places it in the file that is used by the museum to keep track of any loans of museum-owned works of art to its peer institutions. She also dutifully enters this into a computer database that electronically stores this information. She fully intends to return these items when she tires of them, or if she is no longer employed by the museum.

a. Is Allyson's behavior ethical?

ᢦ ᢦ ᢦ   ᢦ ᢦ ᢦ ᢦ ᢦ   ᢦ ᢦ ᢦ

92. Alex runs the Children's and Family Futures Foundation, a 501(c)(3) national think tank based in Washington that provides educational materials and runs seminars to support its public policy agenda. This think tank receives millions of dollars from one particular businessman, and not surprisingly, that businessman supports the organization's public policy agenda, and, also not surprisingly, that agenda favors the policies that will result in the businessman's business making more and more profits. Alex considers his organization to be an educational institution, and he doesn't do any direct lobbying for the policies on the organization's agenda. Rather, he runs educational workshops and develops educational materials to provide background information to member state legislators. The organization is effective; it is not unusual for the think tank to distribute a policy proposal and a sample draft of legislation needed to implement that proposal, and having it introduced (and sometimes even enacted) within days by legislators who are members of the organization. Alex likes to keep the affairs of the organization as close to the vest and out of the public eye as possible, and seeks to avoid having the organization and its staff filing lobbying disclosure paperwork at either the state or federal level. Critics have charged that the organization not only lobbies, lobbying is the *only* purpose of the organization. Alex knows that once the organization admits to lobbying, its 501(c)(3) tax-exempt status would be put at risk.

a. Is Alex's behavior ethical?

ᢦ ᢦ ᢦ   ᢦ ᢦ ᢦ ᢦ ᢦ   ᢦ ᢦ ᢦ

93. Arnold is the executive director of the National Association of Economics Professors and Researchers, a national professional association representing scholars, mostly from educational institutions and government, who conduct research and teach in institutions of higher education about the American economic system. Arnold has just discovered that the trusted staff person who manages the organization's annual conference has been embezzling checks intended to pay for conference exhibits, and has been charging the organization's credit card for personal expenses. The amount of this theft is nearly $50,000. Arnold is very shocked by this news. He fires the employee and refuses to provide him with any severance pay or provide a letter of recommendation. Embarrassed that this occurred under his watch, Arnold decides not to let anyone know

about this discovery—not the police, not his board, not any other staff members, and not even his wife. Eventually, it will all be forgotten, and Arnold will do a much better job investigating future job candidates who are put in a position of trust.

a. Is Arnold's behavior ethical?

ன் ன் ன்   ன் ன் ன் ன் ன்   ன் ன் ன்

94. The "Race to Cure Bladder Cancer" was a complete success, and the race director for this 5K, Bettina, is quite proud of her efforts, which raised $12,000 for the Harristown Bladder Cancer Research Foundation. The race generated lots of good will, race attendees heard her spiel about the organization and the research the foundation is funding, there were scores of pictures taken at the event, and the honorary chair, WCFR-TV anchor Filipina Wilder, would more than likely to mention her participation as the race starter on the 6-o'clock news. Race participants and their supporters were treated to baskets of fruit, bagels, candy bars, and granola bars donated by the local supermarket. Cleaning up wasn't as much of a chore as she had anticipated, and she was able to load the surplus food into her car without the need for assistance. The bananas might not last that long, but the bagels were freezable, and the candy and granola bars would fill her kids' lunch boxes for the rest of the year.

a. Is Bettina's behavior ethical?

b. What alternative behavior might have been available to her?

ன் ன் ன்   ன் ன் ன் ன் ன்   ன் ன் ன்

95. Geraldine does not have a home computer, and recognizes that the world is changing, and email and Internet access has become a necessity. She did set up a Gmail account, but rarely uses it. Instead, she uses the email account provided to her by her employer, the nonprofit 501(c)(3) tax-exempt Wilson Sports Hall of Fame, located at the football stadium at Wilson University, home of the Fightin' Wildcats. Because she does not have her own Internet access, she is forced to do her personal Internet tasks, including responding to email, booking travel, reading movie reviews, shopping for Christmas presents, and so on at the office. To compensate for this, she usually has lunch at her desk. She notices, however, that since she has set up her Facebook account, she is spending much more time on the Internet than she used to, and is having difficulty tearing herself away to do her work for the organization. And since she has discovered Candy Crush, she questions whether she is starting to become addicted to the computer, and thinks about asking for a raise so she could afford to purchase a computer of her own.

a. Is Geraldine's behavior ethical?

ன் ன் ன்   ன் ன் ன் ன் ன்   ன் ன் ன்

96. Bertha is a 60-something executive director of Pennsylvania Privacy Watch, a 501(c)(4) nonprofit organization that seeks to improve state privacy laws. The organization has

20 staff members, including lobbyists, attorneys, and support staff. She recently has developed a fascination with Facebook, having set up a new account. Being unmarried, she has no family of her own, and spends much of her time either in the office or on her computer, entertaining herself by looking up old friends from high school on social networking sites, and Googling names from her past to see what she can find of interest. She has just sent Facebook friend requests to the 15 staff members she manages, and is delighted that three immediately accepted her friend request within a few minutes—although she wonders why they are on Facebook when they should be working.

a. Is Bertha's behavior ethical?

b. Would this situation be different if it was the staff member who is asking her to accept a friend request?

c. Regardless of who initiated the request, is it ethical for those who supervise employees to be Facebook friends with those they supervise?

ఌ ఌ ఌ   ఌ ఌ ఌ ఌ ఌ   ఌ ఌ ఌ

97. Grover, a nurse, has just been called into the office of his supervisor, Rema, the Director of Nursing at the Hospital and Health Center of Greenstown, a nonprofit 501(c)(3) organization, and told that he is fired. Grover has posted on his Facebook page that a certain patient of his, which he names, is certifiably mentally ill, and adds crude, disparaging remarks about this patient. Grover protests that only Rema, and other nurses at the hospital have access to this particular post, since it was posted to a private group. Rema responds that regardless of whether this post constitutes a violation of the Health Insurance Portability and Accountability Act (HIPAA), and whether this page was not an official page of the institution, it was inappropriate and unprofessional for Grover to denigrate any particular patient.

a. Was Grover being unethical by posting about his patient on a "private" social networking page?

b. Was Rema being unethical by firing Grover?

ఌ ఌ ఌ   ఌ ఌ ఌ ఌ ఌ   ఌ ఌ ఌ

98. Matilda is a nurse at the Harristown Home for the Aged, a nonprofit 501(c)(3) tax-exempt organization. The home has a substantial waiting list, because of the reputation it has for providing quality care at affordable fees. Her mother has been getting up in years, and recently suffered a fall and broke her hip. Matilda is unwilling to trust the care of her mother to other facilities that might not have as a good a reputation as the facility for which she works. She recognizes that she cannot afford to take months, if not years, off to care for her mother in her home, and pleads with the executive director, Xeno, to bend the rules and admit Matilda's mom as a patient as soon as there is an open bed. Xeno agrees to accommodate Matilda's request.

a. Is Matilda being unethical by making this request?

b. Is Xeno being unethical by agreeing to the request?

c. Would the situation be any different if it was a major donor of the institution who was making the request rather than a staff member?

⤙⤙⤙   ⤙⤙⤙⤙⤙   ⤙⤙⤙

99. Agnes is the executive director of the Having a Dream Foundation, a nonprofit 501(c)(3) tax-exempt organization that grants "wishes" to disabled children. Agnes, who is attractive, eligible and single, has been schmoozing up a major donor, Winton, an attractive widower who is capable of making a healthy six-figure annual gift to the Foundation according to her prospect research file. She successfully secures his gift in the amount of $50,000. While hoping for more, she knows that these additional funds will make her organization's mission easier to achieve. Without any warning, Winton shyly asks her out. Agnes, flattered, accepts.

a. Is Agnes's behavior ethical?

⤙⤙⤙   ⤙⤙⤙⤙⤙   ⤙⤙⤙

100. Lindsey is the client intake specialist for the Community Health and Human Services Providers of Harristown County, a private 501(c)(3) nonprofit organization that meets social and medical needs of seniors living in Harristown County. Lindsey's job is to meet with new clients of the organization and take down their identifying information, medical history, and screen them for eligibility for services and any financial subsidies for which they may qualify. The clients are quite diverse, being natives of scores of different foreign countries, practicing many different religions, and are diverse with respect to age, gender, race, and sexual preference. Lindsey works in a typical cubicle, with enough space for herself, her desk, and two chairs for her clients to sit in while she enters data into her computer in response to her questions. Lindsey is quite religious, and her cubicle is decorated with crosses, statues of the Virgin Mary, pictures of Jesus, and posters declaring the glory of her Savior. Lindsey feels that in her job, she is doing God's work, even if some of her clients are not worthy of this and are doomed to eternal damnation by not accepting Jesus, who died for their sins and offers them eternal life.

a. Is Lindsey's behavior ethical?

⤙⤙⤙   ⤙⤙⤙⤙⤙   ⤙⤙⤙

101. Morgana is an administrative assistant for the People's Voting Project, a consortium of progressive organizations working to increase voting among populations most likely to vote for progressive candidates. Morgana is riled up about a new dress code that has recently been put into effect by the executive director, Melvin, who put the policy in a formal memo. The policy includes a ban on nose rings, eyebrow piercings and certain other types of decorative piercings that Morgana has spent good money for and for which she is quite proud. Those who violate the policy will be sanctioned, and may be even fired if they fail to honor the terms of this policy. Melvin never discussed the policy with the staff, and it certainly was never considered by the organization's board of directors. She sits down and

drafts an email complaining about new policy and sends it to the entire membership of the People's Voting Project Board of Directors, suggesting that Melvin be fired if he refuses to rescind the policy.

a. Is Morgana's behavior ethical?

b. Is Melvin's behavior ethical?

દ્ય દ્ય દ્ય   દ્ય દ્ય દ્ય દ્ય દ્ય   દ્ય દ્ય દ્ય

102. Riley is an employment specialist for a nonprofit employment and vocational service, and he is delighted that one of his clients, Roxanne, has successfully found a good-paying job after a few counseling sessions with Riley. Today after lunch, Riley returns to his desk and finds a package from Roxanne, which contains a thank-you note, a box of expensive chocolates, and a check for $50 made out to him. Riley pockets the check to be cashed later this week, puts out the chocolates in the lunchroom to share with his colleagues—whose work was partly responsible for his ability to find Roxanne employment, and writes out a thank-you to Roxanne for her gifts, with best wishes for success in her new job.

a. Is Riley's behavior ethical?

દ્ય દ્ય દ્ય   દ્ય દ્ય દ્ય દ્ય દ્ય   દ્ય દ્ય દ્ય

103. Viola is the executive director of The Best Time of Your Life Retirement Community, a nonprofit 501(c)(3) tax-exempt assisted living facility, subsidized by one particular faith community, which has a long waiting list for being considered for residency in the modern, luxury facility. An older couple, Peter and Faith, are meeting with Viola, and are disappointed to learn that the average wait for an apartment in the facility to become available is two years. Viola tells them that if the couple is willing to make a $30,000 donation to the institution, this will entitle them to shave as much as a year off the wait, although there is still no guarantee that there will be an opening as others have made that commitment.

a. Is the waiting list avoidance policy of the Retirement Community ethical?

દ્ય દ્ય દ્ય   દ્ય દ્ય દ્ય દ્ય દ્ય   દ્ય દ્ય દ્ય

104. Gregory is the executive director of a statewide association that monitors legislative and regulatory developments that affect the sports community. Gregory subscribes to lots of sports magazines, including ESPN the Magazine, Sports Illustrated, and Baseball Digest, and many other publications that he subscribed to prior to working for the association. Upon being hired for this position, Gregory began charging these subscriptions to the association rather than paying for them out of his personal funds because they are all now job-related. He also uses the association's credit card to renew subscriptions to three statewide newspapers and the Wall Street Journal, which will continue to be delivered to his home so he can skim them before leaving for work in the morning.

a. Is Gregory's behavior ethical?

⚭ ⚭ ⚭   ⚭ ⚭ ⚭ ⚭ ⚭   ⚭ ⚭ ⚭

105. Shirley is the executive director of a nonprofit 501(c)(4) advocacy organization, the Coalition to Suppress Gun Violence. As a c(4), she recognizes that donors to her organization may not take a charitable deduction on their federal income taxes for donations made to the Coalition. With board approval, she decides to incorporate the Coalition to Suppress Gun Violence Foundation, and apply for c(3) federal tax-exempt status, solely for the purpose of having a conduit for her stakeholders to make tax-deductible donations, with the understanding that all donations made to the c(3) will be funneled directly into the c(4) dollar for dollar.

a. Is the behavior of Shirley ethical?

⚭ ⚭ ⚭   ⚭ ⚭ ⚭ ⚭ ⚭   ⚭ ⚭ ⚭

106. Lance is the Director of the Harristown Bicycle Club, a nonprofit 501(c)(3) tax exempt organization. Lance is dismayed to discover that the winner of the Club's annual professional championship has tested positive for EPO. He meets with the alleged violator, and negotiates an agreement whereby the winner agrees to return the prize money in the form of a donation to the club, not participate in any future events sponsored by the Club, but is not required to admit any wrongdoing. The agreement requires that both parties keep the agreement entirely secret from the public. A reporter calls Lance and starts asking questions about whether there was any evidence that the winner had tested positive for EPO or other performance enhancing drugs. Lance responds with a flat "that is a total fabrication."

a. What behavior described above is unethical?

b. What behavior described above is illegal?

⚭ ⚭ ⚭   ⚭ ⚭ ⚭ ⚭ ⚭   ⚭ ⚭ ⚭

107. Barbara is hired as the new executive director of the Harristown United Way, a nonprofit 501(c)(3) tax-exempt organization. As is typical in Harristown whenever a new executive director is hired, the salary negotiation includes an understanding that the executive director will be making a $20,000 "leadership gift" to the United Way, serving as an example to other staff (and members of the community, as well), and the amount of salary is at a level to accommodate this expected gift.

a. Is the organization acting ethically when it "requires" this donation?

⚭ ⚭ ⚭   ⚭ ⚭ ⚭ ⚭ ⚭   ⚭ ⚭ ⚭

108. The Men's Health Project is a nonprofit 501(c)(3) tax-exempt organization dedicated to education and advocacy relating to diseases that afflict mostly men, including prostate and testicular cancer, but also diseases and conditions that have a broader appeal, such as heart disease, high blood pressure, and obesity. Over the years, the Project has compiled a mailing list of almost 50,000 addresses of donors, and an email list of almost 100,000. A for-profit fundraising organization has approached the Project's executive director, Manny,

about purchasing the lists. He offers the Project $5,000 for it, and Manny finds this quite generous, considering there are no costs involved in electronically transferring the data to this professional fundraiser.

a. Is Manny acting ethically by selling this data to a professional fundraising firm?

⁊ ⁊ ⁊　　⁊ ⁊ ⁊ ⁊ ⁊　　⁊ ⁊ ⁊

109. Jean and Harry are wealthy members of the community who have supported the Fund for a Vibrant Harristown for many years, pledging six figures for as long as anyone can remember. Earlier this year, Harry pledged $250,000 on behalf of his family. But unfortunately, his bookstore business suffered a major collapse and had to be liquidated, following a bankruptcy. The board, which depends so much on the generosity of Jean and Harry, has decided to sue the couple to make good on their pledge, accepting the argument that the Fund has made commitments based on the payment of this pledge, and that there are consequences to those who make pledges and then fail to follow through with their pledge commitment.

a. Is the Fund's board behaving unethically by authorizing a suit against these donors?

⁊ ⁊ ⁊　　⁊ ⁊ ⁊ ⁊ ⁊　　⁊ ⁊ ⁊

110. Juan is the international director for Feed the Big Blue Marble Foundation, an American-based nonprofit 501(c)(3) tax-exempt organization that operates in 30 countries with the mission of alleviating hunger in areas devastated by natural disasters, civil wars, and political unrest, making efforts to avoid taking sides in political disputes. Juan receives a report from his director in Mali, Achmed, that a local village chieftain is blocking the organization's convoy from passing through a road adjacent to his village and reaching residents of a nearby besieged village, and has demanded that the organization pay him the equivalent of $12,000 to let the trucks pass freely. Juan is a realist, and recognizes that this is how business is done in this part of the world. He approves the payment, and arranges to wire the money to a particular unnumbered account in Switzerland.

a. Is Juan's behavior ethical?

⁊ ⁊ ⁊　　⁊ ⁊ ⁊ ⁊ ⁊　　⁊ ⁊ ⁊

111. It's January, and the Harristown Youth Soccer Booster Club, a 501(c)(3) nonprofit, tax-exempt organization, is having its annual flower seed and cookie sale to offset its expenses for the upcoming fall season. As is the case each year, each participating child is expected to raise $200 to fund uniforms, field rentals, soccer balls and other equipment, and insurance. Participating in the fundraising sale is not mandatory, but each youth, or more accurately, their parents, would otherwise be required to pay the Booster Club $200 in participation fees. By selling the flowers and cookies, this fee may be offset, with every $5 in sales equaling $1 in fee reduction. Most children participate in the fundraising effort. (see: irs.gov/pub/irs-tege/booster_club_field_directive_6-27.pdf)

a. Is the Club's fundraising policy ethical?

b. Is the fund's fundraising policy legal?

જ જ જ   જ જ જ જ જ   જ જ જ

112. An animal rights nonprofit organization, Protect Our Animals of Harristown, has received a tip that a poultry farm in nearby Johnson City is raising and slaughtering its poultry is cruel conditions. Its board decides to authorize a member of the staff to volunteer to try to infiltrate the poultry plant by getting a job there, and exposing the conditions by making videos and finding documents that may be incriminating. A staff member succeeds at this, posing as someone with little work experience when in fact the volunteer has a Ph.D. in biology from the state university. The operation is a success, and the local newspaper agrees to cover the story, using pictures and documents obtained by the volunteer.

a. Is the strategy of infiltrating the poultry farm for the purpose of uncovering illegal and or immoral treatment of animals ethical?

જ જ જ   જ જ જ જ જ   જ જ જ

113. Nathan is the regional director for the Progressive Education Project, a nonprofit 501(c)(3) tax-exempt organization. The Project's mission is to provide voter education. It accomplishes this by identifying college student-aged, idealistic volunteers to go door to door with petitions, explaining why voters should be concerned about the environment, and asking for donations to support the organization. Typically, these canvassers get to keep half of the money they raise. A quarter of the money goes to people like Nathan, who supervise the canvassers. The remainder goes to support the state and national offices. Nathan was once a canvasser, and he was hired to become a full-time supervisor based on his success of being a part-time canvasser. The canvassers know about Nathan's story. They hope that some day, their commitment to the organization will result in them being supervisors—having the quarter of the funds raised by the canvassers they supervise go to their own paychecks, and at least indirectly, preserve the environment for the next generation.

a. Is the fundraising model employed by the Project ethical?

જ જ જ   જ જ જ જ જ   જ જ જ

114. The National Association of Biology Teachers is a nonprofit 501(c)(3) tax-exempt organization that represents the interests of 35,000 high school and college biology teachers. Recently, one of its members posted that the endowment of the organization, now nearly $35 million, is invested heavily in a private equity fund that manufactures assault weapons, including the one that was used in the murder of 20 school children in Newtown, CT in December 2012. The executive director insists that the association does not actually own the company, and that the purpose of the investment strategy of the association is to provide the highest, and most stable return possible on its investment. The chairman of the board has taken the opposite position, and advocates that the association should divest itself of any investments in products and services that

are not socially responsible, including tobacco companies, gun manufacturing, and companies that are considered to either pollute the environment or engage in unfair labor practices. The board votes to overrule its board chair and continue with the investment.

a. Is the investment policy of the organization ethical?

ঌ ঌ ঌ   ঌ ঌ ঌ ঌ ঌ   ঌ ঌ ঌ

115. Piperville Community Hospital, a nonprofit 501(c)(3)tax-exempt organization, has always been entrepreneurial in finding sources of revenue to respond to increasing cuts in government reimbursements, and competition from nearby health institutions. Recently, a private laundry service in the community announced that it was closing its doors permanently, and laying off 22 full-time workers, because the hospital was undercutting its business by offering laundry services at a cheaper price; taking advantage of its access to private capital; its exemption from federal, state and local taxes; and its ability to access volunteers. The board is considering launching a similar unrelated business—offering a health club with state of the art Nautilus equipment to compete head-to-head with a private health club that has recently located within two blocks of the hospital's campus. The hospital routinely files a 990-T and pays thousands of dollars in taxes on its unrelated business income.

a. Is the hospital acting ethically by competing for the business of for-profit organizations, even when the operations are outside of the mission of the hospital?

ঌ ঌ ঌ   ঌ ঌ ঌ ঌ ঌ   ঌ ঌ ঌ

116. Sasha teaches economics at the local community college. She is also the author of an economics textbook, which is widely used by some of the leading universities. She has developed the syllabus for Economics 101 at the institution, and requires her textbook for her course.

a. Is Sasha being ethical when she requires her students to adopt the textbook she has authored?

ঌ ঌ ঌ   ঌ ঌ ঌ ঌ ঌ   ঌ ঌ ঌ

117. JoAnne is the Executive Director of the Harristown Homeless Shelter. One of her board members, Ginny, visits JoAnne's office, and asks to see all of the documentation that is related to the organization's credit card issued to JoAnne. JoAnne responds that this is not something that is appropriately shared with every board member and refuses her request.

a. Is JoAnne being ethical by refusing the request to see these documents?

b. Is Ginny being ethical by requesting to see these documents?

ঌ ঌ ঌ   ঌ ঌ ঌ ঌ ঌ   ঌ ঌ ঌ

118. Alma is the Executive Director of the Fund for the Preservation of Historic Rileyville, a nonprofit 501(c)(3) tax-exempt organization whose mission is to advocate for maintaining the downtown area of Rileyville as close to how it looked in the 1950s. It resists attempts to bring in fast food restaurants and other businesses, including adult book stores, that might change the character of the downtown, particularly Main Street. The accountant who audits the organization recently died, and the board is looking for a replacement who will not charge the organization much. Alma suggests that the Board engage the services of her uncle, Bill, who is a retired CPA, and would likely do the audit for the organization for free as a favor. The board gratefully accepts this offer.

a. Is Alma acting ethically by making this offer?

b. Is the board acting ethically by accepting this offer?

c. Is Bill acting ethically by agreeing to audit the organization?

ఆ ఆ ఆ   ఆ ఆ ఆ ఆ ఆ   ఆ ఆ ఆ

119. Oliver is the Vice President of Development for the Hookman School, a nonprofit 501(c)(3) tax-exempt organization that provides K-8 instruction to students with hearing disabilities. The facility will be moving to a new location, and Oliver is organizing an online auction to dispose of surplus goods the school has accumulated over the years. He helps to entice higher bids by noting in the promotional materials that all purchases of goods from this auction will be considered donations, and that those who participate will be entitled to take a tax deduction for the amount of any check they send to the school as a result of what they might purchase during this fundraising event, and the actual goods being provided will be considered a thank-you gift for their donations. Oliver tells those who inquire that he will provide a substantiation letter to document these donations, even if the purchase is less than the amount in the threshold required for these letters.

a. Is Oliver's behavior ethical?

ఆ ఆ ఆ   ఆ ఆ ఆ ఆ ఆ   ఆ ఆ ఆ

120. Portia is the Director of Art and Music Therapy for the West Mountain Heights Nursing Home, a 501(c)(3) tax-exempt organization. She is working on her master's degree online, and spends an increasing part of her day doing classwork. Because of the demands of her family and having a second job at the local supermarket, she finds she is unable to do her schoolwork outside of office hours. Occasionally, she has had to hide what she has been doing from her supervisor, the executive director, because she is not sure whether he would sanction her for doing her school assignments during the working day. But, she rationalizes, what she learns in these classes is often related to her work assignments, and helps her do a better job.

a. Is Portia's behavior ethical?

ఆ ఆ ఆ   ఆ ఆ ఆ ఆ ఆ   ఆ ఆ ఆ

KEY WORD INDEX

ethics,
  approaches, 31, 32, 46, 63, 64, 65, 66, 68, 123, 198
  training, 16, 31, 32, 81, 90, 91, 93, 119, 198
Ethics Risk Index, 37
evaluation, 6, 39, 40, 45, 51, 52, 53, 57, 85, 99, 105, 110, 117, 124, 130, 188, 189, 198, 209, 234
executive director, 11, 25, 40, 41, 42, 52, 84, 85, 86, 92, 94, 98, 107, 109, 111, 129, 156, 195-203, 204, 205, 207, 208, 209, 211, 213, 216, 217, 219, 220, 221, 224, 225, 226, 227, 228, 236, 238, 239, 240, 241, 242, 243, 244, 245, 246, 247
exit, voice, and loyalty, 54
expense accounts, 132, 209, 226
exploitation, 45, 66

F

Facebook, 10, 140, 194, 195, 197, 198, 199, 201, 202, 224, 239, 240
favoritism, 44, 66, 79, 109, 117
  federal tax return (Form 990), 38, 42, 43, 44, 50, 51, 53, 54, 57, 71, 73, 81, 89, 95, 161, 164, 186, 234
financial management, 85, 89-101, 129, 208
financial reports, 91
firing, 13, 14, 16, 17, 44, 49, 58, 63, 64, 93, 110, 111, 113, 130, 135, 136, 137, 140, 141, 143, 145, 151, 169, 170, 171, 174, 176, 177, 178, 187, 201, 202, 208, 209, 211, 225, 229, 238, 240, 241, 242
for-profit, 11, 37, 38, 43, 46, 53, 54, 55, 62, 63, 64, 65, 66, 68, 81, 83, 85, 90, 91, 92, 98, 110, 112, 115, 121, 139, 153, 155, 156, 157, 159, 188, 190, 194, 204, 210, 214, 222, 232, 243, 246
foundations, 5, 6, 13, 15, 16, 38, 50, 55, 71, 89, 97, 106, 107, 121, 122, 129-133, 135-141, 143, 144, 145, 146, 147, 148, 149, 150, 151, 161, 162, 191, 196, 197, 198, 200, 202, 210, 213, 214, 215, 217, 219, 224, 225, 226, 229, 231, 233, 234, 236, 237, 238, 239, 241, 243, 244
founder's syndrome, 138
fraud, 6, 14, 37, 66, 71, 89, 91, 92, 93, 98, 99, 121, 175, 198, 224

free rider problem, 29
fundraisers (professional), 14, 15, 52, 67, 71-77, 104, 107, 114, 122, 123, 125, 127, 131, 133, 154, 155, 158, 159, 209, 210, 214, 217, 222, 229, 233, 244
fundraisers (events), 13, 46, 64, 79, 96, 157, 180

G

gambling, 108, 153-159
Gallup Polls, 61, 68
gays and lesbians, 12, 199
genocide, 11
Gewirth, Alan, 27
gift policies,
  from donors, 73
  from vendors and others, 83, 95
Golden Rule, 21, 22, 29
governance, 25, 44, 71, 79-87, 105, 121, 124, 125, 138, 145, 147, 184
government, 91, 114, 116, 121, 127, 137, 155, 161, 168, 169, 186, 190, 193, 197, 202, 230, 231, 232, 238, 246
  contracts, 98
  regulation, 193
  relations, 85, 208
Grant Professionals Association, 103, 105, 106, 121, 125, 128
grants,
  foundation, 55, 97, 121, 145-151, 162, 196, 200, 226, 234
  general, 40, 50, 54, 74, 85, 96, 124, 125-128, 139, 158, 202, 207, 221, 226, 228, 232
  government, 11, 55, 121, 225-226

H

Hale House, 89
Hammurabi's Code, 113
harassment, 75, 85, 110, 123, 231
  sexual, 15, 37, 64, 109, 117, 175, 193, 209
Health Insurance Portability and Accountability Act (HIPAA), 81, 240
Hershey School, 79-80
Hershey School Trust, 52, 79-80, 81, 82, 86
hiring, 14, 37, 41, 43, 44, 45, 49, 52, 53, 62, 64, 66, 75, 81, 85, 86, 90, 97, 107, 109,

About the Author...

Gary M. Grobman (B.S. Drexel University, M.P.A. Harvard University, Kennedy School of Government, Ph.D., Penn State University) is special projects director for White Hat Communications, a Harrisburg-based publishing and nonprofit consulting organization formed in 1993. The title of Dr. Grobman's doctoral dissertation is *An Analysis of Codes of Ethics of Nonprofit, Tax-Exempt Membership Associations: Does Principal Constituency Make a Difference?* He has taught nonprofit management classes for four universities.

He served as the executive director of the Pennsylvania Jewish Coalition from 1983-1996. Prior to that, he was a senior legislative assistant in Washington for two members of Congress, a news reporter, and a political humor columnist for *Roll Call.* He also served as a lobbyist for public transit agencies. In 1987, he founded the Non-Profit Advocacy Network (NPAN), which consisted of more than 50 statewide associations that represented Pennsylvania charities.

He is the author of *The Holocaust—A Guide for Pennsylvania Teachers, The Nonprofit Handbook, Fundraising Online: Using the Internet to Raise Serious Money for Your Nonprofit Organization* (co-authored with Gary Grant), *Improving Quality and Performance in Your Non-Profit Organization, The Nonprofit Organization's Guide to E-Commerce, The Nonprofit Management Casebook, Just Don't Do It! A Fractured and Irreverent Look at the Ph.D. Culture,* and other books published by White Hat Communications and Wilder Publications (now Fieldstone).

Contact Dr. Grobman at: White Hat Communications, P.O. Box 5390, Harrisburg, PA 17110-0390. Telephone: (717) 238-3787; Fax: (717) 238-2090; Email: gary.grobman@gmail.com.